SELL YOUR BUSINESS SUCCESSFULLY

SELL YOUR BUSINESS SUCCESSFULLY

Tips, Strategies, and Tools

REXFORD E. UMBENHAUR III

JOHN WILEY & SONS, INC.

New York • Chichester • Weinheim • Brisbane • Singapore • Toronto

This publication is designed to provide accurate and authoritative information in regard to the subject matter covered. It is sold with the understanding that the publisher is not engaged in rendering legal, accounting, or other professional services. If legal advice or other expert assistance is required, the services of a competent professional person should be sought.

Library of Congress Cataloging-in-Publication Data:
Umbenhaur, Rexford E.
　　Sell your business successfully / Rexford E. Umbenhaur, III.
　　　　p.　　cm.
　　Includes bibliographical references and index.
　　ISBN 0-471-24516-X (pbk. : alk. paper)
　　1. Sale of small businesses—United States.　I. Title.
　　HD2346.U5U446　　1998
　　658.1′6—DC21　　　　　　　　　　　　　　　　98-20178
　　　　　　　　　　　　　　　　　　　　　　　　　　CIP

Printed in the United States of America.

10 9 8 7 6 5 4 3 2

*To my wife Kathleen, who is a gift of
love from the One who is love.*

ABOUT THE AUTHOR

Rexford E. Umbenhaur III founded and successfully managed the business opportunity division of Harman Realtors, Inc., in La Jolla, California. After many successful years, he joined the largest single-office business brokerage in the country, where he was one of the firm's top brokers. In 1990, Mr. Umbenhaur developed Rexford Business Consultants, a firm that specializes in business appraisals and consulting on all aspects of selling or buying businesses.

After 16 years as a specialist in business appraising, business brokering, and consulting with business-owners and business-buyers about selling and buying businesses, Rexford E. Umbenhaur III takes the lid off all the insider information and know-how of successfully selling a business. He has skillfully combined his education, experience, and original works (forms, checklists, etc.) into a format that is easy to follow and understand.

Mr. Umbenhaur has been through many challenging transactions and has met with various negotiation strategies and ways of selling and buying a business. He has seen and heard many varying ways in which business-owners have been instructed through the sale process. Too many times, the instructions or information was wrong or misleading. Now, in an honest and very straightforward manner, he brings you *Sell Your Business Successfully*.

CONTENTS

CONTENTS

CONTENTS

CONTENTS

CONTENTS

PREFACE

Over the last sixteen years, I have witnessed many variations to the way in which small businesses are sold. There are no formal places of education where a person can learn about selling a small business. For the professional, there is not much training available and many of the business-brokerages do not even provide training. The International Business Brokers Association has made the best effort to organize and provide training to business-brokers in the many facets of selling a business. Quite a few books have been written on the subject of selling a business, but they have been written for the professional business-broker, attorney, CPA, or intermediary; most have been modeled on the sale of publicly traded corporations. There are a few books about selling closely held corporations, but most with gross sales of $50 million dollars and up. I have seen very little written on the many small businesses that are sole proprietorships and partnerships.

With so little information available about selling small businesses, it is no wonder that I have heard from hundreds of people who find themselves involved in the purchase or sale of a business, telling me that they cannot believe the poor representation that they experience. I personally have seen a lack of standard practices and professionalism in the field of business sales, and each time I am very concerned for the unsuspecting client.

There are approximately two million small businesses that are sold each year throughout our country; 70 percent of those sales are done without a business-broker. There is a logical method of progression and details accompanying the sale of a small business. You do not need to feel that you are heading into the abyss when you decide to sell your business. Using a proper guide could drastically reduce the amount of difficulties and lawsuits experienced.

Even if you do prefer to hire a professional to sell your business, you should have a good knowledge of what to expect. If you do not, you will not know how to judge if what you are being told is correct or even the best way of proceeding. Selling or buying a business is like walking through an uncharted minefield; you never know when something is going to blow up underneath you.

I have written this guide because there is no mystery to selling a business. You need to know what to do, and with the proper guidance, any business-owner can succeed in selling his or her own business. The amount of money you can save is substantial: thousands of dollars to tens of thousands of dollars.

Over the last sixteen years, I have helped many business-owners steer a straight course to a successful sale without a major problem. I have put all my experience and knowledge into this guide. I want the information and guidance made available to as many people as it can reach, because I believe that business-owners have made a considerable investment of time and money in their businesses and deserve the best guidance when it comes to selling.

Rexford E. Umbenhaur III

SELL YOUR BUSINESS SUCCESSFULLY

1

BUSINESS VALUATION

INTRODUCTION TO BUSINESS VALUATION

There are many different ways to value a business, depending on the purpose for the valuation and the entity or assets being valued. For our purposes, we are going to discuss determining the value of your business so you can successfully market and sell your business in a reasonable time. Some business appraisers feel that determining a range of value is a better way to represent the value. There are many subjective considerations and many facets of a business, its structure, and performance that can affect the value at any point in time. There are many other appraisers who may consider a range of value which a particular business falls within, but will always decide on the one value that they as professionals determine is the best, given all the information at that point in time. By applying more than one valuation method or varying the capitalization rate (see Exhibit 1.1), also known as the risk factor, or simply called the mul-

Narrower range commonly found

20% 22 25 27 30 32 35 37 40 42 45 47 50 52 55 57 60 62 67 70 72 75 77 80 82 85 87 90 92 95 97 100%

Typical full range of cap rates

Exhibit 1.1 Range of Capitalization Rates

tiple, you will be able to determine the lower end of the value spectrum as well as the higher end. A good thing about determining a range of value is that in this way you will understand the full range within which you will negotiate your sale.

One of the hardest elements for people who are new to business valuation is choosing the capitalization rate or multiple, and thus making that final decision about the one value of the business. There is a fundamental difference in determining a value through appraisal methods and seeing what a business actually sells for. The difference is that the price that a business sells for is a negotiated value. Missing in a business appraisal is the motivation, skill, and emotion brought to the negotiation by both parties. Typically, a business is offered at one particular asking price, but by selling the business anywhere within a range you establish, you can be sure that you did not sell the business for too little. When you are negotiating the sale price and terms, you will have in mind a range and therefore you can rest assured that you will sell the business for a fair price.

Everyone in a negotiated sale likes to feel that they prevailed, that they did their best and were not taken advantage of by the other side. If you understand the range of value that your business is in, then you will know for sure that you ended up selling the business for its true value. You will also know when the buyer is throwing you a low-ball offer. An extremely valuable by-product of going through one or more valuation method is that you will know why you have determined that value. If needed, you will be armed with the ability to explain the reasons why the business is worth what you say it is. The only thing that an uninformed buyer or seller has to hang onto in negotiations is his or her pride and unfounded or misinformed reasoning about the business's value. The better informed you are about the business and why it is worth what you are asking, the better off you will be. As you will see by reading this entire book on selling, both you and the buyer become informed. The better informed you both are about the business, the better the decisions you will make. Of course, we must never forget that pride, emotions, and motivation do affect the negotiations and final sale price.

The valuation methods you will learn are the most commonly used methods for valuing small and very small businesses (under 100 employees and most ranging from one to 50 employees). Business appraisers regularly use one or more of these methods in valuing small businesses; there are many different ways to value a business and perhaps you have heard of a few. Two of the methods discussed here are more commonly used among business-brokers. By applying more than one method you can compare the results and then consider which method is best suited for your needs and type of business.

GROSS-SALES METHOD OF VALUATION

There are valuation methods whereby the gross sales, either annual figures or monthly figures, are used to determine the whole value of the business. I have included this method because some sort of rule of thumb or gross sales formula is included in many books on the subject of valuation or on the sale of a business. Many business-brokers use such methods, and many of these formulas are discussed among business-owners, accountants, and laymen. An example would be a dry cleaner that is valued at 8 to 12 times its monthly gross sales. A survey of individual factors or attributes of the business will determine where in the range of 8 to 12 times the monthly gross the business should fall. There are gross sales multiples that you will hear of or even discover that do not include a range, but are just one number or a percentage. A weakness in this method is that two businesses in the same industry with the same gross-sales volume are usually not worth the same. I have heard many times, from a variety of misinformed sources, that a particular type of business was worth 50 percent of its gross sales (or six times monthly sales), or that one type of business sells for one times its annual gross-sales volume. The problem with such generalized thinking arises because one business may have newer equipment while the other's equipment is much older. One business may have higher rent or offer discounts on products or services and yet have the same gross-sales volume as another business in the same industry. Both factors reduce the net profit and therefore the financial benefits derived from the business and the resultant value. One business can have a very good location that helps bring in business, while the other businesses must spend more on salespeople or marketing and advertising. In other words, there can be and usually are, upon further investigation, many factors that make one business more profitable and more attractive than another business with the same annual gross-sales volume.

For the value-by-gross-sales method to work more accurately, or to use it as a simple check against other methods (I would use it as a check against other methods), you should find out what businesses within the same (same as the business to be valued) industry sold for, in addition to what their annual gross sales were. You will then be able to determine the ratio of the business's sale price to its gross sales. For example, wholesale distribution businesses may have sold for 38 percent of their annual gross sales. This is sometimes stated in different ways such as, "three times monthly gross or eight to twelve times monthly gross."

It is best if you can locate a source of comparable sales of the same or similar businesses in an effort to find out what the sale price/gross sales ratio is, or what the monthly multiplier is. I have included information in the bibliography of this guidebook about where to obtain the only currently available public information that is compiled annually on comparable sales. I would encourage you to also check with a trade association in the particular industry and see if they have knowledge of any ratios that you can use. You can call business-brokers and business-appraisers in your area and ask them if they know of local gross-sales multiples or percentages of gross sales that are used for the specific type of business that you are researching. The publisher of this guidebook, John Wiley & Sons, Inc., publishes computerized databases of this same information. Please see Exhibit 1.3 for a compilation of some percentages and gross-sales multiples that you may find helpful. You will find a compiled list of some businesses and their value as it relates to their annual gross sales or their monthly gross sales.

CHOOSING A GROSS-SALES MULTIPLE

To apply this method of valuation, you must have an idea of a multiplier to use, hopefully based on actual historic business sales information, such as the information that is supplied in Exhibit 1.3. For the business that you will be valuing, you may find that there is a range of multipliers in the historic sales information. If so, you should choose the multiplier that reflects the realities of the attributes of the business being valued. To be more accurate in terms of a realistic value for each specific business, you will need to consider various factors or attributes that exist in the business.

The following details concern the dry-cleaning industry but can easily be applied to most business types. The following will hopefully stimulate some ideas of how you should compare attributes of the business you are valuing to those that have been sold and those that are in current competition with the business being valued.

In the dry-cleaning industry, the range of multipliers typically is from 8 to 12 times the monthly gross sales for the type of dry cleaner known as a retail dry cleaner. A typical retail dry cleaner is a single-location business that does all or most of its business directly with the customer who owns the garment or other dry-cleanable item. Most retail dry cleaners do not launder shirts on site; they typically subcontract the work out to a laundry service. The work performed at a retail dry cleaner consists mostly of receiving the garments, sorting, pre-spot cleaning garments that require such cleaning, dry-cleaning the garments, pressing, and bagging the items. The variety of garments or other items requiring dry cleaning is wide-ranging. Some retail dry cleaners offer cleaning of special items such as wedding dresses or other heirloom items, as well as items such as sleeping bags or quilts.

For the sake of comparison and clarity, a wholesale dry cleaner rarely does business with the garment-owner directly. Typically, they do work for hotels or resorts that do not operate their own dry-cleaning equipment, or they dry clean the items for a business-owner that operates a dry-cleaning store front, better known as a drop-station or agency. There are many dry-cleaning business-owners who operate a location which houses all the dry-cleaning equipment and does retail business, while owning and operating additional drop stations or agencies.

Some dry cleaners are known as "quality" dry cleaners and others may be known as discount dry cleaners. The differences between the two being price, the processes applied, and can include the final packaging of the item. Final packaging differences can be seen in the quality of poly-bags that are used, the quality of the hangers, the use of various paper coverings and fancy ribbons, and so on. A discount dry cleaner may be identified because they advertise prices such as $1.95 for the cleaning of any garment, no limit, or a similar idea in a very low price range. Most dry cleaners offer coupons; they offer them regularly or occasionally. The offering of a coupon does not necessarily make the dry cleaner a discount dry cleaner.

There are specialty dry cleaners too, which clean leather garments, draperies, or specialize in large items such as quilts and various down-filled garments and delicate items including silks and hand-knitted items.

As you can see, all dry cleaners are not the same. Additionally, the dry-cleaning equipment varies by type, size, age, and quantity. Locations also vary greatly. Some dry cleaners are in shopping centers known as strip malls, while others are in stand-alone buildings. Some are located on heavily traveled streets, some have plenty of parking, while others offer drive-through drop-off and pick-up. Some dry cleaners are located in sections of town where more people live who have occupations or jobs that require them to dress more formally than casually. The demographics of the area where a business is located should be considered. Some businesses can be shown to be in superior locations demographically, as compared to a business that sold three months earlier and sold for X times monthly gross sales.

There are dry cleaners that have long-standing reputations in the community as opposed to a competitor that is only two years old. A dry cleaner's reputation may be closely tied to the owner, while some are operated completely by employees and it is the name of the business that has gained the reputation, not a person. Some dry cleaners have great marketing advantages as a result of their very visible locations. Some must spend larger sums on advertising to make up for a poor location. Rent is a factor that must be considered in every case.

No matter what type of business that you desire to value, you need to consider how it compares to its competitors or to standard types within its industry. Many times a business-owner has modified the business in order to be unique among the competitors. The modifications can take the form of offering additional products or services that are not typically found in many of the same type of businesses that exist in the same town or within a wider area. Just as an example, I worked with a dry cleaner that not only operated as a typical retail establishment but also offered shoe repair and special cleaning and packaging of wedding dresses and heirlooms. They could remove smoke from any quantity of fabric-covered household items or garments, they had some wholesale dry-cleaning accounts, they had a separate building and equipment to clean draperies, they had their own laundry equipment, and they had a driver pick up and deliver at people's homes. About the only thing they did not have were several drop stations or agencies. The majority of dry cleaners do fit into being a typical retail operation. Sometimes the differences are slight or few, thus making comparisons easier.

Having laid the foundation for some basic elements to compare, let us take a look at the valuing of a retail dry cleaner using the gross sales method. Keep in mind that this can be applied to most other business types.

First of all, various information about the business should be gathered. To make the job a little easier, use the checklist provided in Exhibit 1.4. Only certain types of information will be useful when applying this type of valuation method. Most important are the business's historical financial statements for the past three to five years. Also the most current year-to-date financial information. Keep in mind that we are applying a method that looks at the annual gross revenues or monthly gross revenues. The definition of gross revenues we are using here is total sales, less discounts, returns, and sales taxes collected. Some refer to this as "net sales." The other information on the checklist will be very useful in creating a marketing package for the business. That is explained in Chapter Two.

Depending on whether you are going to apply the multiple to an annual gross-sales figure or to a monthly gross-sales figure will dictate what data you need to compile. We will start with the use of annual gross sales. Make note of the gross sales for each year. If you are currently within a fiscal or calendar year, as opposed to at the end/beginning or near the beginning of a new year, let's say, past the first quarter, then you should create a current fiscal year. That is, you should create a new whole year out of the months that you have completed in this current year, combined with the months that have not been reached this year, from the previous year. In other words, if the business is being valued in May, then take January, February, March, April, and May of the current year and combine the gross sales of these months with the gross sales from last year's June, July, August, September, October, November, and December to create a new whole year. Now you have not only the previous three to five years of historic financial data, but you now also have an accurate current year or current last 12 months. This is much easier than accurately forecasting the balance of the current year.

Once you have gathered all the financial data and made note of each annual gross-sales figure, you are ready to determine which annual figure, or an average of them, that you should use in the formula. To determine what to use, you will need to consider the performance of the business as represented by the annual figures that you have gathered. Ask yourself whether the business is increasing or decreasing in sales. Is it staying relatively level or are the sales up one year and down the next, only to be up again the following year? If you can create a graph of the gross sales figures, it will be helpful. The more years you include in the graph, the better. Even if each year is opposite the previous year, by creating a graph you will be able to see if the trend over the longer picture is up, down, or level. Perhaps the business showed a multi-year slump and is now back up. The more recent trend is then positive and perhaps is more representative of the current scene than those years of slump. If so, then the most recent years will be the ones to focus on. If, however, the most recent years are down-trending and the business has not yet turned up, then those are the years that represent the most accurate and current trend.

As a note of importance, if the business being valued is on a multi-year down-trend and has not shown recorded signs of turning up, then this is a very difficult matter to deal with when valuing and selling a business. After or while determining the value, you will then need to concentrate on isolating contributing facts that have been responsible for such performance. By doing so, you will then be able to present these facts to a prospective buyer and you can look for a buyer that has the capabilities of turning the business around. For the business will most likely be of interest only to someone that understands the difficulties and believes they have what it takes to turn the business around.

Sometimes the most recent year or the current year is not representative of the historic trend and what you believe the future will be. In those cases, you may either eliminate the most recent year or take a look at what an average of the last several years looks like. No matter what the situation, you will want to arrive at a single gross-sales number that represents the business today. The business's future performance is many times indicated by, or will be a representation of, its past performance or that which is represented by a recent multi-year trend. If a business has been increasing by 10 or 15 percent each year, then it would be reasonable to predict the same in the future, provided there are no current or coming situations that will alter that prediction.

Once you have determined the single gross revenue figure that you want to use, you must look up what multiples are applied to annual sales of businesses like the one you are valuing. Look over the list in Exhibit 1.3. Try to find as close a match as possible to the type of business you are going to value. If you cannot, then look to see if the business is a member of a trade association and call on behalf of the business. If the business is not a member, just call the main or larger trade association of that type of business and see if someone knows of a multiple or range of multiples used in that industry. In the resource section at your local main library, you will find some directories that will be of help in locating trade associations. One to look for is the *National Trade and Professional Associations of the United States.* Try calling some local business-brokers, certified public accountants (CPAs), or other business-owners in the same type of business. It is good to compare several opinions and judge, in light of your knowledge of the business, which one is more reasonable. Keep in mind that this is only one method of valuation and you can apply all the methods explained in this book and then see which outcome is most representative of the business.

Some businesses on the list in Exhibit 1.3 only have one multiple or one percentage, not a range. When this is the case for the business that you are valuing and the attributes of the business are seen as negative or below normal, you should decrease the multiple or percentage that is given in Exhibit 1.3, or any other one that you have researched. Conversely, if the attributes of the business are very good, appreciably above average, then you should increase the multiple or percentage. The increases or decreases should be very slight, depending on the number of attributes that are above or below normal or average for that business type. Sometimes there is an accumulative affect, again either positive or negative. What I mean by accumulative affect is that a particular business may have more than one attribute that is very good or bad. If the business has several attributes that are very good, then the increase above the average may be more than very slight, but only in rare cases of extremely good attributes should the increase be more than very slight. The increases or decreases should be fractional. For example, if the single multiple for the business that is being valued is five times the monthly gross and the business has a very good attribute or an accumulation of very good attributes, then increase the multiple by .12 to .25. Some people increase the multiple by .25 for each positive attribute or decrease the multiple by the same increment.

When there is a range of multiples and you have to consider what multiple to use, the amount of incremental change depends on the size of the range from the lower end to the upper end. For example, if the range is from three to six times the monthly gross, then we are only dealing with four whole numbers, three, four, five, and six and two whole numbers between the extremes. If there are several attributes that are very good and the rest of the attributes of the business are normal, then you should be at the higher end of the range. Similarly, if there are several attributes viewed as negative, then the lower end should be used. In the example of the three to six range, 4.5 would be the normal or average multiple. That would be for a business that does not have any particularly negative attributes and does not have any particularly outstanding attributes either. The narrower the range, the more the movement should be fractional, perhaps no smaller than .25 to .5. In ranges that are wider, the change can be in halves to whole numbers. Most of the ranges are narrow.

In the event that the business you are valuing is valued by using percentages, then a similar methodology should be used. If the business has above average attributes, the changes should be in small increments. Similarly, if the business had negative attributes, the percentage should be decreased by small increments.

As a basic guideline for this method of valuation, if the business has a range from which you must choose, then follow the advice given above. If the business has only one multiple or one percentage, then only make increases or decreases conservatively.

When you find that the multiples are in a range, like the dry cleaners' 8 to 12 times monthly gross sales, then you can approach this by applying several of the multiples within the range to the annual gross-sales figure you have decided to use. This will show you a range of value. You may find yourself asking, but what multiple is really the best to use? There may well be certain intrinsic attributes of the business that should invariably put the business in the lower or higher end of the range. Some of the intrinsic attributes you need to consider are the various elements of the business, as mentioned previously. You should consider applying the information you know or can learn about the business in the following.

The main idea in choosing the multiple that best represents the business, in light of the attributes or shortcomings of that particular business, is to carefully consider all the different positive attributes and deficiencies, weighing each as a positive or a negative, then plot the business in light of all the elements within the range of multiples.

ATTRIBUTES THAT AFFECT THE CHOICE OF A MULTIPLE

The following considerations are provided as a guideline, not as attributes that exist without variance in quality. You will be able to draw from all that follows in this section and apply what is imparted here to your decisions and analysis when determining the value of the business by the other methods also. The analogies offered are drawn from the dry-cleaning industry and several other industries; they should serve the purposes of giving you good examples you can apply to most businesses.

The Unique or Above-Average Business

If the business to be valued has been in business for five years or more and consistently earns profits above a market-rate salary for the owner, and it is likely from all indications that it will continue doing so, then this is an obvious attribute that would contribute to pushing the business incrementally past the median toward the upper end of the range, making it a positive attribute. If the typical dry-cleaning business is a single-location retail operation and the business that is to be valued has been made more complex by offering untypical services or products, or has multiple locations, then this must be viewed as a negative. I know that this can be argued as a positive attribute, but there exist elements within businesses that can be seen from both points of view, and well they should be.

When the owner adds locations and offers more and diverse services or products, they create an abnormal, albeit good, business. The industry dictates the standards of normal or abnormal, not the owner, business-broker, or business-appraiser. In most business industries, there is a typical or standard model for what a business looks like and how it operates. If the business has lowered its standards or becomes below standard, then its value will drop in the marketplace. Conversely, if the business has exceeded the standard model, it can negatively affect the value. In other words, if the marketplace is most robust for typical dry cleaners, then a dry cleaner that has become untypical is much of the time harder to sell, even if it does earn more than the typical competing dry cleaner. The majority of buyers may not desire the added complexity, or typically have the ability to manage a multi-location business, or have the expertise to competently offer the added services or products that the current owner provides. Because a business-owner is more educated or gifted enough to create an untypical business in a particular industry does not necessarily mean that the business will be highly sought after by buyers.

There are some businesses, especially those that are very small, that will not typically find a buyer who even desires to own a more complex entity. Therefore, the dry cleaner, or other type of business that has become an untypical style is many times viewed in the marketplace as a more negative attribute. Keep in mind that we are speaking about the marketplace. The more that a business has untypical elements, the more it is a candidate for a much narrower market. To put it another way, it will appeal to only a few buyers instead of the larger segment of the marketplace. This usually requires drawing from a much larger pool of buyers than is typical for such a business. This also applies to business industries themselves. For example, a radio station is a unique enough business within its own town or city that prospective buyers will be sought from outside the area, perhaps from an area as large as the whole country.

I once worked on valuing and selling a sky-diving business that also offered glider rides and some other services and products. Because of the uniqueness, I did not find a buyer from the normal pool of local business-buyers and had to search nationwide for a qualified buyer. There were local buyers that could easily afford the business, so that was not the reason for the wide search. It was not typical for the marketplace and therefore dictated a much greater effort to sell. The uniqueness actually gave a slight negative to the value of the business. If you have a business that has plenty of excess earnings, yet you have a very difficult time locating a buyer, then some attribute of the business is negative as far as the marketplace is concerned.

Another example concerned a small chain of hair salons. The owner controlled six locations that were spread over a few parts of one city. The pool of buyers most knowledgeable about running that type of business and who had the desire to be an owner did not want, and in most cases could not purchase, six units. The buyers typically want a single location that they can manage themselves. It is one thing to start out with one location in a particular business and, as one's abilities and knowledge increases, slowly expand to multi-locations; it is clearly another to buy into a multi-unit operation at the start. In that case, the owner sold off each unit separately. By the way, it pays to investigate whether the business is worth more to the seller sold in individual units, or as a whole. Each situation is unique and should be so judged.

Reputation

In addition to the elements mentioned so far, you should consider if the business's reputation is tied to the business itself or is attributed to the owner or a key employee or two. The transferability of the business's reputation with its customers, in the community, and with its competitors and vendors is very important. If the good reputation is attached to a person or persons apart from the business as a whole, then the value will be negatively affected. For most businesses, there is not really a positive side to this aspect. If the reputation is on the business, then that is as it should be and is not viewed as a special positive attribute. That is, unless the typical business in that industry is based on the reputation being tied to a person and the reputation of this particular business is not. This enables the business to success-fully transfer the reputation along with the business, allowing the business to be sold into a larger marketplace. One caution, though. If the typical business in that industry is built on the reputation of the owner or other individuals employed there, then often buyers are uncomfortable with the unusualness of the business not structured in the typical fashion and will shy away. Although, I have always found success while selling a business or consulting on the sale of a business structured so that the reputation was on the business, as a whole, and not on the owner or a particular employee.

There are several types of businesses that can fall into this type of situation. Usually, the more personal the service involved, the more such concerns will need to be considered. A few examples will help make the idea completely clear. In a doctor's medical practice, we usually find more personal reputation involved, yet doctors sell their medical practices on a regular basis. How the transition between owners is handled and maintaining as much of the patient base as possible are very important. People need medical care; the need by the public is addressed not only by the personal reputation of the practitioner, but also by the fact that the medical office is open to the public, can be known about, and does not contribute to the ill health or death of those that visit there. Doctor's practices that have a lot of personal goodwill are sold to doctors who will establish their own reputation and there are doctor's practices that are owned by those who do not work in the business and are sold to others who will not work the business or to those who may.

Automotive-service businesses fall into this category, too. Many automotive-service businesses are built on the reputations of the owner or a particular mechanic. This can make the transfer of the good reputation more difficult. However, there are automotive service businesses that are built on the reputation of the business name and not on an individual. Wilhelm's Transmission Shop may not have had a Wilhelm involved in the business for the last 25 years. Those businesses that enjoy a reputation built on attributes of the business as a whole or based on product recognition are easier to sell and it's easier to maintain the reputation after the sale has taken place than those businesses with lots of personal goodwill. They are more common, too.

Location

Location is a factor that can contribute toward the business being placed higher in the range of multiples, too. Of course, each element that can have a positive effect can also cast the business toward the lower end if the attribute is viewed as negative. Keep in mind that some attributes may not be real positive factors, but are viewed as normal, as what should be expected of a business of that type. The results of a normal attribute on the choice of a multiple are of no effect, it is a neutral. If the normal attribute is absent, it should have a negative effect. Location is one of those attributes that can have a normal, positive, or negative effect on the choice of a multiple within a range.

Each business must have a location. There are some locations that are exceptional and really contribute to the business being much more successful than many of the competitors. Other factors get involved in the location, too. You can have a business in what is considered to be an outstanding location, yet the rent is high as a percentage of sales and renders the profit margins into a less than satisfactory range. Or, the location is leased and the term on the existing lease contract is short, thus making the stability of the location questionable. Perhaps the landlord will want to substantially raise the rent when the lease is due to be renegotiated. If that is the case, then the future rents will have a negative effect on the profits, driving them lower. Lower future profits are a negative, despite the wonderful location. Good locations are better than average if they contribute to greater profits and the location will remain extra-profitable for the foreseeable future.

There are various ways in which a location can affect a business's value, sometimes things are not as they seem at first glance. Many times such concerns affect retail-type businesses and restaurants, although it seems as though every business is subject to its location to a greater or lesser extent. Some location concerns involve distribution issues and accesses to highways, airports, railways, or waterways that provide public access to the business. Of course, the location's effect on profits is the real issue.

I had the opportunity to value and sell quite a few businesses in an area where there are many businesses of a wide variety that are located on prime retail-traffic streets in monetarily viable areas that surprisingly make little to no real profits. The rents were the culprit. On the outside, the businesses looked great, they have many patrons, and sell a lot of merchandise and services. Yet, examination of the profits causes one to wonder why the owners put themselves through the exercise of going to work each day. This type of situation is one reason that valuing a business solely by using a gross-sales multiple can be misleading. Rare are the buyers that will hand over tens of thousands or even hundreds of thousands of dollars for a business that has a good reputation, an outstanding location, and a very brisk business which racks up sizeable gross-sales figures, just to pay for all the employees and end up with little or no real profits.

Location is a factor that can contribute to putting the business on the higher end of the multiple range, but you must be careful to identify that the results of the location are in fact above normal. Perhaps the location is good or just average. If the rent is lower than market rate, thus creating greater profits, and it will continue as such in the future, then when applying this method of valuation, it will have a positive effect on the choice of multiple. When applying a different method that uses excess earnings or net profits as a major indicator of value, then the low rent will have no real effect on the choice of the multiplier or capitalization rate, as it is called in those methods.

An inferior location will generally be taken as a negative factor that can contribute to the choice of a multiple in the lower end of the range, or at least move the choice more to the middle if most other factors are positive. An inferior location cannot only affect lower sales, but can create the need to increase advertising expenses over what might be considered to be a more optimum amount to spend for that size of business, thus impacting the percentage of profit.

If the business is in an inferior location and the lease has a short time remaining, it may be wise to look into the cost of relocating the business. If moving is a possibility, then provided that any losses in revenue due to the move are negated as much as possible, the impact on the choice of a lower multiple may be mitigated.

To provide an example of how location can affect a business's success and its subsequent sale, the following is offered. A client who wanted me to assist in selling her business called me. I had helped her to purchase real property for her business site some five years earlier (she had been directly across the street). She had built her own building and continued to operate a very successful business. The business was one of the most profitable businesses of its kind in the whole city. The city had a population of over two million and competition was plentiful. The reason the business was so successful was directly related to the location. In fact, it had a very unique location, one of a kind. No competitor could ever have such a superior location without actually having this very site. Despite the obvious superiority of the location and the likewise obvious effect upon the profitability of the business, the location was viewed by prospective buyers to be in the wrong part of town. All the buyers who could afford such a business did not feel comfortable doing business in that part of the city. The owner had been running the business there for 16 years, she is a woman and only women worked in the business, usually no more than two women were on the site at a time. So here we were faced with a business that was very small, extremely easy to operate, had take-home earnings over $90,000 annually, the owner worked part-time, the location was the reason for the success, yet the location was the stumbling block to selling the business. The business was also priced extremely well. In fact, we lowered the price a few times to compensate for the reactions of the buyers. When compared with the price of other businesses making a similar amount of money, this business was a real bargain. This goes to show us how location can be a very important factor.

The Lease

Briefly mentioned within the discussion of location was an important element that requires further explanation, that being the lease and some of its provisions that affect the choice of a multiple, and thus the value of the business. Most small and very small businesses lease the property or space that they occupy, thus giving great weight to the lease's effect on the continuance of the business and its profits, or lack thereof.

There are a very wide variety of lease contracts. Within them, there are certain sections or clauses that have a direct influence on the value of the business. How much these particular clauses affect the business dictates what influence they should have toward choosing a multiple. The entire lease is a very important contract and all the stipulations are important to the lessee. I will point out those that should have the greatest impact on the value of the business.

As larger companies like real estate investment firms own more and more rental space, the more restrictive and more uniform the leases are getting. Those people in the business of leasing, selling, and managing commercial real estate are sharing more information and are becoming more involved in larger trade organizations than in the past, therefore access to more complex leases continues to grow.

The first issue is the term of the contract. How many years are left until the lease is over? In times past, many leases were longer in the length of years than is typically seen today. The average lease term seems to be from three to five years. There are the occasional leases of 10 years or more, but they are rarer today. When you are valuing a business, look up the number of years left on the lease. The number of years left can inform you of a few things, such as how long can you count on the business being in its present location, and how much time there is until the cash flow of the business will be affected by a likely increase. If the years left are few and a renewal is not likely, then the ability to sell the business at all can be a question. I have seen a short lease that, if renewed, the rent would go up substantially and actually render the business not saleable. The increase in rent would have rendered the profits so marginal that it was not worth staying in business. To move the business would have been very costly and as it was coupled with an unknown loss of business due to the move, the idea of moving was not considered too valid.

Some leases have a section that grants an option to renew the lease for a certain amount of time. This is very helpful, provided that the rent increase is not too much for the margins of the business to bear. Some options indicate that the rent will increase only the amount of previously agreed-to annual rent increases, or that the increase will be a factor of the cost of living or consumer price index. Those are more commonly seen in leases, but you must carefully read the option section. I have seen options which say that the rent will be adjusted upward at the commencement of the option, but the amount of increase will not be determined until then, and if both parties cannot come to a mutual agreement on the increase, then either the lease will end or some third party will set or arbitrate the amount. It is not good to have such an important issue unresolved. Such an issue can injure the sale of the business, or minimally lower the value. If the business's lease contains such an open-ended stipulation, it should be treated as a negative and cause the choice of a multiple to be toward the lower side of the mid-range, if you have a range to consider. Occasionally, I have seen leases that contained multiple option periods, such as three five-year options. If the stipulations within the lease stay the same and the annual rent increases are standard for the area and economy, then the lease can be viewed as a positive attribute. The amount of credit that it contributes to the increase in the multiple will be small, though. It is a positive selling point.

Look to see if the lease is assignable. In many leases, there is a section that addresses the issue of assignment. It is the absence of this clause that would be of concern. The absence would mean that the current lease is not transferable to a buyer of the business. This would be considered a negative attribute. The effect is the same as having the current term of the lease end when you sell the business. This puts the future of the business into an area of uncertainty. It means that the business may need to be moved or at best it puts the landlord into a very positive position as far as asking for an unscheduled rent increase. It can provide the landlord with the opportunity to eliminate some aspects of the lease that are viewed by the landlord as unfavorable to his or her position. The only way to alter the effect of the absence of such a clause is to speak to the landlord and ask what his or her position on assigning the lease to a buyer would be. Find out as many details as you can from the landlord on what they will want. Is it only a rent increase or does the landlord desire a different tenant? When you have found out what the landlord wants, you will be able to determine the impact on the choice of a multiple.

There are some leases that state that the lease may be assigned to some other party, but the other party must be equally qualified, financially, to the current tenant. This can pose an initial problem especially when you are still in the stage of determining the value of the business so you can sell it. The difficulty is that you do not know anything about what the potential buyer's financial abilities will be. Perhaps the current business-owner is very qualified financially, or is a corporation that has a very strong balance sheet. When looking for buyers, we certainly plan on them being financially qualified to purchase the business. However, that does not mean that they will be as qualified as the current tenant.

I have seen this type of difficulty more in leases at large malls. I have had clients who owned chains of stores and desired to sell off selected locations. Since they were very well qualified and represented good security for the landlord, the prospect of an individual buying the store and qualifying for the lease assignment was less than assuring. The point is that such a stipulation limited the market for the business. Of course, the landlord does not share the concern of the sale of your business. Just the presence of such a clause affects the business-owner's ability to freely sell the business to whoever is able to pay an acceptable price on acceptable terms. Therefore, such a clause is more of a negative. It is not necessarily a big negative, but depending on the circumstances, such a clause can negatively affect the price of a business.

The solution to such a stumbling block is to speak to the landlord or property manager and inquire about the clause. See how strictly they adhere to it. Some landlords or property managers have had bad experiences with tenants and desire to stick to the clause strictly and some will indicate a degree of flexibility and may be willing to work with you. The point to discuss is the qualification of a potential buyer being equal to or stronger than the current tenant. In many cases of lease assignments, the out-going party remains secondarily liable for the payment of rents, and the like. If you or the current tenant will remain on the lease after the sale of the business is complete, then I would try and leverage that fact, since it is similar to the landlord having a co-guarantor. Sometimes the landlord knows that by law, depending on your state laws, the out-going tenant must remain on the lease in a secondary position. They may see your offer to remain on the lease as an advantage they already have. If the lease has a clause stating that the assignee must be equal in financial capability to the current lessee and there is no flexibility, then the lease will create a negative effect on the choice of multiple.

Management

Management in the business is an important area to consider. If all the essential expertise is in the person of the owner, this can very well affect the value, thus the multiple. In many small businesses, the owner applies general business skills. That is, if there is such a thing. I believe that small-business–owners are some of the most multitalented people around. By general business skills, I meant that the owners are not applying themselves in the business as the

24

head design engineer, head auto mechanic, or even the top salesperson. When the owner is the general manager of the business, it is easier to locate a buyer with skills in managing. There are obvious differences between running a restaurant and running a manufacturing company. Depending on the knowledge specific to any particular industry, trading general management personnel (the owner) is easier than when that same person is educated in a more specific field of expertise. This can be seen very clearly in the printing business. Most printing businesses are small. Some of the owners operate as pressmen or perform pre-press operations and exhibit skills in art and design. There are printers where the owner is the general manager. They may do some of the selling or at least sales management. The printing business that has an owner who performs general management or sales management will find it much easier to locate a buyer for the business than the one in which the owner runs the printing press or is the best artist in the shop. When it is easier to find a buyer that can trade places with the out-going owner, it is possible to get more for the business, and thus increase the multiple used.

In fact, this is especially noticeable in a business industry where many of the owners are involved in a particular skill in the business and the one you are valuing does not. If the business has employees who do the various skilled positions, the business can be seen as having an advantage when it comes to selling. A buyer who might not have considered buying such a business can consider such a venture, thus expanding the buyer market.

Longevity

Another element that can affect the choice of multiple is how long the business has been in existence: the longer, the better. This attribute coincides many times with the length of time for which a business can show its financial viability, although not always. If the business has been around for one to four years and is not selling because success is nearly impossible there, then depending on the reasons for the sale, the short length of time may be less of a factor. A business that has been in existence for 10 years or more, even with up- and down-trends in their financial history, shows the business can withstand the competitive pressures. Thus, the business is looked on with a sense of less risk. Of course, there are always many factors in play at all times that affect a business's viability.

Some businesses may be seen as trendy, and since they have only been around for a short time, their life expectancy is uncertain to potential buyers. If the business you are going to value has been in existence for a short time, under five years, then this factor should be viewed as a slight negative. Only if the future of the business can be demonstrated as being secure should this not be considered as a slight negative. By looking at an extensive historic track record, we can be more confident in the future of the business. We must keep in mind all the attributes mentioned in this book to truly get the complete picture of future viability.

Competition

Another factor to look at is from the outside of the business. That is, whether there are new competitors coming into the area who will pose a threat to the future of the business. Businesses change constantly. There are many industries that have been changed by the idea of "mega." The hardware business used to be made up of small businesses, many mom and pop businesses. Today, the huge do-it-yourself home and garden centers have taken center stage. In some cities, the small hardware stores do not exist anymore. There is a trend to go "mega" in the pet-store industry. This will probably affect some of the smaller pet stores in the areas where the big stores locate. If the business you are valuing is one of those that may be affected by the changes in competition such as in the examples previously mentioned, it will have a negative impact on the multiple you choose. Sometimes the threat of a giant competitor is not the only threat from competition that can affect the choice of multiple.

If a local chain, franchise, or other independent competitor is opening in a location in your market area, this should be judged as a factor that will affect the choice of a multiple toward the lower end of the scale. At least, it should impact the choice by a slight margin, depending on the perceived effects of the competitor.

Some businesses represent certain brand-name products. This is usually on the wholesale distribution or retail level. If the business you are going to value represents certain brand-name products, the basis of the representation should be examined. In some cases, the representation is exclusive for a given territory. If this is the case, then the stipulations in the agreement are of special interest. The overall evaluation of the relationship will determine what effect it will have on the choice of multiple. If the relationship is in writing, it is better. It is very good if the representative contract is assignable. In some cases, the contract may be between the manufacturer and the corporation doing business as the distributor or retail-sales location, and not the owner personally. That can be good, too. The overall business relationship between the two is most important. Is the business being valued fulfilling the expectations of the manufacturer? Can the contract be transferred to a new owner? If the contract can be transferred, will the quotas or discounts change? Is there territory protection, or will the manufacturer allow just about anyone to represent the company in the area? You must get the answers to these questions. The effect on the choice of multiple depends on the answers.

In some cases, there is a seemingly exclusive representation relationship, but nothing is in writing. I had this happen when I was working with a small representative of the Coleman Camping Equipment Company. The relationship had been in existence for years and no one else in the area had such a relationship. In fact the area was huge, covering the better half of a large, populous state. We looked into getting the relationship in writing, but the manufacturer did not want to do so. The distributor had been doing a good job and Coleman verified this. It appeared that as long as sales of Coleman equipment and supplies keep going at an acceptable pace, there would remain a good relationship. For a buyer who does not have the long-term relationship experience the current owner has, it can be an uncertain future. Of course, now we can also see how important a business is with a long history and established relationships. A quite new business would be looked at with greater uncertainty than one that had been representing a particular manufacturer for 10, 15, or more years. In the case of the distributor mentioned, the lack of a written contract did negatively impact the value of the business. Fortunately, the company had been around for quite some time.

A similar thing can occur with a gas station where the owner owns the land and facilities, and contracts with a major brand oil company. In these cases, the station-owner is under a certain type of supply contract with the oil company for exclusive representation and he or she must buy all the station's fuel from the major brand supplier. In turn, the oil company provides signage and in some cases, the overall look of the station. The contractual relationship must be looked into. The choice of a multiple depends on the particulars in the contract. The questions are similar to those set forth previously. How long is the contract, is it assignable, do the quota or discounts change when transferred, what is the history on renewal, what trends exist in the supplier's business? To help get an idea of what the standards are in your area, to better judge the elements of the contract, speak to the oil company and see what other contract conditions exist for other stations. Seek someone in the same town with a similar situation and compare the contract stipulations. If there is a trade association, call them and seek some comparative information. When you have a good idea as to the quality of the elements of the contract, you will be in better shape to judge it. Of course, if the contract has obvious flaws it will negatively impact the choice of multiple.

You should apply the same type of investigation and considerations any time the business has contractual relations with others, be they suppliers, buyers, or perhaps a sales organization.

I worked with a company that had a sister company which did all the sales. The companies were under different ownership and the sales organization did not sell exclusively the other's products. In other

28

words, it sold other companies' products as well. What made this particularly interesting was that the sales organization was the only avenue that the other company had for getting its products sold. Obviously, the relationship between them was vital for the manufacturer. It did affect the choice of the multiple used when an appraisal took place.

Equipment

It is important to consider the equipment in the business. Depending on the type of business you may be valuing or selling, the importance of equipment differs. Service-type businesses generally have less equipment, but not always. For example, a real estate sales office uses basic office equipment such as telephones, photocopy machines, computers, faxes, and office furniture. Some pure sales organizations may use slightly less equipment than that. There are service businesses that depend on a larger quantity and variety of equipment such as a direct-mail company. Service businesses such as these employ the use of various types of machines that fold paper, sort or collate paper, drill holes in paper, and staple paper, and so on, in addition to their office equipment and furniture. Even a small deli or sandwich shop has equipment that is important to the smooth operation and must be considered. If you are selling a deli and the meat slicer does not work, the toasters do not work, or perhaps the steam table, then the value could be negatively affected.

Most business-brokers are specialists in sales and negotiations, most business-appraisers specialize in valuing the intangibles of the business. In both cases, very few have any depth of knowledge or expertise in equipment. I say this only to reassure you that you, like those mentioned, can obtain an understanding of the condition of the equipment in the business you are valuing or selling. Our purpose is to be aware that looking over the equipment for condition and functionality is very important. The greater the business's dependence on equipment and the greater the investment in the equipment, the more this is true.

Not only is condition and functionality important, but quantity matters, too. Does the business have the equipment it should have to do a competitive job? We must keep in mind here that we are presently discussing a valuation method that is broad in scope and therefore, we are not concerned with the valuing of individual pieces of equipment. There are other valuation methods that take a detailed approach to each of the components involved in the valuation of a total business. That does not negate the importance of what is said here.

Look over all the equipment the business uses. Ask about the age, find out if the equipment was purchased as pre-owned or new. Find out about the typical life of the equipment and compare the information. Check out the condition of the equipment by turning it on or asking to have it operated. It is good to see the equipment in regular use. Ask the operators of the equipment, they usually have a good knowledge or sense of its condition. Also be aware if the business lacks a piece of equipment they should have. If you feel the need, ask to speak to the person responsible for the maintenance of the equipment. You may need to seek someone to come out and give all or some of the equipment a look-over. In some small businesses, there may not be any regular maintenance scheduled, or any equipment maintenance company under contract. Make a list of all the equipment that will be valued and sold. Get an idea of the quality and condition as previously mentioned and then add your conclusions to all the other information you have to help you make a decision about the proper multiple to use.

With the previous discussion about the attributes that need to be considered when making a decision about which multiple to be used, you should be able to make a wiser choice.

CAPITALIZATION OF NET EARNINGS METHOD OF VALUATION

Some accountants, business-brokers, and other individuals use a method called *price/earnings ratio, capitalization of net earnings,* or SDCF (**S**eller's **D**iscretionary **C**ash **F**low). Those are basically three names for the same method, depending on the complexity one wants to pursue. This method is used widely. One of the major drawbacks of this method is that it does not take into account the amount of fixed assets in the business (fixtures and equipment), their condition, or generally any individual characteristics of the business. It is almost a one-size-fits-most kind of approach to value. I say that because if the market research says that a particular business type, say a delicatessen, has an average capitalization rate or multiple of two, and we apply that multiple to your business and to the same business across town and to the same business in the next town, we are saying that they all are the same. Of course, the profits are usually different, thus we get varying sale prices. The truth of the matter is that each business is different and has attributes, positive and negative, that should affect the multiple used and thus the resultant value. A modified method would take into consideration the various attributes or characteristics of each business to which this method is applied. The outcome of considering not only the market-derived information leading to the choice of a multiple, but also the particulars about the business, allows a more realistic multiple to be used. At least the multiple would then have some correlation to the specific business other than just being in a particular industry that has a certain multiple attached to it, or at least a narrow range. This method is more useful for businesses that have total net earnings—including the owner's wages—that roughly equal what it would cost to hire a manager, and therefore be a business with an absentee owner.

In other words, the business makes enough profits to say that the owner has a job and nothing more. Technically, there are no real profits or returns on or of the investment in the business above a wage for the labor of the owner. The business pays its overhead expenses and some wages for the owner's time, plus some perquisites. There are many businesses that fall into this category. To apply this method to all businesses is absurd, although many people try. If you are selling an ice-cream shop and its annual net profit—including owner's wages—is between $25,000 and $45,000, and the owner is working 50 to 60 hours or more per week, then this method will apply. Technically speaking, there is little to no goodwill value based on a net profit. The owner is selling a job. Do not misunderstand, there is a market for such businesses. In select cases, a business of this kind can grow into a business with much greater profits. Some by their nature will not get much bigger, for example, a mailbox and small office-supplies business, or an ice-cream shop. Expansion through multiple locations is something other than increasing the revenues, gross and net, of a particular business.

There are many people who would rather pay for a job (buy a small business) and control their own businesses and daily routines than work for someone. In addition, there are many people who for various reasons would find it difficult to get a job earning $25,000 to $45,000 or more.

This method of valuation, price/earnings ratio, capitalization of net earnings, or SDCF, usually employs a multiplying factor which is applied to the annual net profit before an expense for the owner's labor has been deducted; the multiplier used is best determined by the marketplace. When applying the modified formula, the information derived from the marketplace should be added to your consideration of the particulars about the specific business. Not all businesses in a particular industry are the same. They all have strengths, weaknesses, and attributes that are specific to each one, and should be judged accordingly. In the information that is available from the marketplace, the usual multiplier is 1.5 to 2 times the annual net profit (depending on the industry). The full range of multiples are from one to five, including fractions. The lower the multiple, the riskier the business. Examples of businesses that would typically be in the lower range would be an auto-repair shop, a beauty salon, a personal service business, or a wholesale-distribution business. Some of the factors that will help to put a business in the higher range are as follows: a business that has been established and profitable over a long time, a business that is easier to transfer ownership (requires investment and management ability, not a highly trained skill), and a business that has some sort of competitive edge. There are many, many examples that can be made with higher multiples. Some general types of businesses would be a well-established manufacturing business or businesses that have earnings over $100,000, and a well-known hamburger franchise. Some studies of sales of small businesses that I have seen put the average adjusted net profit multiplier at two; that is the average across the nation and over many years, for all types of businesses. Do keep in mind that just because a certain business has market-derived information that points to a multiple of say, 1.75, does not mean that the business you are valuing must use that same multiple. There are many factors, as stated before, that are particular to each business. These things should not be overlooked when applying this method. Adjust the multiple accordingly.

Multiplying the seller's discretionary cash flow, also known as the adjusted net profit, determines the value for the entire business (all fixtures, furniture, equipment, supplies, and goodwill). The SDCF is the earnings of the business after all business expenses except depreciation, amortization, one-time unusual expenses, owner's salary or draw, personal expenses that the owner has running through the business (also known as perquisites), and any income taxes have been deducted. For this valuation method, you would add to the value, so derived, the salable inventory which would then give you the total value. I have included information in the bibliography at the end of this guidebook about where to obtain the only public information currently available on comparable sales. This study gives individual multipliers for specific businesses and average multipliers for classes of businesses. One difficulty I had is that I could never understand why, when applying this method, a business that requires a lot of machinery as opposed to a pure service business would sell for approximately the same amount. As an example: a business has $85,000 in fixtures and equipment and net earnings (including the owner's salary) of $55,000, compared to a service business with $20,000 in office furniture and computers with a net earnings of $55,000 (including the owner's salary). The asking price would be the same when applying the SDCF or business-broker method. Nevertheless, this method is used extensively.

For those who have businesses that fall into this category and want to apply this valuation method, please read the section in this chapter called Determining the Adjusted Net Profit. The adjusted net profit will include any wages or salary attributed to one working owner. When you are determining the net profit for your business, if you have a partner or spouse working in the business, be sure to leave in or add in a market-rate salary for them. Many times in very small businesses, the owner's wife is doing all the accounting work—without pay. This creates a false profit picture. In that case, you should increase the expenses by the cost of a bookkeeper/accountant. When you have finished figuring out the adjusted net profit, apply an appropriate multiplier to the adjusted net and you will then have your value. Offer the business for the value determined, plus the inventory. Be sure to adjust the inventory value for obsolete or nonsalable merchandise. If you have accounts receivable, you can include them in addition to the value. Some people sell both accounts receivable and accounts payable, offsetting the accounts receivable by the accounts payable. Some people choose to pay off all the accounts payable and liabilities and collect the accounts receivable—post closing of the transaction. There will be much more about structuring the sale in Chapter Four.

When considering the multiple to use, read over the information titled Attributes that Affect the Choice of a Multiple, presented in the previous section about the gross-sales method of valuation. Keep in mind that by varying your decisions about the multiplier or capitalization rate, including small fractional changes, you can develop different values, thus a higher and lower range or value.

The following is an example of this valuation method, applied to a printing shop. The first case is of a small printing shop. They produce small to medium two-color printing, copying, graphic design, and typesetting services for businesses or individuals. The major product lines are manuals, bookbinding, custom three-ring binders, letterheads, envelopes, business cards, brochures, flyers, and newsletters. The business has been established for 10 years, and its focus is on commercial accounts that make up 60 percent of the company's gross revenues. The business is located in 2,500 square feet of rented commercial/industrial space. The lease is assignable and the rent is fixed at $1,600 per month for three years. There is an option to extend the lease for an additional five years. If the option is exercised, the rent will increase to $2,000 per month with an annual cost of living increase that will be no greater than 6 percent in any one year.

The business employs eight people, plus the owner. The owner is the general manager and occasionally makes sales calls on the largest customers, or large potential customers. One of the employees is the production manager. The employees have been with the company for no less than three years and everyone is planning to stay, at the present time. The business owns all the equipment except one 5390 Xerox duplicator that is leased for $2,110 per month. All the furniture, fixtures, and equipment are in good operating condition and have a total market value of approximately $95,000. At this time, there are no competitors known to be moving into the market area of the business.

The inventory runs about $7,000. The annual gross sales were approximately $592,000. The most recent year produced a seller's discretionary cash flow of $103,000. Based on the type and quantity of the foregoing information and not much more, many small businesses are valued and sold. I think the information is insufficient for a good analysis of a business's value. Nevertheless, many businesses are listed by brokerages and sold with little more.

The research data on market-derived multiples for printing shops showed that other printing shops with similar SDCF, ranging from $100,000 to $114,000, sold within a range of multiples of .8 to 3.2 times the SDCF. The average multiple of those printing shops in that range is 2.28. The gross sales of these print shops ranged from $235,000 to $840,000. The printing shop that is the subject of the valuation is within the ranges of SDCF and gross sales. In the market information, there were many more printing shops that were not as close in SDCF or gross sales. The full range of multiples went from a low of .8 to a high of 5.6 times the SDCF and the overall average multiple is 2.2 times the SDCF with the median multiple being 2.0. So the question is, what multiple should be applied to the printing shop we want to value? If we simply take the average multiple of 2.28 times the SDCF of our print shop, we may not be providing a fair and reasonable value.

On closer examination of the market-derived information of actual sales of small businesses, there are two that are quite close in comparability in SDCF to the printing shop we want to value. One has a SDCF of $106,000 and the other has a SDCF of $100,000. Our shop's SDCF is $103,000. Having two comparable businesses is not an abundance of information, surely not enough to form conclusive market studies. In the full range of market information that was researched, there are a total of 30 printing shops. I found five that were fairly comparable, with two being quite close. I used the five closest to come up with the average of 2.28 as an SDCF multiple. The average of the two closest comparable businesses was 2.95. The question remains, what multiple should be used to apply to our printing shop?

We can go one of two ways. We can use the information I have provided about the printing shop and apply one of the several choices of multiples to the SDCF of our printing shop. Or we can gather more information and research about our printing shop and then adjust the best choice of multiple, based on the total information we have studied about our printing shop.

The latter approach should be done. Instead of just looking at the last year's SDCF, we should consider the last five years of SDCF and see what kind of a trend shows up. Additionally, we need to consider all the attributes of the business. We do this because each business is unique and has its own positives and negatives. If we apply the average SDCF multiple from our larger findings, 2.2, to our printing shop's SDCF of $103,000, we may actually be over- or under-valuing the business. Our justification for doing so would only be the strength that a comparable study containing 30 businesses would give us. As I mentioned in the opening paragraph of this valuation method, it would then be a one-size-fits-most method. I do not deny that taking the easy way out will produce a value and that the business can be marketed for that value and may well sell, too. What I do believe is that we should consider all the information we can gather about the business and adjust the multiple upward or downward according to our considerations of the research about that specific business. The multiple that we start with is also important. The market data of comparable businesses sold gets us into the ballpark of multiples for that type of business.

After looking over five years of financial information about the printing shop we can now see that the five-year SDCF trend is down. The following figures in Exhibit 1.2 are historic. In 1991, the business' SDCF was $105,000; in 1992, the SDCF was $150,000; in 1993, it was 135,000; in 1994, the SDCF was $114,000; and in our most recent year, 1995, it was $103,000. So we now have some important questions to ask regarding the future viability of the business. As you can see, if we just took the last year and applied a multiple that did not take further investigation results into consideration, we could very easily have used too high a multiple.

We need to ask such questions as why is the business's annual SDCF shrinking? Are the gross revenues shrinking too, or is it more a matter of increased costs and thus smaller margins and smaller net profits? Is the problem from within the business or is it an effect of changes in market conditions or overall economic conditions in the region? The answers to questions such as these are very important

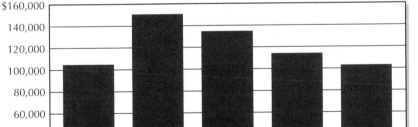

FIVE-YEAR SDCF CHART

Exhibit 1.2 SDCF

when we consider what multiple we should choose. It is best to always look at and consider all the information and attributes of the business when choosing a multiple to apply. Certainly, if the answers show us that the cause or causes for the four-year down-trend are incurable, the resultant value will be much different than if we see that the trend is breaking and all indications are that the business should begin to trend upward.

It is a good idea to compare the profitability of this business to other businesses in the same industry. Getting this kind of information is not always easy. You can contact the trade associations for any particular industry and ask if they have some industry standards or norms. If 12 to 15 percent is the usual profit percentage and this business is achieving profits greater or lesser than the industry's average, we want to know why. Depending on the degree of variance, it is a good idea to look at the cost of labor and the cost of goods sold to see if they are in line historically and in line with industry averages.

For our didactic purposes, we shall say that the printing shop is now showing signs of a break in the downward-trend. This is not depicted in the chart shown above because we only have seven months of the current year. If the performance of the business as depicted in the current year-to-date information continues through the balance of the year, it will be a much better year. After investigating the reasons for the four-year down-trend we have discovered both internal and external causes. The external causes were due to the growing recession causing poor regional economic conditions, as well as downsizing in companies doing U.S. government work (due to cutbacks) who are customers of this printing shop. A few large customers were getting fewer government contracts. Internally, the causes were due to the owner taking an eighteen-month sabbatical, thus the follow-up and overall supervision was lacking. Additionally, in late 1994, the top salesperson left to pursue other goals.

The business began turning around when the owner refocused his attention on growth and hired new and additional sales staff. The owner also personally made sales calls on all the largest customers. New copy equipment was leased that enabled the business to compete for business it did not try for or had subcontracted out. After four years, the economy was beginning to turn up, too. All this change was accompanied by a change in location resulting in a substantial savings in rent while obtaining a larger space. The changes were working and the gross revenues and profits were climbing each month.

With the preceding information now known, we must choose a multiple that will be applied to the SDCF. Even though the business seems as though it is turning around, seven months of better sales and profits do not make for a totally reliable long-term picture. What we do have going for us is that the business has been in existence for 10 years and it appears to have weathered the present storm.

Going back to the multiples from the market-derived comparable information we recall that the multiples gotten from a study of the larger pool of businesses (the 30 printing shops) were 2.2, as average. The smaller number of more comparable businesses had an average of 2.9. The full range of possible multiples is .8 to 5.6. Considering all the attributes of the business in the present time and the idea that the business has been on a four-year down-trend, with seven months of increase, we would not necessarily want to be in the higher end of the range. The average of 2.9 may be a little high since the turn-around time is less than a year or more. The business is fully staffed and its equipment is in good condition. The business did show a $103,000 SDCF last year. The business was never in the red. You should take the time to carefully consider all the information and weigh everything carefully before making a final decision. After much deliberation, I determined that the most representative multiple was 2.3.

The next thing to be done is to apply that to the SDCF. We should use the $103,000 from the year-end 1995. To see what effect the turn-around in performance has on the value, we can create a fiscal statement ending July 31 from the actual SDCF. In this way, we do not have to create a pro forma and make projections on the future performance, we can take actual performance and use that in the valuation. Using the $103,000, we come up with a value of $237,000, plus the inventory of $7,000, for a total value of $242,000.

To create a fiscal year ending July 31, we must take the monthly financial statements from August 1, 1995, to July 31, 1996, and combine the information. We must determine the SDCF by adjusting the fiscal statement's net profit to include the depreciation, amortization (if any), the owner's salary and any personal expenses of the owner, any one-time unusual expenses, and income taxes. You can use the form provided in Exhibit 1.5 for the purpose of figuring the SDCF (also known as the adjusted net profit). In this case, the result is a SDCF of $124,000. The resultant value when applying the very same multiple is $285,000, plus the inventory, for a total value of $292,000. In the case of a business such as the one in our example, I would probably go to market at the higher number. In fact, I would suggest marketing it at $300,000, including the inventory. This allows for some negotiating room.

There are many factors that should influence your decision as to what multiple you choose. Keep in mind that the present value is the result of expected future earnings, which should be based on actual historic performance. There are times when projections must be made, but I would avoid that if possible.

This method of valuation is usually applied to the most recent year's SDCF as opposed to creating a fiscal year. You should consider creating a fiscal year at times such as described in the previous example, or when you want to have the valuation as of a certain date. Even if your business's financial year is already a fiscal year instead of a calendar year, you can create an artificial fiscal year. Since the purpose for valuing the business in this book is to put the business on the market, there will be far less need to create a fiscal year than if you just wanted to get an idea of the business's value at a particular point in time.

As you can see, this method of valuation can be applied to many types of businesses, and so it is. This method is used most often for businesses that have a SDCF of less than $100,000 per year. As previously mentioned, it is applied to businesses where the buyer is, for all practical purposes, buying a job. The SDCF represents the total package of compensation available to one owner. How they decide to expense it is up to the owner and his or her tax advisors.

If the business has two owners, we must make some adjustments before we multiply the SDCF. For those businesses that have two owners, we do not include the compensation for both in the SDCF. You should make sure that the SDCF is the earnings net of all business expenses, which include the market-rate compensation for one of the owners in a two-owner business. The same thing goes for any employees that are not on the payroll. This usually means a wife or other family members, but can be a partnership. The business must be charged a market-rate compensation for each person supplying labor, except one owner. In the excess earnings method, we deduct everyone's compensation while in the SDCF method we do not.

When applying this method, be sure to add back any debt service that is paid by the business, prior to using the multiplier. This usually is expensed as interest payments. You want to value the business as if it owned nothing. Do this even if there are debts that will be assumed by a buyer. The business is providing the capital to pay the debt and we want the value of the business to also reflect its ability to pay such debt. Some people teach that the rent on equipment should be added back, too. I do not agree with this, unless the rental was temporary. It would be similar to adding back the cost of the electricity. If it is a regular monthly cost, it should not be added back. Leased equipment that will be paid off and owned outright should be added back, but not leased equipment that will remain on lease and will be replaced by newer equipment according to the lease.

If your valuation process determines a multiple that is higher than the average for your industry, keep in mind this important thing: if you have done the research and have come up with what you feel is a soundly reasoned multiple, thus value, do not allow buyers or their representatives to try to sell you on the idea that "a business such as you have sells for only two times the net profit." I have heard arguments such as that so many times. That is why I mention it. You just need to ask if they have compared your business to the businesses they are referring to. Get specific. Your knowledge and research allows you to do that. Usually, they do not have any specific business in mind. They are just going off of what they have been told is average, or have seen in one of the studies that I mention in this guide-book. They have not done their homework. You should be prepared to ask questions such as: Does *the business* (this is being specific) you are referring to have a lease as good as mine? Does the business you are referring to have the excellent location that my business does? Does the business you are referring to have a profit margin as good as what we are getting, which none of our competitors do? Does the business you are referring to have the long history of sustained prof-its that mine does or the growth rate that mine does? You need to pin them down. Quite soon, it will be evident that they know little about your business and even less about those that made up the statistics leading to the industry average multiple of two.

All this discussion leads me to tell you that the weakness in all the current studies of comparable sales of small businesses is that there is a great lack of information about the businesses that were used in the studies. Only the most basic information is gathered and in some cases all that is known is the asking price, the sale price, the gross sales, and the net profit (and there are many definitions of that). We know nothing of all the various elements that combine in each business to create those few statistics that are gathered. Additionally, a business-broker or sales agent in the vast majority sold the businesses that get into the studies. In some studies, there are none sold through attor-neys or sold by owners directly. In all those cases, a commission was paid and the broker or sales agent set the asking price. Strangely, very few were ever appraised or studied at any depth. A very large per-centage of small and mid-sized businesses are sold through owners or representatives outside the real estate industry.

By applying this valuation method, you will be using one of the business-broker's main methods for valuing a small business. Unfor-tunately, many business-brokers or sales agents do not go into the depth that this guidebook goes into, and this is not a technical man-ual; it is for the lay person. The facts that make up such a critical com-ment are changing. The business-brokerage industry is working to improve the education and competence of those in the industry. Armed with the information contained in this guidebook, you will be able to judge the education level (in good business-brokerage practices and valuation) and competence of any sales agent or business-brokers that you meet.

WHAT TO DO IF THERE ARE LITTLE TO NO EARNINGS

If a business has little to no real net earnings, then when it is sold it will most likely be a fixed asset sale (just the value of the furniture, fixtures, and equipment) or liquidation sale. There will not be any goodwill or intangible value paid. When the business cannot be sold as a going concern due to a lack of profit, then an orderly liquidation or forced liquidation sale will mostly likely be the result.

An orderly liquidation sale is where you sell off the assets, getting as much as you can for the assets in used condition. This would be done in an orderly fashion over enough time to receive the highest price you can for the assets. The cost of selling the assets is deducted from the total proceeds received to arrive at the net value of all the assets.

Forced liquidation is where the assets must be sold as quickly as possible. There would not be time to locate a buyer willing to pay top dollar. The assets must just be sold for what can be gotten in a short time. This is going to end up resulting in the lowest overall value, both for individual assets and for the total of all the proceeds received for all the assets sold.

Even though a business may have no profits, this does not always mean that a liquidation sale must take place. For example, I once talked to a man who owned a small deli. He worked in the business part-time; his wife and children worked in the business too. The wife and children were not compensated for their labor. The total money that the family withdrew from the business—including all wages for the owner and family—was $20,000 to 25,000. This business's goodwill had no real economic value on the open market. In fact, the business may not be salable, but it did not have to be sold. The difference between this example and a business that has an SDCF of $38,000 is quite a bit. This deli had several family members working for the $20,000 to 25,000, including the owner. When the earnings were divided among the family members who worked in the business and the hours they worked were calculated, they were earning at or below minimum wage.

Whether a failing business or one that has very low profits is salable is somewhat determined on whether the business can be turned around or expanded. If you can demonstrate to a buyer that the business's failure or very low profitability is due to mismanagement or real lack of capital, then a buyer may be interested. If the location is good and the market for the products or services is adequate, then a buyer may be able to see that they can make a real go of it. The buyer's risk factor will be very high, in so much as they are taking over a business that has been in business and yet is not generating true profits. The business usually sells for much less than the owner has invested in it, or the cost to recreate it to its current state.

If you have serious doubts whether your business is salable, you can always give a sale a try. I would not try to list the business for sale. Brokers may not want to handle it as their buyers are looking for a viable business that minimally earns enough to support them and their families. If a broker does want to list the business, he will probably not work too hard on it. There are some brokerages that have a quota of businesses that each broker must list per month, regardless if they sell or not. The surefire way to determine if the business can be sold is to offer it for sale. Follow my instructions in this guidebook and run some ads as I suggest in Chapter Three. If there is a buyer out there, you will find them. The buyers in the market will give you feedback and their questions will indicate their concerns. If you show the business to several prospective buyers and they all feel that the business cannot be turned around, it is time to consider selling off the equipment and getting out that way. I would suggest giving the market a good try, though. Advertise the business and try hard to sell it for as long as you can. One or two ads or a couple meetings with buyers will not accurately tell you if you will succeed in selling. Before giving up, because there is a lease involved and your liability extends to the end of the lease, it may be better to try to find a buyer who feels he or she has the ability to turn it around and sell the business to that buyer for what you would piecemeal out the equipment, provided they assume the lease.

EXCESS EARNINGS METHOD OF VALUATION

A very popular valuation method among business appraisers, and I think a more accurate method of determining the value of a small business, is the *excess earnings method,* also known as the *investment method.* This method is valid for any business larger than those that fall into the category described in the preceding valuation methods. The SDCF method previously mentioned can be applied to any business as a sort of check against other methods. In the excess earnings method, we take into consideration all the pertinent factors and assets in the business that contribute to the business's success. The mathematical process is fairly simple. It is the depth of research and attention to detail that make this method more or less accurate. One of the major strengths of the excess earnings method is that it uses and considers actual performance of the business and considers the various assets individually, not combined as in the SDCF method.

There is another valuation method commonly used. It is known as the *discounted future earnings method.* To apply this method, it is required to project the gross income, expenses, and net profit for three to five years. A pro forma profit and loss statement must be created for each year, plus a final "terminal" year. This is a more complex method allowing for greater mistakes. Professional appraisers must use extreme caution and diligence when using this method. The main weakness is in predicting the future. I only mention this because you may have heard about such valuation methods. This method is good to apply to a business that expects tremendous future growth—such as has not been seen in any historical years, or to a business that has very radically fluctuating performance, year to year. If you are interested in this method, look up the books I have cited in the bibliography at the end of this guidebook.

All businesses have the same basic components. Whether it is General Motors or your business, the same basic components make up the business. They are the tangible assets including: the personnel, the inventory, accounts receivable, furniture, fixtures, and equipment, and the intangible assets which include goodwill. General Motors just has a larger quantity of these assets than your business. They may also have patents, real estate, and intellectual property which your business does not have, but many of the same classes of assets exist in all businesses. I have found through experience that when I apply this method of valuation, it is the most accurate. That is, of course, if one is objective and approaches the information and considerations honestly. I have had many businesses sell within pre-calculated ranges from the appraised value. By doing the research that this method requires, you get to understand the business better and from a different angle than you may ever have before. Therefore, when it comes to preparing your marketing materials, you will be able to do a spectacular job.

A brief overview of the method will aid in understanding the method and its components before we proceed into the detailed instruction of how to actually perform this method of valuation. You will be determining a realistic picture of the monetary benefits of your business by adjusting your financial statements to reflect a non-personalized and normal operating scene. This is similar to what is done in the SDCF method with the exception that returns of and on the investment in the various assets are deducted before the true net income is shown, and the proper labor for the owner is not left in the net income. In order to do this, you will need to consider the value of your labor. In many small businesses, owners do not take a salary, they just take what is left over each month, or if the business is very lucrative, they only take what they need and they try to figure out creative ways of expensing the rest to themselves. If the business is a corporation, there are double taxes to be paid. Taxes are paid on the salary that the owner or corporate officer(s) take and on any profits that the corporation shows.

When making these normalizations to your expenses, you may actually need to increase the payroll because you have family members working who are not being paid directly through the business, or who are not being paid market rates. For businesses that can afford it, I usually see family members being paid over market rates. You will then take a look at the different types of assets that the business has, basically they are tangible and intangible assets. They generally consist of inventories and furniture, fixtures, and equipment. You should determine the market value in-place for these assets. There are more details regarding these assets in the detailed instructions. You will then determine the value of the intangible assets, or the goodwill. If there are other assets such as intellectual properties, those will be considered, too. When you have completed all the aforementioned work, it will be time to do the final math and see the resultant value.

There are complexities that can be added to the processes involved, but this guidebook tries to present a less complicated, yet no less effective and accurate approach than a professional may use. Our purpose here is not to teach a course in appraisal to professional appraisers, but to instruct small-business–owners and men and women from other professional fields in what they need to successfully sell a business while getting the best price for it they can. In some cases, the salesperson hired to sell the business is more interested in just getting the business sold than in selling it for a good value. Questioned about it, they will not admit it, but succeeding in selling the business is more important than their concern for getting you what the business is really worth. The rationale is that pricing a business is so subjective that just getting it sold validates the pricing of the business; of course, no sale—no commission.

Selling businesses for a living is a very difficult and trying career. As a business-owner, you only go through the process once or a few times, not as a living. When a sales agent lists a business for sale, they are very happy if it closes, no matter what the price. Most brokerages have a minimum fee. If every business sold that the sales agent or brokerage listed, things might be different. The business-brokerage industry says on average that only 2 out of every 10 businesses sell.

With odds like that, it is not difficult to understand why the focus is on selling the business at practically any cost as opposed to being so concerned that the sales agent gets the best possible price for the seller. This is mentioned to inform you of the realities so you are wiser when you venture into the world of selling a business.

DETERMINING THE ADJUSTED NET PROFIT

Most small businesses are operated to create benefits for the owner, as a by-product of producing products, or of offering services for others. Those benefits are realized in a variety of ways. The greater the amount of future benefits that the business will produce, the greater the value of the business. Of course, the amount of assets that the business has are part of the total value, too. In valuing your business, we want to make sure that we value the full amount of benefits that the business produces. To do this, we must adjust the net profit as reported on your financial statements so it reflects all the monetary benefits that the business generates.

To help you be more organized in the evaluation of your business and in the creation of your marketing information, there is a checklist provided in Exhibit 1.4. This checklist has been very helpful in the collection of all the information that is necessary to the sale of a business. To determine the true profitability of your business, you will need to look carefully over your financial information and make some adjustments. Of the financial items on the checklist in Exhibit 1.4, you will need either of the following:

- The last year-end financial statement or tax return
- Three to five years of year-end financial statements or tax returns
- A 12-month statement (fiscal year statement) for the last 12 months you have been in business

To create a 12-month statement (fiscal year statement) that ends on the last date you want the value to include, you must use the monthly financial statements from the current year, ending the month closest to the date of value. Next, add that to those monthly statements, the months from the previous year that will make a last 12-months statement. For example, if you want the value to be as of April 30, 1997, use the monthly financial statements from January 1, 1997, to April 30, 1997, and add to those figures the monthly financial information from May 1, 1996, through December 31, 1996. This will create a statement of the last 12 months ending April 30, 1997.

It is possible that the most recent year was not as good as the business historically performs. You may want to use the year that best represents your business, as long as the year you choose is indicative of the true current status. In other words, last year may not have been too good, but it was a one-year slip, not a trend. To value your business of say, 10 or more years, on the basis of last year, which was poor, would not do justice to the quality of business that you have established. If your business is on a multi-year downward-trend and it has not turned up, then I would not pick one of the years when things were good as representative of your current business. If you decide to look at multiple years, then you may determine that a three- or five-year average annual adjusted net profit is the best representative of your business, for valuation purposes. I would not suggest using a one-time unusually high-profit year to determine the true value of the business, especially if the next year will not produce the same results.

Look over the financial statement(s) and make a list (an adjustment worksheet is provided in Exhibit 1.5) of any expenses the business had that were one-time costs, such as a purchase for equipment or repairs that were nonrecurring. An example of a nonrecurrent expense might be if your business moved and the business had added expenses related to the move, plus doubling of some overhead expenses that occurred during the time of transition. Another example would be if the air-conditioning system went out and you had to replace the system. That would be an unusual one-time expense and should be adjusted to create a more normal picture of the overhead. Another example of one-time unusual expenses might be if the hot water pipes broke and the costs of the natural gas and water went up due to the break. You would want to identify this added expense and adjust the financial statement's net income to reflect them in profits as opposed to expenses.

Look for items such as contributions, donations, or dues and subscriptions that were not really necessary or typical ongoing expenses. Also look for any and all perquisites that you expensed in any category. Some examples of an owner's perquisites are personal auto insurance, life insurance, your medical coverage, your car expenses, such as fuel or repairs (include any for your spouse or family), personal travel and meals, excess telephone expenses, credit card expenses charged to the business that were personal, purchases from stores such as Costco or Sam's Club that were really personal.

In addition, look for and put on the list any interest expenses, depreciation, and amortization costs. For those not too familiar with amortization expenses, it is an expense recognized by the Internal Revenue Service (IRS) that is for such things as goodwill, the cost of a noncompete agreement, copyright or patent, or other such type of contract, intangible, or intellectual property that has definable value. The cost of the intangible or intellectual property is spread out over a period of time that is recognized by the IRS. The expense shows up on the profit and loss statement but is a noncash expense. A non-cash expense is an IRS-recognized expense not accompanied by a monthly disbursement of funds.

Also, include any rental or lease payments (not the property rent or lease payment). These would be for any equipment you may have rented for a short time because you had a special need. It could be for payments on equipment leases that were recently paid off or any payments on equipment that will be paid off either before or during the sale of your business. In some businesses, renting or leasing equipment is a permanent cost of the business. If that is the case, do not put the expense on the adjustment sheet. An example of a more permanent lease or rental situation is a restaurant that perpetually leases their dishwashing equipment, or a printing business that always leases photocopiers; they just lease a newer model when the lease is up.

Include any payroll expenses for yourself. Do not forget the payroll taxes associated with the owner's compensation and income taxes. Add back any debt payments, even if a new owner will assume the loans. If the business has income from interest or from some non-operating entity, such as the sale of a piece of equipment, then exclude that from the statement. The idea is to normalize the statement.

When you have identified all the types of adjustments and their amounts, total them up and add that total to the net profit that is shown on the profit and loss statement. Exhibit 1.6 is an example of how the adjustments look when using the worksheet provided in Exhibit 1.5. The new total is your adjusted net profit. At this point, this is also known as the SDCF, as discussed in the previous valuation method. You should do this for each of the last three to five years. Look at the trend of adjusted net income over these years to see where it is going. This information will be useful later in your analysis and presentation of your business.

DETERMINING THE LABOR COMPONENT AT MARKET VALUE

If you have a partner, spouse, or other family members working in the business, you should determine what it would cost you to replace them with nonrelated employees. In those cases where owners have spouses and family members working in the business, if they are being paid at market rates (what it would cost you to replace them with nonrelated employees), no adjustment would be necessary. However, if you are under-paying or over-paying them, you will need to make any adjustments needed on the adjusted form in an effort to bring the pay rate to market standards. The adjustment to be put on the list may be an increase in the payroll expense or a decrease. On occasion, an owner has staff or employees (family or not) on the payroll who are excessive and are not needed in the business. If this is the case, make note of the excess payroll. If the reverse is true, you may want to note down any extra payroll that there should be.

The next step is to objectively determine what it would cost in today's market to hire a replacement for yourself as owner-operator, and for any partners you have. One of the most notorious understated or overstated expenses in a small business is the value of the owner's services to the business. In some cases, such as those where the owner is also a salesperson, you might need to determine what it would cost to hire two people; one full-time manager and a part-time or full-time salesperson. Include whatever it takes to figure out a realistic replacement cost for the working owner(s).

For one business I worked on, the two owners were not only the general managers, they both divided secretarial duties, bookkeeping duties, and they spent quite a large amount of time performing the skilled tasks that many of their employees and subcontractors did to service the clients. A market-value salary rate, or hourly wage for each task was determined, then that information was applied to the amount of time each partner spent doing the various tasks. In this way, we came up with what it would realistically cost to replace each owner. It was only through this exercise that the owners realized whether they were really making some profits from the business. Without such research, it is difficult sometimes to really know what the score is. I know that in many small businesses, the owner is almost irreplaceable, or at least with reasonable cost, but this is exactly why this is done. This is the method of valuation that determines if there are excess earnings or not.

Research and write down all of the items and their related expenses that you can find, as mentioned in the preceding paragraphs and in all the information in the section about Determining the Adjusted Net Profit. Once you have done that for the year(s) you are using for your study, we can determine the adjusted net profit. You can use the worksheet provided in Exhibit 1.5 for your calculations. By following the form, you will arrive at your adjusted net profit—pre-tax.

When done, you will have determined the totality of the normalized net earnings or cash flow available to an owner of this business. It does not matter what you have shown for tax purposes. Almost all closely held corporations and sole proprietorships try to decrease their taxable net profit by increasing expenses and are more or less "living through their business." That is one of the benefits of owning your own business.

DETERMINING THE VALUE OF THE CURRENT ASSETS

Just as you reconstructed the picture of the performance of your business through the profit and loss statements, you will also need to make adjustments to the balance sheet. Many times, the closely held corporation will not sell the balance sheet per se. They select certain assets to be sold. Much of the time, only a very select few of the liabilities are transferred. The balance sheet is comprised of two major areas. The two areas are *current assets*, which is comprised of the cash, accounts receivable, notes receivable, and the inventory. The other area is *fixed assets*, comprised of the building and property if it is owned by the corporation, the furniture, fixtures, equipment, vehicles, and other similar assets. There is also the category called *other assets*, which usually contains such things as goodwill, non-compete covenants, copyrights, and so on. Just as the balance sheet contains assets, it also contains a record of the liabilities. These are generally listed under two categories called *current liabilities* and *long-term liabilities*.

In the sale of many small businesses, the cash in the bank is usually not included in the price, nor is it sold, although it can be. The accounts receivable are included in about half of the small business transactions. Sometimes the determinant is whether the amount is large, and whether you will sell the business free and clear of all liabilities or include the liabilities in the sale. Many times, all the liabilities are paid off during or through the escrow proceedings (closing proceedings), and the accounts receivable due are collected and passed on to the seller over the 30 to 60 days following the close of escrow or consummation of the transaction. If you decide to include the accounts receivable in the value and thus the sale of the business, then you will want to adjust the amount of accounts receivable for any doubtful accounts.

The inventory is usually valued at cost, less any obsolete, old, or nonsalable inventory. In many businesses, this is at least 10 percent of the inventory on hand. The asking price of a business is usually stated as the value, plus the inventory and accounts receivable (if you are including the accounts receivable). This is done because of the fluctuation from moment to moment in these two assets. Notes receivable, if there are any, are generally collected. If this is not possible, some people take them with them. Such notes may be due from employee advances and therefore must be settled in some fashion, perhaps the amount can be offset by another element in the sale.

If you are selling your corporation, then you will most likely be selling everything, all assets and liabilities. In some cases when selling the corporation, you may decide to select certain assets that would not be sold with the business; you can also select certain liabilities to pay off or not transfer to the buyer. The asking price will be the total value of the assets, not the amount of equity. When someone sells a home, the home-owner does not offer the home for sale at the equity value, he or she asks the value of the total asset. The liability assumed, or to be newly established, is a part of the financing that is carried out during the sale process.

If you have any miscellaneous assets, or other assets such as lease deposits, they are included in the total value. If any assets in these categories are not transferable or important to the ongoing business, do not include them. An example would be a vehicle, boat, a company motor home, or equipment that you want to take. A liability that most times is not sold with the business is a loan to corporate officers. Check with an accountant or your tax preparer for their advice on these matters. Exhibit 1.7 is an example of the foregoing assets as they appear on the balance sheet. The example is divided into "actual" and "adjusted," the actual column is what you might see from your accountant and the adjusted is what it looks like in preparation for the valuation and sale. What is not included here is the value of the business's goodwill, also known as the intangible asset.

DETERMINING THE FIXED ASSET VALUE

The next step is to determine the fair market value in-place of all of your fixtures, furniture, and equipment. This can be very difficult and time-consuming, but it need not be too hard, especially since your goal is to market and sell the business, not produce a comprehensive professional appraisal report to be used in court where there may be a need to defend each decision and value in the appraisal. The accuracy of the whole valuation is determined by the degree of detail you apply to each step. If you want the fixed asset value to be quite close to the actual market value in-place (it may be right on), then estimate closely and objectively. For even more accuracy, you will need to confirm the values through various sources such as used-equipment dealers, equipment appraisers, auctions, newspapers, catalogs, and manufacturers. For most purposes, the close and thoughtful estimate is adequate. I would suggest that you give each asset careful consideration. I would not spend much time trying to determine the market value in-place of your three-hole paper punch, but I would research the current market value of all the larger equipment and furniture. I would be accurate as possible about the value of the four-drawer file cabinets and the photocopy machine, as well as the display cases, and the like. I would not be concerned with the plastic trashcans, brooms, and so on.

The procedure involves making a list of all the furniture, fixtures, and equipment. There is a sample list shown in Exhibit 1.8. Later, you will need the same compiled list to sell your business, only I would not put the values of the items on the list that I provide to a buyer. If the values are left for the buyer to see, then in some cases this gives the buyer a reason to go item by item and negotiate the price they will pay. We do not want to do this because they are buying the business as a whole, not piecemeal. Some people set up the list into sections such as "office equipment and furniture," "shop equipment," or they divide the list into the rooms or departments of the business. To see an example of a list, look at the list provided in the sample marketing package in Chapter Two.

Once you have the list or while you compile the list, you should assign a value to each item. (For those who do not want to go through all this, I will explain later a bulk method you can use.) One very helpful thing to do is to use your depreciation schedule to locate the original costs of items. It is generally easier to begin with listing the price you paid for the item. You then have a starting place. The value you want to reach is either what it would cost you to replace the item with one in similar condition and age (not new), or to estimate the fair market value in-place. The fair market value in-place is the value of the item as it is, in-place, in the business as part of the cohesive group of tangible assets assembled and contributing to the production of excess earnings. The value is typically less than what it cost new, unless the item has appreciated. The value is greater than what you would get by selling it at a garage sale or out of the classified ads. For example, the cost of your desk may have been $500; if you sold it piecemeal then you might get about $150 to $200 for it. But, in-place as part of your whole business, the value is a little higher, say $300 to $350. Be careful you do not increase the items too much. Of course, the value you use has a lot to do with the condition. If the item is really old and in poor condition, then it may only be worth what you could get for it at a garage sale. Items like telephone systems lose quite a lot of their value after installation (if you were to rip it out and try to sell it). Selling the system in-place does help retain the value. Put a value next to each item on your list and make a grand total. Compare this total to the value of the fixed assets shown on the balance sheet. The balance sheet shows the original cost of only the items you declared for depreciation, and are still being depreciated, then subtracts the depreciation and gives you a remainder called the book value. That is the value of the fixed assets for tax purposes.

In most cases, there are a lot of assets that are not included in that value. I am sure that many items you have bought have been expensed and therefore are not included in the value shown on the balance sheet. Nonetheless, the assets exist in the business and should be sold as part of the whole business. Walk around to each office and each section of the business. If there are some assets around that are not worth fixing or are going to be sold with the business, do not include them in the value. This would be seen more in a business that is incorporated. Some corporations have cars, boats, snowmobiles, and the like, on the books. I would not include the non-operating assets unless you are sure that you want to sell them with the corporation.

For a quick and dirty bulk method, just use the total original cost of everything and subtract (depending on age and condition) 10 to 30 percent of the total cost. This will give you a value for the fixed assets of the business. Even this very quick and dirty method does require starting from the original cost, which means that you will need to gather that information about everything in the business. Depending on the amount of assets in the business, this is one of the more tedious tasks involved in the valuation process.

For those of you who bought your business, there is a good possibility your accountant or someone else made a decision about how much the value of these assets were for tax purposes. That means that if you use your depreciation schedule as a beginning point for the cost of the equipment, there may be no basis in reality for that number. As an example of this, I was working on a business and was told that the owner had bought the business five years earlier. The accountant had allocated the purchase price and the amount allocated for the furniture, fixtures, and equipment was $15,000. This number was chosen because the buyer (now the seller) did not want to pay too much tax on the value of the equipment when he bought the business. You see, buyers had to pay 7.75 percent tax on the total value of all the equipment bought in the business. Therefore, I would see all sorts of low values for the fixed assets of the business. It was advantageous when he had to pay the tax but when it comes to selling, the owner–seller would like to be paid the true value of all the furniture, fixtures, and equipment. That the owner paid tax on $15,000 worth of equipment does not mean that he paid less than the market value of the equipment when he bought the business. He actually spent about $35,000 for the equipment, furniture, and fixtures. He just paid tax on $15,000 of it. When that is done, the value of $15,000 or whatever the allocated value, is where your depreciation begins.

Therefore, if you bought your business and do not have an individualized list of all the furniture, fixtures, and equipment with realistic costs to start from, you need to do one of two things. You can either skip the idea of starting to figure out the current market value in-place from the original cost, and just determine or find out what the current market value in-place of each piece is. Or, research the original costs and then determine the current market value in-place by age and condition of the item at present, and then subtract the appropriate amount of wear and tear. The process would look like this: we have a piece of equipment that cost $7,500 brand-new. This piece of equipment is five years old. It has been maintained well and has a life expectancy of 20 or more years. The IRS allows you to depreciate this particular piece of equipment over 10 years. According to the accounting procedures, the equipment has a present book value of $3,750. But, in the world of real economic life, not tax-based life, the piece of equipment may be worth $5,625 or more. Some equipment actually appreciates. If that piece of equipment cost $7,500 new five years ago, maybe that same piece of equipment costs $9,125 today. If so, then used in-place it may be worth more than the $5,625. In fact, it is installed and is working quite smoothly in the business. When it comes to the fixed assets of the business (the furniture, fixtures, and equipment) it can pay to get a good, accurate understanding of the value.

DETERMINING THE INTANGIBLE VALUE OR GOODWILL

The second major component contributing to the overall value is the intangible asset or goodwill. Goodwill is generally considered to exist as a result of reputation, longevity of the customer base, length of time in business, technology or other factor of superiority employed over the competitors, profitability, proprietary processes, and other attributes that may have an economic value. Since most all businesses have some element of goodwill, the pertinent issue is whether the goodwill of a particular business has economic value.

The existence of intangible asset value (goodwill) can be upheld in either of two ways. From the perspective of the marketplace, goodwill exists if the business entity can be sold for an amount in excess of its net tangible asset value. Alternatively, goodwill has economic value if it produces income above and beyond the income produced and associated with other factors employed in the business such as capital and labor.

You are now ready to begin applying the figures you arrived at in all the previously described categories. I have provided an excess earnings worksheet in Exhibit 1.9. Begin with the business's adjusted net profit. Subtract from the adjusted net profit a rate of return on the total fair market value in-place of the fixed assets (the furniture, fixtures, and equipment). It works like this: let's say the total fair market value in-place of all your fixed assets is $100,000. In today's market, what would you expect to receive as a reasonable return on your investment into the total fixed assets? The range of rates of return can depend on the type of assets included in the business. For example, if you have a lot of computers or other electronic equipment that go down in value rapidly, you might want a quicker return on your capital, say 25 to 30 percent. Desks and other items that hold their value longer would rate a return of 10 percent. If you are using the total for all classes of fixed assets combined instead of breaking the assets into various category types, then you might use 15 to 18 percent as an overall rate. Therefore, you would subtract 15 percent of the $100,000 or $15,000 from the adjusted net profit.

A more technical process is to determine a rate of return *on* the value of the fixed assets and a return *of* the investment into the fixed assets, then subtract those from the adjusted net profit. The return *on* is the rate you would want to receive for investing in equipment as opposed to keeping your money in the bank or other investment vehicle, and therefore the rate fluctuates with the market and the times. The return *of* is the amount of money you should put away each year so you can replace the asset when it has worn out. In other words, the business should be able to replace each fixed asset. For example, some furniture or equipment may have a real life of 10 to 20 years, therefore you divide the cost of the item by 10 or 20 and that gives you the amount you would need to set aside to replace the assets. Keep in mind that costs do go up for some types of assets. Not everything goes down like consumer electronics equipment.

Once you have subtracted the return on the fixed assets from the adjusted net profit, you are now ready to subtract the value of labor for yourself or what you would have to pay to hire someone to replace you. The remainder, if any, is the excess earnings of the business and is a basis for determining the value of the business's goodwill or intangible asset value.

To determine the intangible value, take the excess earnings and capitalize them. This is done by choosing a capitalization rate and dividing the excess earnings by the rate, usually shown as a percentage. A capitalization rate converts earnings into value. Some appraisers and business-brokers refer to the capitalization rate as a risk factor. Capitalization rates are typically determined by the marketplace. They are the rates of return on the investment in intangibles that buyers in the marketplace are willing to accept, in relation to the risk of return.

The full range of rates is typically between 20 and 100 percent. I have personally not seen a small business sell with a 20 percent capitalization rate, and I may have seen one or two exceptional situations where 25 percent was used. Sometimes the intangible assets of a business are only worth a return of 150 percent (a high-risk business). A tighter range found across the entire country is from about 40 to 67 percent. This is on pre-tax excess earnings. If you are using after-tax earnings, the rates will be lower than those stated. Sometimes plotting a return on a line may be easier for some people, as in Exhibit 1.1.

There are many theories on how to determine what the capitalization rate should be. For our purposes, keep in mind the range in Exhibit 1.1, especially the narrower range. You can seek market information from the source I have cited in the bibliography at the end of this guidebook. The study cited gives average multiples for different types of businesses. You will need to consider if your business fits the average range, or adjust the multiples to reflect the attributes both negative and positive of your business.

When deciding where to plot the capitalization rate, consider the following: the greater the risk of getting your invested money back, the greater the return. A business that has been in business for only one year or so, sells trendy items, and has an owner who does all the sales and management would tend to be placed at 100 percent return or even higher. Businesses that require special trade skills such as beauty salons and auto repair shops tend to be in the range of 67 to 100 percent. Much of the clientele may follow the practitioner if they move down the street or even to the other side of town, leaving the business with a potentially low or nonexistent profit picture. A retail business with a very short lease and strong potential for a new higher rent factor, or relocation, will tend to warrant a higher risk factor. Of course, if the business is one that is not dependent on its location then the risk involved in a move is negligible. Moves are costly, so a business that must be moved can have its value decreased.

If a business has a long track record of growing revenues and profits, the employees are stable, the owner is easily replaced without losing customers, the lease is of sufficient length and is at or below market rates, the bookkeeping is in good order, the products or services are well accepted, there are no known detrimental major competitor changes occurring now or in the near future, no changes in local, state, or federal laws that will be detrimental to the business or its profits, then the capitalization rate will be in the lower ranges, more likely 29 to 45 percent. Determining a capitalization rate is clearly where a more subjective judgment is made. Just consider as many factors, or attributes, about the business as possible and then decide where on the scale you would place the business.

Manufacturing businesses will be found to be near 33 to 38 percent, wholesale/distribution businesses are in the range of 53 to 67 percent, food services are found to be around 48 percent with retail businesses closer to the wholesale businesses at 53 to 67 percent, and service businesses averaging about 50 percent return on intangible value. It is important that you judge the business individually. Each business has unique characteristics that must be considered when choosing a capitalization rate. Businesses that are on the larger side of small businesses, say, $3 million to $15 million in revenues, tend revenues toward the lower end of the scale.

Once you have decided on a capitalization rate, divide the excess earnings by that percentage. This will give you the intangible value of the business. Next, add to the goodwill value (or intangible value) the value of the fixed assets and any current assets that you will be selling. The total will give you the value of the business. Exhibit 1.10 shows the process in a mathematical form. If you want to know the value of a corporation including all its assets, then total all the current assets with the value of the fixed assets, any other assets, and the intangible assets, less any liabilities. Historically, goodwill has been a nondepreciated or non-amortizable asset. This was due to IRS codes. As a result of this, most businesses, when sold, reported low amounts of goodwill and carried low amounts of goodwill on their balance sheets. Now goodwill can be written off and I suspect that we will see an increase in the amounts value-allocated to goodwill. I mention this because I have heard buyers try and negotiate the price of a business down by saying that businesses, especially the particular type they are looking at, do not historically have very much goodwill. I heard it enough times, and it was being said about businesses that were valued quite well, that I suspected that either it was a total ploy on the buyers' part or they had heard from an accountant that most businesses do not show much goodwill, or at least this particular type did not. The inability to write off goodwill definitely kept the amount of goodwill that was officially reported to minimums. This did not by any means indicate that goodwill was not a major portion of the purchase price, or that it was figured in different ways than showed in this guidebook. It was only for tax reporting.

PROVIDING NEGOTIATION ROOM IN THE ASKING PRICE

When it comes to publishing or orally telling a potential buyer what you want for the business, you should add some negotiating room to the final value figure. If you add too much, then you risk turning off the potential buyers. If buyers feel a business is over-priced, many times they will not inquire further than the asking price and the adjusted net. I have seen many buyers who do not have a clue as to what the real value was in a business pass on a very good opportunity because they were applying some rule of thumb that an uninformed business-broker or accountant had told them. So it is a good idea to find out why they felt the price was too high, if in fact they did. If they were misinformed about how to understand the value of a business such as yours, it could create a sale where there would have not been one.

The following will give you an idea of the negotiating room found in various industries. Manufacturing businesses have seen as much as 15 percent, wholesale/distribution 23 percent, food businesses about 17 percent, retail comes in around 18 percent, and service businesses have had up to 13 percent negotiating room. If your business is valued objectively, you will not need to build in as much room as reported above; perhaps 8 to 10 percent is all that you will need. The proceeding information was for broad types of industries, some specific types of businesses and the average differences from their asking prices to the actual sale prices are as follows: printing businesses 8 to 10 percent, travel agencies 17 percent, gas stations 24 percent, convenience stores 18 percent, dry cleaners 11 percent, beauty salons 17 percent, liquor stores 13 percent, auto repair 8 percent, videotape rental 20 percent, janitorial services 12 percent, and delis 10 to 20 percent. As a point of reference, the businesses that contributed to the preceding information were not formally valued and most were valued via some sort of rule of thumb or business-broker method, thus the larger ranges of fluctuation from asking price to actual sale price. Businesses with profits above $100,000, or those that have been valued professionally or have been valued by a method more than a rule of thumb, typically end up with a negotiation range of approximately 10 percent. A very important element to remember is that many small businesses that are sold are not presented very well at all. By applying the information as set forth in this guidebook, you will be able to properly present your business and therefore get what the business is worth. Additionally, you will be able to price it more correctly, thus the negotiation range will be more narrow, around 8 to 10 percent.

When you are marketing your business, keep notes about what the buyers are saying about the offering. You can and should, if there is sufficient evidence, make adjustments to the asking price. Do not be too anxious to make changes, though. It is better to indicate to the buyer that you are a reasonable person and will look at any serious offer they would like to make. Do not accept verbal offers. Too many important points can be left out. I will speak about this in more detail in the chapters on marketing the business (Chapter Three) and negotiating the sale (Chapter Four).

EXHIBIT 1.3 VALUES AS A PERCENTAGE OF GROSS SALES AND MULTIPLES

Type of Business	Pricing Based on a Percent of Gross Sales	Pricing Based on Gross Sales
Food Services	39%	
Manufacturing	52%	5 × Monthly Gross plus Inventory
Retail Businesses	33%	
Service Businesses	61%	4 to 4½ × Monthly Gross + FF&E and Inventory
Wholesale Distribution	38%	
Accounting Practices	100% (a range would be 90% to 150%)	
Advertising Agency	75%	
Answering Service—Full Service 24 hr.	90% to 125%	13 to 16 × Current Monthly Billings (Range is 2 to 4 × Monthly Gross)
Auto Parts—Retail		4 to 6 × Monthly Gross plus Inventory
Auto Repair	34%	2 to 5 × Monthly Gross plus Inventory
Bakeries	69%	4 × Monthly Gross plus Inventory (Range is 2 to 5 ×)
Beauty Salons	43%	4 × Monthly Gross plus Inventory (Range is 2 to 5 ×)
Beer Tavern		6 × Monthly Gross plus Inventory
Bicycle Shop		2 to 4 × Monthly Gross plus Inventory
Bookkeeping	50%	4 × Monthly Gross plus Inventory
Car Wash—Full Service w/gas	40% to 100%	10 × Monthly Gross plus Inventory
Cocktail Lounges	50%	4 × Monthly Gross plus Inventory and Current Value of Liquor License (range 2 to 7 ×)
Coffee Shop		4 × Monthly Gross plus Inventory
Coin Operated Laundries	63%	7 to 10 × Monthly Gross plus Inventory, Less Depreciation on Equipment

Exhibit 1.3 Values as a Percentage of Gross Sales and Gross-Sales Multiples

Type of Business	Pricing Based on a Percent of Gross Sales	Pricing Based on Gross Sales
Computer Service	57%	
Convenience Stores	31%	3 to 6 × Monthly Gross plus Inventory
Delicatessens located in Office Bldg. or Office Complex	58%	6 × Monthly Gross plus Inventory (Range is 3 to 6 ×)
Delicatessens (located in strip malls or other retail type locations)	39%	4 × Monthly Gross plus Inventory (Full Range is 3 to 6 ×)
Donut Shops	85%	8 × Monthly Gross plus Inventory
Dry Cleaners	87%	8 to 12 × Monthly Gross plus Value on Tickets of Finished Goods
Employment Agency	50%	2 to 4.5 × Monthly Gross
Fast Food—Hamburgers	69%	6 × Monthly Gross plus Inventory
Fast Food—Pizza	32%	3 to 7 × Monthly Gross plus Inventory
Florist	25% plus FF&E	4 × Monthly Gross plus Inventory (Range is 3 to 5 ×)
Food Products Distributor	55%	
Frozen Yogurt Shops	32%	4 to 6 × Monthly Gross
Gas Stations	18%	3 × Monthly Gross plus Inventory
Gift Shop		4 × Monthly Gross plus Inventory
Hobby Shop		4 × Monthly Gross plus Inventory
Ice Cream Shop		5 × Monthly Gross plus Inventory (Range is 4 to 6 ×)
Industrial Supply Distributor	28%	
Insurance Agencies		125% to 200% of Gross Commissions
Janitorial Services	61%	4 × Monthly Gross plus FF&E
Janitorial Supplies Distributor	40%	

Exhibit 1.3 *(Continued)*

EXHIBIT 1.3 VALUES AS A PERCENTAGE OF GROSS SALES AND MULTIPLES

Type of Business	Pricing Based on a Percent of Gross Sales	Pricing Based on Gross Sales
Landscape Maintenance	41%	
Linen Supply		25 × Weekly Gross
Liquor Stores	37%	5 × Monthly Gross plus Inventory (Range is 4 to 7 ×, includes License)
Lock & Key Shop		4 × Monthly Gross plus Inventory (Range is 3 to 5 ×)
Lube & Tune-Up Shops	50%	
Mail Box & Shipping	44%	
Medical Equipment Distributor	48%	
Office Supplies		4 × Monthly Gross plus Inventory (Range is 3 to 5 ×)
One Hour Photo Business	60%	
Parking Lot Sweeping	68%	4 × Monthly Gross plus FF&E
Photo Studio	52%	3 × Monthly Gross plus Inventory
Plastics Manufacturing	45%	
Pool Service		4 × Monthly Gross plus FF&E
Pest Control	100%	
Printing Businesses	62%	4 to 6 × Monthly Gross plus Inventory
Publishing	71%	
Restaurant w/Cocktails	32%	4 × Monthly Gross plus Inventory and Current Value of Liquor License (Range is 2 to 5 ×)
Restaurant—Family	29%	4 × Monthly Gross plus Inventory (Range is 2 to 5 ×)
Restaurant—Full Service	33%	2 to 5 × Monthly Gross plus Inventory
Retail Pet Store w/o Grooming	36% plus FF&E and Inventory	3 × Monthly Gross plus Inventory

Exhibit 1.3 (Continued)

Type of Business	Pricing Based on a Percent of Gross Sales	Pricing Based on Gross Sales
Retail Pet Store w/Grooming	50% plus FF&E and Inventory	4 × Monthly Gross plus Inventory
Retail—Bicycles	22%	
Retail—Florist	40%	
Retail—Women's Clothes	23%	
Travel Agencies	10%	Range is 5 to 15%
Uniform Rental		35 × Weekly Gross
Video Tape Rentals	63%	

Exhibit 1.3 *(Continued)*

EXHIBIT 1.4 CHECKLIST FOR BUSINESS INFORMATION NEEDED

Business Information Needed

You will need all or most of the following information so you can value your business and create a presentation package.

Need   Have

Need	Have	
_____	_____	*Year End* financial statements and/or Business Tax Returns for up to the last 5 years.
_____	_____	*Year to Date* financial statement.
_____	_____	Most recent Balance Sheet.
_____	_____	List of all furniture, fixtures, machinery, equipment, and company vehicles (if any), with name and model. You can use a depreciation schedule to help. Add any assets that have been fully depreciated and may have fallen off the records. If any items are on a lease and the buyer should take over the lease, then make a separate list or create a sub-section to your main list. Include the lease information: original date of lease, total dollar amount of the lease, payment amount, interest rate, payoff date or number of months the lease is for.
_____	_____	Any leases or rental agreements (premises or equipment). You will need to record the particulars of these leases in the presentation package.
_____	_____	Leasehold improvements—if significant—complete list with name and age.
_____	_____	Brochures or other printed materials about the business (ads, coupons, flyers, etc.).
_____	_____	Information about the inventory and quantity (raw materials, work in progress, finished goods). What percent of inventory is not salable or obsolete?
_____	_____	Account list and accounts receivable aging report. You can write a brief mention about the condition of the accounts receivable in your Business Summary Section of the presentation package.
_____	_____	Information about employee benefits, if any. Use this information in the Employee paragraph in the presentation package.
_____	_____	Copies of patents, special licenses, permits, and contracts that are assumable or required. If your business has any of these, be sure to mention the particulars in the Business Summary Section of the presentation package.

Exhibit 1.4 Checklist for Business Information Needed

Need   Have

___	___	Number of employees: designate position held, wages/salaries, and if full- or part-time.
___	___	Hours of operation and explain how work shifts/business hours are manned.
___	___	List working family members, designate position held, compensation, and schedule.
___	___	Explain owners/partners duties or responsibilities, hours, compensation, and benefits.
___	___	Prepare a history of the business.
___	___	Prepare a description of the business operation (describe the flow of the products/services).
___	___	Prepare an outline of the future for your business. You may mention needed improvements, discuss any future trends you see, and include any outside factors which do or will effect the business.
___	___	Marketing: describe what you do and have done.
___	___	List your competitors and mention something about the nature of the competition in your industry.
___	___	List any Trade Associations you belong to or those that are available for your industry.
___	___	You can include any price lists or schedules you have.
___	___	Provide information about your market, who are they, where do they come from, what type of mix do you have, that is, commercial accounts (business to business), government, private industry, private individuals, etc.

All the information mentioned above is vital to the creation of the presentation package. All the above is what every buyer will want to know about your business. Putting the information into a presentation package saves a lot of time in the long run. Many, many sales of businesses do not succeed because the information set out above was not put together and given to the buyer before an offer was made. A business sale was never lost because the information provided was too detailed.

Exhibit 1.4 *(Continued)*

EXHIBIT 1.5 WORKSHEET FOR ADJUSTED ANNUAL NET PROFIT

Worksheet
Adjusted Annual Net Profit

For Year Ending_____

Net profit per tax return or profit or loss statement $_____

Adjustments: (Noncash expenses, Nonrecurring
expenses, personal expenses, unusual
one-time expenses, excessive expenses, etc.)

Depreciation	_____
Amortization	_____
Interest	_____
Owner's Salary	_____
Payroll Taxes (owner's)	_____
Donations	_____
Leased Equip. Cost	_____

(for any equip. that will not continue as an expense
for a new owner)

_____	_____
_____	_____
_____	_____
_____	_____
_____	_____

Personal Expenses

Telephone	_____
Insurance	_____
Travel & Entertainment	_____
Meals	_____
Auto Expenses	_____
Legal & Professional	_____
_____	_____

Total Adjustments $_____ $_____

Total Annual Adjusted Net Profit $_____

Exhibit 1.5 Worksheet for Adjusted Annual Net Profit

For Year Ending December 31, 1997

Net profit per tax return or profit or loss statement   <u>$29,000.00</u>

Adjustments: (Noncash expenses, Nonrecurring expenses, personal expenses, unusual one-time expenses, excessive expenses, etc.)

Depreciation	$4,148.00
Amortization	897.00
Interest	1,646.00
Owner's Salary	
Payroll Taxes (owner's)	
Donations	
Leased Equip. Cost	6,288.00

(for any equip. that will not continue as an expense for a new owner)

Contributions	125.00
Subscriptions	47.00
Sam's Club	1,456.00
Real cost of wife's bookkeeping	<6,000.00>

This cost had not been expensed.

Personal Expenses

Telephone	
Insurance	3,336.00
Travel & Entertainment	431.00
Meals	
Auto Expenses	3,675.00
Legal & Professional	

Total Adjustments	$16,049.00	$16,049.00
Total Annual Adjusted Net Profit		$45,049.00

Exhibit 1.6 Example of Completed Adjusted Annual Net Profit Form

	Actual	Adjusted
CURRENT ASSETS	12/31/95	12/31/95
CASH	1,658.00	0.00
ACCOUNTS RECEIVABLES	82,783.19	0.00
INVENTORY	145,023.25	134,000.00
NOTE RECEIVABLE	325.00	0.00
TOTAL CURRENT ASSETS	**229,789.44**	**134,000.00**
FIXED ASSETS		
MACHINERY AND EQUIPMENT	75,089.65	30,000.00
FURNITURE AND FIXTURES	31,247.90	11,000.00
LEASEHOLD IMPROVEMENTS	18,098.70	5,000.00
VEHICLES	38,104.32	14,000.00
LESS: ACCUMALATED DEPRECIATION	(51,765.42)	0.00
TOTAL FIXED ASSETS	**92,676.45**	**60,000.00**
OTHER ASSETS		
RENT DEPOSIT	2,000.00	2,000.00
GOODWILL		756,000.00
TOTAL OTHER ASSETS	**2,000.00**	**758,000.00**
TOTAL ASSETS	324,465.89	950,000.00

LIABILITIES AND OWNER'S EQUITY

	Actual	Adjusted
CURRENT LIABILITIES		
ACCOUNTS PAYABLE	40,051.25	0.00
PAYROLL TAXES	8,975.35	0.00
SALES TAX PAYABLE	1,324.56	0.00
TOTAL CURRENT LIABILITIES	**50,351.16**	**0.00**
LONG-TERM LIABILITIES		
NOTE PAYABLE	10,500.00	0.00
TOTAL LONG-TERM LIABILITIES	**10,500.00**	**0.00**
TOTAL LIABILITIES	60,851.16	0.00
OWNER'S EQUITY	236,614.73	950,000.00
TOTAL OWNER'S EQUITY	**236,614.73**	**950,000.00**
TOTAL LIABILITIES AND OWNER'S EQUITY	324,465.89	950,000.00

Exhibit 1.7 Example of an Adjusted Balance Sheet

Item	Make	Cost	Date Pur- chased	Market Value "In-Place"
SHOP EQUIPMENT				
Pick-up Truck	Ford-Ranger	$4,927.08	12/92	3,000.00
Pick-up Truck	Toyota	5,642.17	8/94	4,000.00
Copier	Cannon	1,027.43	4/90	750.00
Fax Machine	Sharp	375.54	9/94	275.00
Computer	Triad	25,795.00	2/89	15,000.00
Pager	Motorola	49.95	9/94	35.00
Modem	Universal	475.00	9/94	425.00
Phones	2-Radio Shack, 3-4 line GE	806.36	6/95	800.00
Telemoney Mach.	Verifone (2)	63.60	11/94	60.00
Scope	ESI	4,315.15	4/95	4,300.00
Emission analyzer	Allen	1,337.50	1/95	1,200.00
Engine cleaner	Motorvac	3,779.00	1/95	3,700.00
Bead Blaster (leased)	Trico	1,099.42	10/94	850.00
Battery Charger	Schumacher	99.00	12/94	90.00
2 Shop Fans	Granger	463.84	2/95	450.00
Shelving	misc.	1,680.00	2/89	1,400.00
Air Compressor	w/extra tank	600.00	2/89	400.00
Mitchell Manuals	Mitchell	2,400.00	10/94	2,200.00
(33) Video Training Programs	Sorrenson	29.95 ea. 988.00	11/94	950.00
OFFICE EQUIPMENT				
(4) Desks				
Table				
(14) Chairs		$1,400.00	various	1,100.00
Computer Table			ages	
(4) File Cabinets				
(3) Cupboards				
Typewriter				
Refrigerator	Kenmore	140.00	8/95	125.00
Toaster	Proctor Silex	15.00	3/93	10.00

Exhibit 1.8 List of Fixed Assets, Cost vs. Market Value In-Place

EXHIBIT 1.8 LIST OF FIXED ASSETS, COST VS. MARKET VALUE IN-PLACE

Item	Make	Cost	Date Pur-chased	Market Value "In-Place"
Microwave	Goldstar	79.95	6/92	50.00
Coffee Maker	Proctor Silex	29.95	3/93	15.00
(2) Vacuum	Eureka	69.50	3/93	50.00
(3) Heat Dish	Presto	74.95	11/93	65.00
(2) Fans	Tantung	69.90	11/93	40.00
(5) Trash Cans	Rubbermaid	49.75	10/94	35.00
Lamp w/Stand	Edge	29.95	11/94	25.00
Lamp		19.95	10/94	15.00
Creeper	Roll-Over	16.95	11/94	15.00
Floor Jack	allied	54.45	11/94	50.00
Bench Grinder	Delta	69.95	10/94	65.00
Vise	Olympia	19.50	10/94	15.00
(5) Fire Extinguishers	Amerex	214.75	5/93	200.00
(7) Work Benches			2/89	200.00
(3 sets) Shelving		150.00	12/94	125.00
MISC.	various	500.00		500.00
Total		**$59,543.54**		**$42,585.00**

Exhibit 1.8 *(Continued)*

75

Excess Earnings Worksheet

Annual Adjusted Net Profit $_ _ _ _ _ _ _ _ _ _

Less: return on and of fixed assets   –

                                         $_____

Subtract Owner's Labor @ Market   –_____

Remainder is Excess Earnings . . . . $_____

Divide by the Capitalization Rate   ÷_____

Goodwill or Intangible Asset Value $

Fixed Assets Value @ FMV in-place   +_____

TOTAL THE VALUE OF THE BUSINESS **(before adding the Inventory or Accounts Receivable)**

TOTAL VALUE OF BUSINESS $_____

The asking price is usually stated as the value, plus the inventory. Be sure to add some negotiating room in the asking price, before the inventory. See the chapter titled "Preparing the Presentation of Your Business"

Inventory @ Cost, Less obsolete inv.   +_____

{add in any other assets included in the sale, such as accounts receivable or cash}

_____   +_____

_____   +_____

_____   +_____

TOTAL PRICE OF THE BUSINESS $_____

Exhibit 1.9 Excess Earnings Worksheet

EXHIBIT 1.10 MATHEMATICAL DEPICTION OF CALCULATING GOODWILL

$410,000.00	**Adjusted Annual Earnings**
− 89,000.00	Labor for owner/mgr.
321,000.00	
− 11,000.00	18% return on and of investment in fixed assets of $60,000.00
$310,000.00	**Excess Earnings**
÷ .41	Capitalization Rate
$756,000.00	**Goodwill or Intangible Asset Value (rounded off)**
+ 60,000.00	Fixed Assets @ fair market value in-place
$816,000.00	
+ 134,000.00	Inventory @ cost, net of obsolete or nonsalable merchandise
$950,000.00	**Total Value**

Exhibit 1.10 Mathematical Depiction of Calculating Goodwill

Standard Industrial Classification

The following is a summary listing of the Standard Industrial Classification (SIC) Codes by major industry groups, followed by an alphabetical listing of the major industries comprising the four digit codes. For a complete listing of all industries comprising each SIC code refer to the Standard Industrial Classification Manual published by the Office of Management and Budget. For a summary listing of SIC codes by industries and applicable size standards, refer to the Federal Acquisition Regulations (FAR) Subpart Part 19.1

Titles and Descriptions of Industries by Major Industry Groups

Major Group

Division A. Agriculture, Forestry, and Fishing
01. Agricultural production crops
02. Agricultural production livestock
07. Agricultural services
08. Forestry
09. Fishing, hunting, and trapping

Division B. Mining
10. Metal mining
12. Coal mining
13. Oil and gas extraction
14. Mining and quarrying of nonmetallic minerals, except fuels

Division C. Construction
15. Building construction general contractors and operative builders
16. Heavy construction other than building construction contractors
17. Construction special trade contractors

Division D. Manufacturing
20. Food and kindred products
21. Tobacco products
22. Textile mill products
23. Apparel and other finished products made from fabrics and similar materials
24. Lumber and wood products, except furniture
25. Furniture and fixtures
26. Paper and allied products
27. Printing, publishing, and allied industries

Exhibit 1.11 List of Businesses by Standard Industrial Classification

EXHIBIT 1.11 LIST OF BUSINESSES BY STANDARD INDUSTRIAL CLASSIFICATION

28. Chemicals and allied products
29. Petroleum refining and related industries
30. Rubber and miscellaneous plastics products
31. Leather and leather products
32. Stone, clay, glass, and concrete products
33. Primary metal industries
34. Fabricated metal products, except machinery and transportation equipment
35. Industrial and commercial machinery and computer equipment
36. Electronic and other electrical machinery and equipment, except computer equipment
37. Transportation equipment
38. Measuring, analyzing, and controlling instruments; photographic, medical and optical goods; watches and clocks
39. Miscellaneous manufacturing industries

Division E. Transportation, Communications, Electric, Gas, and Sanitary Services
40. Railroad transportation
41. Local and suburban transit and interurban highway passenger transportation
42. Motor freight transportation and warehousing
43. U.S. Postal Service
44. Water transportation
45. Transportation by air
46. Pipelines, except natural gas

Standard Industrial Classification
Titles and Descriptions of Industries By Major Industry Groups

47. Transportation services
48. Communications
49. Electric, gas, and sanitary services

Division F. Wholesale Trade
50. Wholesale trade durable goods
51. Wholesale trade nondurable goods

Division G. Retail Trade
52. Building materials, hardware, garden supply, and mobile home dealers
53. General merchandise stores
54. Food stores
55. Automotive dealers and gasoline service stations
56. Apparel and accessory stores

Exhibit 1.11 *(Continued)*

57. Home furniture, furnishings, and equipment stores
58. Eating and drinking places
59. Miscellaneous retail

Division H. Finance, Insurance, and Real Estate

60. Depository institutions
61. Nondepository credit institutions
62. Security and commodity brokers, dealers, exchanges, and services
63. Insurance carriers
64. Insurance agents, brokers, and service
65. Real estate
67. Holding and other investment offices

Division I. Services

70. Hotels, rooming houses, camps, and other lodging places
72. Personal services
73. Business services
75. Automotive repair, services, and parking
76. Miscellaneous repair services
78. Motion pictures
79. Amusement and recreation service
80. Health services
81. Legal services
82. Educational services
83. Social services
84. Museums, art galleries, and botanical and zoological gardens
86. Membership organizations
87. Engineering, accounting, research, management, and related services
88. Private households
89. Miscellaneous services

Division J. Public Administration

91. Executive, legislative, and general government, except finance
92. Justice, public order, and safety
93. Public finance, taxation, and monetary policy
94. Administration of human resource programs
95. Administration of environmental quality and housing programs
96. Administration of economic programs
97. National security and international affairs

Division K. Nonclassifiable Establishments

99. Nonclassifiable establishments

Exhibit 1.11 *(Continued)*

EXHIBIT 1.11 LIST OF BUSINESSES BY STANDARD INDUSTRIAL CLASSIFICATION

Standard Industrial Classification
SIC Alphabetical Listing {nec = not elsewhere classified}

0115 Corn
0119 Cash grains, nec
0131 Cotton
0134 Irish potatoes
0139 Field crops, except cash grains, nec
0171 Berry crops
0172 Grapes
0174 Citrus fruits
0175 Deciduous tree fruits
0179 Fruits and tree nuts, nec
0182 Food crops grown under cover
0191 General farms, primarily crop
0211 Beef cattle feedlots
0212 Beef cattle, except feedlots
0213 Hogs
0219 General livestock, nec
0241 Dairy farms
0251 Broiler, fryer, and roaster chickens
0252 Chicken eggs
0271 Fur-bearing animals and rabbits
0272 Horses and other equines
0273 Animal aquaculture
0279 Animal specialties, nec
0291 General farms, primarily animal
0721 Crop planting and protecting
0722 Crop harvesting
0723 Crop preparation services for market
0724 Cotton ginning
0751 Livestock services, exc. veterinary
0752 Animal specialty services
0761 Farm labor contractors
0762 Farm management services
0781 Landscape counseling and planning
0782 Lawn and garden services
0831 Forest products
0851 Forestry services
0912 Finfish

0919 Miscellaneous marine products
0921 Fish hatcheries and preserves
0971 Hunting, trapping, game propagation
1011 Iron ores
1021 Copper ores
1031 Lead and zinc ores
1041 Gold ores
1061 Ferroalloy ores, except vanadium
1081 Metal mining services
1099 Metal ores, nec
1221 Bituminous coal and lignite surface
1222 Bituminous coal underground
1231 Anthracite mining
1241 Coal mining services
1311 Crude petroleum and natural gas
1381 Drilling oil and gas wells
1411 Dimension stone
1422 Crushed and broken limestone
1423 Crushed and broken granite
1429 Crushed and broken stone, nec
1442 Construction sand and gravel
1446 Industrial sand
1455 Kaolin and ball clay
1459 Clay and related minerals, nec
1479 Chemical and fertilizer mining, nec
1499 Miscellaneous nonmetallic minerals
1541 Industrial buildings and warehouses
1611 Highway and street construction
1622 Bridge, tunnel, & elevated highway
1629 Heavy construction, nec
1731 Electrical work
1741 Masonry and other stonework
1751 Carpentry work
1752 Floor laying and floor work, nec
1771 Concrete work
1793 Glass and glazing work
1794 Excavation work

1796 Installing building equipment, nec
2011 Meat packing plants
2021 Creamery butter
2022 Cheese, natural and processed
2023 Dry, condensed, evaporated products
2024 Ice cream and frozen desserts
2026 Fluid milk
2032 Canned specialties
2033 Canned fruits and vegetables
2034 Dehydrated fruits, vegetables, soups
2037 Frozen fruits and vegetables
2038 Frozen specialties, nec
2041 Flour and other grain mill products
2043 Cereal breakfast foods
2047 Dog and cat food
2051 Bread, cake, and related products
2052 Cookies and crackers
2053 Frozen bakery products, except bread
2062 Cane sugar refining
2063 Beet sugar
2064 Candy & other confectionery products
2066 Chocolate and cocoa products
2067 Chewing gum
2074 Cottonseed oil mills
2077 Animal and marine fats and oils
2079 Edible fats and oils, nec
2082 Malt beverages
2083 Malt
2085 Distilled and blended liquors
2086 Bottled and canned soft drinks
2087 Flavoring extracts and syrups, nec
2091 Canned and cured fish and seafoods
2092 Fresh or frozen prepared fish
2097 Manufactured ice
2098 Macaroni and spaghetti
2099 Food preparations, nec
2111 Cigarettes
2121 Cigars
2131 Chewing and smoking tobacco
2211 Broadwoven fabric mills, cotton
2221 Broadwoven fabric mills, manmade
2231 Broadwoven fabric mills, wool
2252 Hosiery, nec

2253 Knit outerwear mills
2254 Knit underwear mills
2258 Lace & warp knit fabric mills
2259 Knitting mills, nec
2261 Finishing plants, cotton
2262 Finishing plants, manmade
2269 Finishing plants, nec
2273 Carpets and rugs
2295 Coated fabrics, not rubberized
2298 Cordage and twine
2311 Men's and boys' suits and coats
2321 Men's and boys' shirts
2322 Men's & boys' underwear and nightwear
2323 Men's and boys' neckwear
2325 Men's and boys' trousers and slacks
2326 Men's and boys' work clothing
2329 Men's and boys' clothing, nec
2342 Bras, girdles, and allied garments
2353 Hats, caps, and millinery
2361 Girls' & children's dresses, blouses
2369 Girls' and children's outerwear, nec
2371 Fur goods
2381 Fabric dress and work gloves
2386 Leather and sheep-lined clothing
2387 Apparel belts
2389 Apparel and accessories, nec
2391 Curtains and draperies
2392 House furnishings, nec
2394 Canvas and related products
2396 Automotive and apparel trimmings
2399 Fabricated textile products, nec
2411 Logging
2426 Hardwood dimension & flooring mills
2431 Millwork
2435 Hardwood veneer and plywood
2451 Mobile homes
2514 Metal household furniture
2515 Mattresses and bedsprings
2519 Household furniture, nec
2591 Drapery hardware & blinds & shades
2599 Furniture and fixtures, nec
2653 Corrugated and solid fiber boxes
2655 Fiber cans, drums & similar products

2657 Folding paperboard boxes
2673 Bags: plastics, laminated, & coated
2674 Bags: uncoated paper & multiwall
2675 Die-cut paper and board
2677 Envelopes
2679 Converted paper products, nec
2731 Book publishing
2732 Book printing
2741 Miscellaneous publishing
2752 Commercial printing, lithographic
2754 Commercial printing, gravure
2759 Commercial printing, nec
2761 Manifold business forms
2771 Greeting cards
2782 Blank books and loose-leaf binders
2789 Bookbinding and related work
2812 Alkalies and chlorine
2813 Industrial gases
2816 Inorganic pigments
2819 Industrial inorganic chemicals, nec
2823 Cellulosic manmade fibers
2833 Medicinals and botanicals
2835 Diagnostic substances
2836 Biological products exc. diagnostic
2861 Gum and wood chemicals
2865 Cyclic crudes and intermediates
2869 Industrial organic chemicals, nec
2875 Fertilizers, mixing only
2879 Agricultural chemicals, nec
2891 Adhesives and sealants
2892 Explosives
2895 Carbon black
2899 Chemical preparations, nec
2951 Asphalt paving mixtures and blocks
2952 Asphalt felts and coatings
2992 Lubricating oils and greases
3053 Gaskets, packing and sealing devices
3061 Mechanical rubber goods
3069 Fabricated rubber products, nec
3083 Laminated plastics plate & sheet
3087 Custom compound purchased resins
3111 Leather tanning and finishing

3131 Footwear cut stock
3142 House slippers
3143 Men's footwear, except athletic
3149 Footwear, except rubber, nec
3151 Leather gloves and mittens
3161 Luggage
3199 Leather goods, nec
3211 Flat glass
3221 Glass containers
3241 Cement, hydraulic
3251 Brick and structural clay tile
3253 Ceramic wall and floor tile
3255 Clay refractories
3271 Concrete block and brick
3272 Concrete products, nec
3274 Lime
3275 Gypsum products
3281 Cut stone and stone products
3291 Abrasive products
3292 Asbestos products
3295 Minerals, ground or treated
3296 Mineral wool
3312 Blast furnaces and steel mills
3313 Electrometallurgical products
3316 Cold finishing of steel shapes
3321 Gray and ductile iron foundries
3322 Malleable iron foundries
3351 Copper rolling and drawing
3353 Aluminum sheet, plate, and foil
3354 Aluminum extruded products
3355 Aluminum rolling and drawing, nec
3363 Aluminum die-castings
3365 Aluminum foundries
3366 Copper foundries
3398 Metal heat treating
3411 Metal cans
3412 Metal barrels, drums, and pails
3421 Cutlery
3423 Hand and edge tools, nec
3429 Hardware, nec
3431 Metal sanitary ware
3433 Heating equipment, except electric

3441 Fabricated structural metal
3442 Metal doors, sash, and trim
3443 Fabricated plate work (boiler shops)
3446 Architectural metal work
3449 Miscellaneous metal work
3452 Bolts, nuts, rivets, and washers
3462 Iron and steel forgings
3465 Automotive stampings
3466 Crowns and closures
3469 Metal stampings, nec
3479 Metal coating and allied services
3483 Ammunition, exc. for small arms, nec
3491 Industrial valves
3492 Fluid power valves & hose fittings
3496 Misc. fabricated wire products
3497 Metal foil and leaf
3498 Fabricated pipe and fittings
3499 Fabricated metal products, nec
3519 Internal combustion engines, nec
3523 Farm machinery and equipment
3524 Lawn and garden equipment
3531 Construction machinery
3532 Mining machinery
3534 Elevators and moving stairways
3535 Conveyors and conveying equipment
3536 Hoists, cranes, and monorails
3537 Industrial trucks and tractors
3541 Machine tools, metal cutting types
3542 Machine tools, metal forming types
3543 Industrial patterns
3545 Machine tool accessories
3549 Metalworking machinery, nec
3556 Food products machinery
3562 Ball and roller bearings
3563 Air and gas compressors
3564 Blowers and fans
3567 Industrial furnaces and ovens
3569 General industrial machinery, nec
3571 Electronic computers
3572 Computer storage devices
3575 Computer terminals
3577 Computer peripheral equipment, nec

3578 Calculating and accounting equipment
3581 Automatic vending machines
3582 Commercial laundry equipment
3586 Measuring and dispensing pumps
3592 Carburetors, pistons, rings, valves
3593 Fluid power cylinders & actuators
3594 Fluid power pumps and motors
3599 Industrial machinery, nec
3621 Motors and generators
3624 Carbon and graphite products
3629 Electrical industrial apparatus, nec
3631 Household cooking equipment
3632 Household refrigerators and freezers
3633 Household laundry equipment
3634 Electric housewares and fans
3635 Household vacuum cleaners
3639 Household appliances, nec
3641 Electric lamps
3643 Current-carrying wiring devices
3646 Commercial lighting fixtures
3648 Lighting equipment, nec
3651 Household audio and video equipment
3669 Communications equipment, nec
3671 Electron tubes
3675 Electronic capacitors
3676 Electronic resistors
3677 Electronic coils and transformers
3678 Electronic connectors
3679 Electronic components, nec
3694 Engine electrical equipment
3695 Magnetic and optical recording media
3699 Electrical equipment & supplies, nec
3711 Motor vehicles and car bodies
3714 Motor vehicle parts and accessories
3716 Motor homes
3721 Aircraft
3724 Aircraft engines and engine parts
3728 Aircraft parts and equipment, nec
3732 Boat building and repairing
3751 Motorcycles, bicycles, and parts
3761 Guided missiles and space vehicles
3821 Laboratory apparatus and furniture

3822 Environmental controls
3824 Fluid meters and counting devices
3825 Instruments to measure electricity
3826 Analytical instruments
3829 Measuring & controlling devices, nec
3843 Dental equipment and supplies
3845 Electromedical equipment
3911 Jewelry, precious metal
3915 Jewelers' materials & lapidary work
3942 Dolls and stuffed toys
3944 Games, toys, and children's vehicles
3952 Lead pencils and art goods
3953 Marking devices
3955 Carbon paper and inked ribbons
3961 Costume jewelry
3965 Fasteners, buttons, needles, & pins
3991 Brooms and brushes
3995 Burial caskets
3996 Hard surface floor coverings, nec
3999 Manufacturing industries, nec
4111 Local and suburban transit
4119 Local passenger transportation, nec
4131 Intercity & rural bus transportation
4141 Local bus charter service
4142 Bus charter service, except local
4173 Bus terminal and service facilities
4212 Local trucking, without storage
4214 Local trucking with storage
4215 Courier services, except by air
4221 Farm product warehousing and storage
4225 General warehousing and storage
4412 Deep sea foreign trans. of freight
4424 Deep sea domestic trans. of freight
4432 Freight trans. on the Great Lakes
4481 Deep sea passenger trans., exc. ferry
4482 Ferries
4491 Marine cargo handling
4493 Marinas
4512 Air transportation, scheduled
4513 Air courier services
4522 Air transportation, nonscheduled
4581 Airports, flying fields, & services

4612 Crude petroleum pipelines
4731 Freight transportation arrangement
4785 Inspection & fixed facilities
4841 Cable and other pay TV services
4899 Communication services, nec
4911 Electric services
4923 Gas transmission and distribution
4925 Gas production and/or distribution
4931 Electric and other services combined
4932 Gas and other services combined
4939 Combination utilities, nec
4971 Irrigation systems
5012 Automobiles and other motor vehicles
5013 Motor vehicle supplies and new parts
5015 Motor vehicle parts, used
5021 Furniture
5023 Homefurnishings
5031 Lumber, plywood, and millwork
5032 Brick, stone, & related materials
5039 Construction materials, nec
5045 Computers, peripherals, & software
5046 Commercial equipment, nec
5047 Medical and hospital equipment
5051 Metals service centers and offices
5052 Coal and other minerals and ores
5063 Electrical apparatus and equipment
5064 Electrical appliances, TVs, & radios
5065 Electronic parts and equipment
5072 Hardware
5082 Construction and mining machinery
5083 Farm and garden machinery
5084 Industrial machinery and equipment
5085 Industrial supplies
5094 Jewelry & precious stones
5099 Durable goods, nec
5113 Industrial & personal service paper
5122 Drugs, proprietaries, and sundries
5136 Men's and boys' clothing
5139 Footwear
5141 Groceries, general line
5143 Dairy products, exc. dried or canned
5145 Confectionery

5146 Fish and seafoods
5147 Meats and meat products
5148 Fresh fruits and vegetables
5149 Groceries and related products, nec
5153 Grain and field beans
5154 Livestock
5159 Farm-product raw materials, nec
5169 Chemicals & allied products, nec
5181 Beer and ale
5191 Farm supplies
5192 Books, periodicals, & newspapers
5193 Flowers & florists' supplies
5211 Lumber and other building materials
5251 Hardware stores
5271 Mobile home dealers
5311 Department stores
5399 Misc. general merchandise stores
5411 Grocery stores
5421 Meat and fish markets
5431 Fruit and vegetable markets
5441 Candy, nut, and confectionery stores
5451 Dairy products stores
5499 Miscellaneous food stores
5531 Auto and home supply stores
5541 Gasoline service stations
5551 Boat dealers
5571 Motorcycle dealers
5599 Automotive dealers, nec
5611 Men's & boys' clothing stores
5641 Children's and infants' wear stores
5651 Family clothing stores
5699 Misc. apparel & accessory stores
5712 Furniture stores
5713 Floor covering stores
5714 Drapery and upholstery stores
5719 Misc. homefurnishings stores
5722 Household appliance stores
5734 Computer and software stores
5736 Musical instrument stores
5812 Eating places
5813 Drinking places
5912 Drug stores and proprietary stores

5921 Liquor stores
5942 Book stores
5944 Jewelry stores
5945 Hobby, toy, and game shops
5946 Camera & photographic supply stores
5947 Gift, novelty, and souvenir shops
5948 Luggage and leather goods stores
5961 Catalog and mail-order houses
5962 Merchandising machine operators
5963 Direct selling establishments
5983 Fuel oil dealers
5984 Liquefied petroleum gas dealers
5989 Fuel dealers, nec
5992 Florists
5999 Miscellaneous retail stores, nec
6011 Federal reserve banks
6019 Central reserve depository, nec
6029 Commercial banks, nec
6035 Federal savings institutions
6061 Federal credit unions
6081 Foreign bank & branches & agencies
6082 Foreign trade & international banks
6099 Functions related to deposit banking
6111 Federal & fed.-sponsored credit
6159 Misc. business credit institutions
6162 Mortgage bankers and correspondents
6163 Loan brokers
6221 Commodity contracts brokers, dealers
6282 Investment advice
6311 Life insurance
6321 Accident and health insurance
6324 Hospital and medical service plans
6331 Fire, marine, and casualty insurance
6399 Insurance carriers, nec
6411 Insurance agents, brokers, & service
6513 Apartment building operators
6514 Dwelling operators, exc. apartments
6515 Mobile home site operators
6553 Cemetery subdividers and developers
6712 Bank holding companies
6719 Holding companies, nec
6722 Management investment, open-end

6726 Investment offices, nec
6732 Educational, religious, etc. trusts
6799 Investors, nec
7011 Hotels and motels
7041 Membership-basis organization hotels
7212 Garment pressing & cleaners' agents
7213 Linen supply
7215 Coin-operated laundries and cleaning
7216 Dry-cleaning plants, except rug
7217 Carpet and upholstery cleaning
7218 Industrial launderers
7219 Laundry and garment services, nec
7231 Beauty shops
7241 Barber shops
7261 Funeral service and crematories
7299 Miscellaneous personal services, nec
7311 Advertising agencies
7319 Advertising, nec
7322 Adjustment & collection services
7323 Credit reporting services
7331 Direct mail advertising services
7335 Commercial photography
7336 Commercial art and graphic design
7342 Disinfecting & pest control services
7349 Building maintenance services, nec
7352 Medical equipment rental
7353 Heavy construction equipment rental
7359 Equipment rental & leasing, nec
7361 Employment agencies
7363 Help supply services
7371 Computer programming services
7373 Computer integrated systems design
7374 Data processing and preparation
7375 Information retrieval services
7376 Computer facilities management
7377 Computer rental & leasing
7378 Computer maintenance & repair
7379 Computer related services, nec
7381 Detective & armored car services
7389 Business services, nec
7521 Automobile parking
7533 Auto exhaust system repair shops

7536 Automotive glass replacement shops
7537 Automotive transmission repair shops
7538 General automotive repair shops
7539 Automotive repair shops, nec
7542 Car washes
7549 Automotive services, nec
7629 Electrical repair shops, nec
7694 Armature rewinding shops
7812 Motion picture & video production
7822 Motion picture and tape distribution
7829 Motion picture distribution services
7832 Motion picture theaters, exc. drive-in
7833 Drive-in motion picture theaters
7911 Dance studios, schools, and halls
7929 Entertainers & entertainment groups
7933 Bowling centers
7993 Coin-operated amusement devices
7996 Amusement parks
7997 Membership sports & recreation clubs
7999 Amusement and recreation, nec
8052 Intermediate care facilities
8062 General medical & surgical hospitals
8071 Medical laboratories
8072 Dental laboratories
8082 Home health care services
8092 Kidney dialysis centers
8099 Health and allied services, nec
8111 Legal services
8211 Elementary and secondary schools
8221 Colleges and universities
8222 Junior colleges
8231 Libraries
8243 Data processing schools
8244 Business and secretarial schools
8322 Individual and family services
8331 Job training and related services
8351 Child day care services
8412 Museums and art galleries
8422 Botanical and zoological gardens
8611 Business associations
8631 Labor organizations
8641 Civic and social associations

8699 Membership organizations, nec
8711 Engineering services
8712 Architectural services
8721 Accounting, auditing, & bookkeeping
8731 Commercial physical research
8732 Commercial nonphysical research
8741 Management services
8742 Management consulting services
8744 Facilities support services
8748 Business consulting, nec
9111 Executive offices
9121 Legislative bodies
9131 Executive and legislative combined
9199 General government, nec

9211 Courts
9222 Legal counsel and prosecution
9223 Correctional institutions
9224 Fire protection
9311 Finance, taxation, & monetary policy
9411 Admin. of educational programs
9431 Admin. of public health programs
9441 Admin. of social & manpower programs
9451 Administration of veterans' affairs
9511 Air, water, & solid waste management
9512 Land, mineral, wildlife conservation
9531 Housing programs
9611 Admin. of general economic programs
9721 International affairs

2

PREPARING THE PRESENTATION OF YOUR BUSINESS

A word of advice while you are offering your business for sale: when it comes to making decisions for the business that have future consequences, make the decisions as if you were not selling. Do what is best for the future of the business.

In this chapter you will find an outline of a presentation package and some examples of presentation packages. By following the outline and the examples, you can create your own presentation package. Putting together a proper presentation package on your business is one of the two most beneficial things you can do toward the successful sale of your business.

WHAT SHOULD BE SOLD, ASSETS OR THE CORPORATION?

If your business is a regular corporation, you must decide if you are going to be selling the assets of the corporation or the stock in the corporation. This decision is very important. If the business is a sole proprietorship or a partnership, then you have no decision to make, you will be selling the assets. You may decide to only sell selected assets, but there is no entity like a corporation to sell or to even be concerned about. If your business's structure is a corporation, you may want to discuss what it is you will be selling with your certified public accountant (CPA) or tax advisor. Generally speaking, most small businesses, if incorporated, are sold for the assets only. Buyers are consistently advised to buy only the assets. Due to the significant loss in any buyer's ability to write off the purchase price through an allocation, the fair market value of a closely held corporation is reduced. Likewise the owner/seller of a regular corporation is faced with a possible double tax. It is far better, when it comes to selling, to have owned the business as a Sub-Chapter S corporation, sole proprietorship, or partnership than a regular corporation. The double taxation will occur if you cannot find a buyer to purchase the stock in the corporation and you (actually it is the corporation) end up just selling the assets. In that case the actual seller is the corporation. The corporation is assessed a tax on the gain produced by the sale (if there is gain). When you, the stock holder/employee, withdraw funds from the corporation you can be taxed personally on the same funds taxed for capital gain. This is not a good situation. If your corporation has depreciated its assets to zero or near zero, the buyer will be getting the assets with no more depreciation left. In addition, the buyer will inherit the liabilities of the corporation. Most of the buyer's advisors will not want the buyer to buy into such a situation, especially when the buyer can purchase many other businesses without the hassles associated with buying stock in someone's corporation. You should check with your tax advisor about the best way to proceed if you do own a regular corporation.

CREATING A PRESENTATION PACKAGE IS VITAL

The purpose of creating a presentation package is to inform the buyer enough to be able to make a decision to go ahead with buying the business or to decline to go further. The time you spend making a complete and detailed presentation package will pay off throughout the entire process of selling your business.

With your presentation package, you will reduce the average time of explaining your business to a buyer thoroughly enough to have them make an intelligent decision to go forward in the process of buying your business or to stop, from 2 to 3 hours to 15 minutes. You are busy and you have a business to run. Most business-owners I have met do not have an extra two to three hours to spend with each potential buyer who wants to consider buying the business. It does only take one interested party to make the sale happen, but in most cases it takes introducing several parties before you locate the right buyer. It is not uncommon to interview 10 or more prospective buyers. This package will set forth all the essential information that the buyer needs to know at this time. When buyers read the material provided in your presentation package, they will either ask to see the business (and ask a few more questions for clarification), or they will not be interested in going further. It will be fairly cut and dry. A presentation package will eliminate, almost entirely, the need to "sell" your business to a buyer. With a presentation package created as I have laid out, you do not have to have any selling skills in order to sell your business; the package does the work for you.

After many years of selling and consulting on the sale of businesses, I would say that a key reason I was much more successful in closing a business sale than the business-brokerage's industry average was because I had taken the time to investigate and communicate as much as I could about the business—even the weaknesses. That is why a complete presentation package is so important. Putting a price on the business that represents its value is, along with the presentation, the most important factor in selling the business. With those two vital elements accomplished, the rest of the sale is mostly just a process of marketing and advertising until you meet that buyer who is suited for your business.

AN HONEST PRESENTATION IS A KEY TO SUCCESS

When you are creating the presentation package, be sure to be completely honest about all the information. Do not worry about some imperfections in your business—all businesses have them. It is far worse to cover up a flaw than to expose weaknesses so the buyer can understand and accept them. You will not only be successful in selling your business, but you will save a possible lawsuit.

Flaws or weaknesses in your business are golden opportunities to a buyer; they are opportunities to improve the business. Most buyers will have a sense of enthusiasm or eagerness when they see things they can do to improve the business. Not only are expectations of future growth via outside influences a positive, but expectations of results for improving the very business itself from within are powerful influences on a buyer. Many buyers can see opportunities to improve the business and they develop a very positive attitude about their ability to improve on what you have set in motion, on what you have accomplished while owning the business. *One word of caution:* do not try to charge the buyer (in a price too high) for the results they may accomplish with your business. You should get paid for your results—not for what they may accomplish.

I cannot stress enough to communicate everything to the potential buyer honestly. From all the material in the presentation package to anything you say to the buyers or additionally show them, be consistently straightforward. If you misrepresent anything at one point, you will lose integrity; everything you say and the materials you provide will be taken with suspicion. Everything will be discovered— sooner or later. Later could mean a lawsuit. Some buyers look for inconsistencies so they can gain justifications for offering you a lower price. Providing correct information about the business, information that when confirmed will check out just as it had been presented, will not only help the sale happen, but will help it go more smoothly.

FATAL FLAWS TO A SUCCESSFUL SALE

What many owners, business-brokers, or other intermediaries fail to understand is that imperfections are not deal-killers, unless they have been hidden. Of course, there are some elements that can be fatal flaws. Fatal flaws are things such as: laws or regulations that render the business obsolete or marginally profitable, very negative press or reputation, growing competition which makes it very difficult to make a livable profit margin, a bad location (too expensive to overcome by lots of advertising), and rent that is too high (especially when it will go even higher). The main idea is, if there exists or will exist factors that cannot be changed which render the business unprofitable or increasingly less profitable, then you have a serious deterrent to successfully selling the business as a going concern. If the problem can be corrected, explain inside the presentation package how it can be done. You want to anticipate any question that someone might have and answer it in the package. Included in Chapter Three of this guidebook is a list of over 120 questions that a buyer may ask you. Read this list over and make sure to answer all the questions that pertain to your business inside the presentation package. The list of questions does not contain anything directly specific to your actual business. (This book would have to be very large to include the specifics of many business types.) You should add any information that is specific to the business where appropriate.

To create the presentation package, you can use a computer. You can have a secretary or a typing service prepare it (there are a lot of them around, especially with the advent of the computer and word processor). If you do not have a computer, you can type the package on a typewriter or locate a business that has computers you can rent at their premises.

THE IMPORTANCE OF THE FINANCIAL
INFORMATION SECTION

The financial information about your business's performance is a very critical element to the successful sale of the business. The financial information is your record of how well the business has performed. Without understandable, reliable records, it will be very difficult to sell your business. As stated in other areas of this guide, everything must be presented with integrity. If the buyer finds inconsistent, false, or misleading information once, they will question *everything* from then on.

CREATING A PRESENTATION
OF THE FINANCIAL INFORMATION

For those who know how to use a computer and spreadsheet software, the job of presenting the business's financial information will be easy. Just recreate the pages as I have shown in the sample presentation package titled "Perfect Press" in Exhibit 2.1—but with your financial information.

For those who cannot create the information themselves, or who do not want to have an accountant prepare the information as I have provided in the sample presentation package, there is a solution. Use the profit and loss statement (P&L) from your business as your CPA or bookkeeper prepared it. In the financial section of the presentation package you create, put a page following the P&L that shows the adjustments you made to arrive at the adjusted net profit. There is an Adjustment to Financial Statement sheet provided at the end of this chapter in Exhibit 2.2 for just such purpose. You can make copies of that page to use in your presentation package. Use one adjustment sheet after each annual P&L you use, and after the most recent year-to-date P&L. If you use monthly financial statements, then use an adjustment after each month.

KNOW WHAT YOU ARE REALLY SELLING AND SELL IT

Some people make the mistake of thinking that buying or selling a business is an unemotional event, that the sale is just facts and figures. That is very far from the truth. Of course, facts and figures are involved and are crucial to the sale. A business is where most owners spend a lot of time. Their livelihood is dependent on the business's success. Buyers can and do get as emotionally involved as the seller can. I am not talking about emotionally charged negotiations, although that can happen. I am talking about the emotional relation that develops for the perceived benefits of small-business–ownership. The more you consider the following and use the power contained therein, the more receptive you will find the buyers.

Whenever you discuss your business with a potential buyer, remember that you are really selling, and the buyer is really buying, all the benefits of the business. You are selling an opportunity to do, have, and enjoy certain rights and benefits from what you have created or developed, you are not guaranteeing them. The ability to enjoy the benefits and rights of your business can be realized by a buyer, provided they manage all the elements of the business at least as successfully as you have. You are selling income and the ability to increase the amount of income the owner will have. You are selling the independence that comes from owning and operating one's own business (as opposed to working for someone). You are selling an identity. All business-owners have some of their identity tied up in the work they perform or the business they own. You are selling flexibility; even though business-owners are the hardest working people I know, they have the ability to develop the business in such a way as to achieve the type of work schedule and time off they need or want.

Some businesses are even considered lifestyle businesses. That is because the owner has enough flexibility in his schedule to more or less develop the business around his desired lifestyle.

These elements are what you are really selling. Remember to accent some or all of these issues to the buyers when speaking to them. Keep in mind that the value of a business is equal to the present worth of the future benefits of ownership. When you compose parts of your presentation package, write the sections with all the above in mind.

THE TOOLS FOR CREATING AN EFFECTIVE PRESENTATION PACKAGE

To create an effective presentation of your business, follow the outline provided on page 102. Look at the example of a completed presentation package provided in Exhibit 2.1 so you can see how the whole presentation package is laid out and how the material is written and presented. Once you have created your own presentation package you can take a master copy to a photocopy business and have them make as many copies as you want. I would suggest making at least 5 to 10 copies of the entire package. Keep your master copy so you can produce additional copies if needed.

There are many local businesses such as Postal Annex, Mail Boxes, Etc., instant print businesses, and some of the large office-supply stores that will make copies of the package for you. The cost is only a few dollars.

I have found that the best way to bind the package is to three-hole punch each page and put the information into a half-inch three-ring binder. Of course, if you create a large volume of information, then a half-inch binder may not be large enough. You can purchase a half-inch three-ring binder with a plastic cover for less than three dollars each. The three-ring binders that have plastic covers allowing you to slip a cover page with your business's name, address, and logo into them work best, but are not essential. By using a three-ring binder for the presentation package, the information can be viewed flat, and changing pages, making additions, or updates will be much easier.

Everything contained in the outline and completed sample presentation package (Exhibit 2.1) is important. You should try to make the best package that you can. The process does take some time to complete, but is worth every moment spent.

AN EXPLANATION OF THE PRESENTATION PACKAGE OUTLINE

This explanation of the presentation package follows the outline so you may want to refer to it, beginning with a cover page. This refers to the outside cover page that you can slip into the plastic cover of the three-ring binder. The first page inside the presentation package can be one or more pages of photos of your business; a picture of the outside and three or four pictures of the inside should be sufficient. The photo page is one of the few optional pages to the whole package; a map page can follow the photo page.

I have found that many buyers like to see where the business is located on a map. In this way, they can relate their home and many other factors to the geographic location of the business. Depending on how large of an area the business supports or a buyer may come from, I sometimes use two maps.

One map shows the business's location and the surrounding one to three miles; another map I use is one showing the business's location as it sits in relation to the entire county or half of a county. Not all potential buyers are familiar with your business's location and how it relates to the larger neighborhood or the entire county. This page is another optional page.

Following the map page, we have the table of contents. This is not the last page in the package, but is the last page created. You can organize the table of contents page easier once you have put together the entire basic package. For those who do not have the ability to create a presentation package with a typewriter, computer, or someone to type it for you, then you can omit the table of contents page. I would recommend some sort of table of contents page if you could produce one.

The Offering Page

The next page is important. It is called the offering page and contains the basic information that the buyers will need to know about the asking price and the terms you will be offering. There are three main headings on the offering page: Offering Price, Available Financing, and Total Price Includes. Each main heading has subheadings, such as Asking Price or Balance of Total Price and should be typed to the right of the main heading or underneath the main heading. (Look at the sample presentation package in Exhibit 2.1 for a clear depiction.)

After the creation of the offering page, the remaining contents of the presentation package are divided into three sections. You should use tabbed dividers to separate each section. You can buy tabbed section dividers today that can be written on with pen or purchase the ones that allow you to slip the title into the clear tab. If you are creating a very simple presentation package and do not want to use tabbed dividers, then you can use some colored paper to separate the sections. If you choose to use the colored paper section dividers, then type, in very large letters, the name of the upcoming section on the colored paper.

Section One: The Business Summary

Section one is called Business Summary and contains an abundance of important information that all buyers will want to know about your business. The Business Summary section is set up with headings such as Type of Business, Lease Location and Facilities, and Business Description. Fill in the information about your business under each heading. If you have any articles that have been written about your specific business or its industry, include all support information at the end of this section.

Section Two: The Financial Section

Section two is the Financial Section. You can just tab the section Financial Section for a simple yet effective title. In the outline, I have put the order of the financial information as it should appear. You do not need to separate the information with dividers, but you can use a colored piece of paper with the title of the financial data that is coming up. For example, between each year's information, you can put a colored piece of paper that identifies the upcoming year; that way the readers of the presentation package will not get confused and mix up the data they are reading.

Section Three: Promotion and Marketing

Section three is called the Advertising, Marketing Samples, and any Additional Support Information Section. I would title the tab "Promotion and Marketing." In this section, you should include copies or extra originals of any flyers you have sent out, brochures, direct mail letters, photocopies of your Yellow Pages ads, and photocopies of any other types of ads you have run. You can also include any additional information that you think will be informative to the buyer or that will create interest in your business.

The More Detail, the Better

You can get as detailed in the creation of your presentation package as you are able. Some of the best ones I have created contained a lot of detail. The work was time-consuming but paid off because it really helped to sell the business.

The more information you put into the package, the better. The more you describe your business in each section, the better. Anticipate what the buyer should know about the business and write it out. You are not teaching the buyer your business when you detail everything. You are explaining the business and its varying elements. After all, that is what you are selling. Selling a business is not like selling anything else. It is much more difficult to successfully sell a business without a detailed presentation. There are many business-brokers and intermediaries that try to sell businesses with very little information; the published success rate for selling businesses, by the business-brokerage industry, is a dismal 20 percent. Putting together these types of presentation packages put my success rate over 95 percent. You, too, will succeed because you will take the time to put together a proper presentation of your business.

AN OUTLINE OF A BUSINESS PRESENTATION PACKAGE

The First Five Pages

Cover Page

Refer to the example package for a representative cover page.

Photo Page

If desired, this is an optional page. You can mount a few photos of your business on this page. It helps give the buyer a feel for the business prior to going there.

Map Page

This is an optional page which shows the county or a large section of it, and mark your location. Many people may be unfamiliar with how the location of the business relates to where they live or to the rest of the county. This gives a good, quick, visual reference.

Table of Contents Page

The table of contents is a good idea, but is optional for those who are trying to create a very simple presentation package.

Offering Page

Put the name and address of the business centered at the top of the page. The following headings are to be put in the order shown. Look at the presentation package example to see how this should look all filled out. The following list of heading titles, "Offered For" all the way to "Total Price Includes" and the relevant information should be on one page, if possible (see the example package).

- Offered For:
- Asking Price
- Inventory Amount
- Total Price
- Down Payment Required
- Balance of Total Price
- Available Financing

This is where you put the terms of a note you will carry. If there are any assumable notes or equipment leases, you should put the specifics about them here (see the example package for ideas). Include a line specifying the security required for the loan such as: *Security on loan amount: The note shall be secured by a security agreement and UCC-1 filing on all securable assets of the business and shall be personally guaranteed by the buyer. Note Holder reserves the right to qualify and approve the buyer for assumption of financing.*

- Total Price Includes (lists all the assets being sold.)

For example:

- Lease
- Noncompete agreement
- Goodwill
- Leasehold improvements
- Furniture, fixtures, and equipment
- Customer lists

- Training/consulting
- Vehicles (list the make, model, and year)

The Business Summary Section

You should create different sections. Business Summary is the first section. You can separate the sections by tabbed dividers or just a sheet of paper with the title of the section typed on it. Use the following titles and fill in the information below the title (see the example package).

Type of Business

Describe your business's industry. You can include your SIC (Standard Industrial Classification) code, too. Look at Exhibit 1.11 for your business's SIC code.

Example: Industrial Supply Distributor (wholesale) sells tools, abrasives, cutting devices, and lubricants. SIC code: 5085.

Location

Give the address and any other helpful particulars.

Organization

Mention the form of business, for example, sole proprietorship, Sub-Chapter S Corporation, and so on. If you are incorporated, mention the number of shares issued and outstanding, who the officers are, if there are any other classes of stock or restrictions, and so on.

Key Points of Interest

Mention several (one to five) key factors that are of special interest to someone concerning your business or its industry. Example:

long lease with no annual cost of living increase, established 15 years, and the like.

Reason for Selling

Write why you are selling (this will establish motivation and credibility).

Business Established

Tell when the business was founded and when you took over or bought the business.

Business Hours

Write out what hours and days the business is open. Include any after-hours work offered to customers.

Lease and Location and Facilities

Here you should describe in more detail the key elements to the lease. Examples: when the lease was originated and became effective, the term and expiration date, any options along with any important elements of how to exercise the options, whether the lease is assumable, and if there is any fee charged by the landlord to handle the assignment. Give the current base rent and any extra charges, such as common-area fees, property taxes, and maintenance fees, if any. Mention any rent increases such as cost of living and if there are any maximums or minimums to the increases. Mention the amount of security deposit required. If the lease specifies what the permitted uses for the premises are or limits the type of business or products sold at the location, mention them here. Mention if there is a noncompete clause. Say where the business is located, and describe the facilities, for example, 3,000 square feet of combined office and warehouse space, with the office taking up about 200 feet of the facility. You can point out any specific responsibilities mentioned in the lease in regard to repairs or maintenance.

History of the Business

In this section, you should write a brief overview of how the business began and any major changes it went through.

Business Description

This is where you should describe in more detail the nature of your business specifically. This can take the form of relating the typical routines or processes the business goes through on a daily or weekly basis. This is also where you can mention the way your business does things that you feel make it different and special. Mention all the attributes of the business and the services it performs. In this section, you can describe your product lines and if they are proprietary or not, and if there are any territorial rights you have for representing any products or services. Point out any unique or distinctive elements about your products or services. (Include any product brochures, flyers, or information in support of this section in the section following the Company Summary main section and refer to it in this subsection). If there is a seasonal cycle to your business, then you should mention it, or any slower periods of business that recur annually.

Employees

Include in this area how many people are on staff and how many are full-time and part-time. Mention the various job titles or positions held. Set down the wages per position and mention how you schedule the labor to cover the daily needs of the business and its customers. You can say how long various people have been with your company (this can be viewed as a big positive in many cases). You should describe the owner's or partner's various responsibilities and duties performed, such as bookkeeping, ordering of inventory, sales and marketing, the major bidding, customer complaints, and so on. Put down the hours the owners or partners spend working each week. (50 to 80 hours) If the business has a manager in addition to the owner or partners, then specify the differences and the duties for each.

You should mention any personnel that should be replaced or who will not be staying with the business after the sale. This could be a family member, one of the partners, some employee that has given notice, and so on.

Mention any employee benefits and programs offered; this includes vacations and sick leave. If you have promised any raises, this should be mentioned. You can relate any pay scale differences that exist, such as paying certain people eight dollars per hour when the going rate is only $6.50 or vice versa. If you have a good staff of employees, accent this.

The Market

In this section, you should describe who uses your services or buys your products. Are they other businesses, consumers, or both? If you can relate how the area demographics support your business, then it is good to explain the demographic data in relation to your business and its growth. If your business sells to other businesses, you can add some information about the growth of *their* industry and how it relates to your sales; you can set out some strong reasons for buying your business. As you know, what goes on with your customers directly effects your sales level. Therefore, show the positives and how it all relates to your business. Include any demographic reports or articles from trade magazines or other sources in support of your statements.

Marketing and Competition

Describe all the types of advertising you have done and what you feel has worked the best; also mention all the ways you feel the business generates new customers. You can accent any special elements that set your business apart from the competition. Mention why you feel you keep the customers you have. (Mention that examples of your marketing materials can be seen in the last section of this package).

Regarding the competition, you should say something about how competitive the industry is, and say how many competitors you feel you have. If your industry is not too competitive, I would mention that. You can also describe this in geographical terms, such as within a three-mile area there are 16 similar businesses; or within the 92109 zip code, there are 10 similar businesses and our location is superior due to the following reasons. You can relate your strengths to the weaknesses of the competitors and point out why doing business in your part of town is superior to that of other places. This gives you a place to really draw a distinction between your business and the others. You can include an area map and identify the location of your business and the competitors. Place it in the package after this section.

Future Expectations

In this section, you should explain how you see the future for not only your business, but also your industry (you can point to the effect created by the changes in your customers). You can mention what changes the new owner should make to cause improvements in the business. If you can set forth specific elements and their positive effects and demonstrate the positive future of your industry and business, it will help a lot.

Why You Should Buy This Business

In this section, you should summarize and accent the main positive elements of your business as set out in the various sections above. You can mention how your business is unique and unlike any other. You can mention how well the business is priced. It's a real value! This is your opportunity to sell the best elements of your business. You should gather all the support documentation and articles in support of your statements you can find.

You can call your local chamber of commerce; they usually have a tremendous amount of information about many businesses and their industries, as well as demographics information. Contact your trade association for interesting information. Check the Internet for any information that could be helpful.

List of Furniture, Fixtures, and Equipment

Prepare a detailed list of the furniture, fixtures, and equipment that is included in the sale. You can also make a list of the things that do not go with the business, like a special antique desk, artwork, a special clock, or anything else that you will take with you.

Support Information

This is a place to put any supporting information you might have. Items such as magazine or newspaper articles about your business or its industry, maps identifying competitors' locations in relationship to your location, and the like. This is the end of the first section. Do not include examples of your marketing here. The last section of the package will be better for such things.

The Financial Information Section

If you have access to a spreadsheet program, you should prepare a summary of the financial history of your business (three to five years) and also a graphic depiction (a chart) of the history. You can place the graph at the beginning of this section right after the balance sheet (see the example presentation package).

If you cannot have your financial information put into a spreadsheet and presented in the way shown in the example package, then use the business's P&L as prepared by your accountant. Place an Adjustment to Financial Statement sheet behind each P&L you use (an example and a blank adjustment sheet is provided).

The financial section is very important and must be communicated properly so the buyer can understand the economic benefits of your business. As with most privately owned businesses, the owner's financial information is reported so they will pay the least amount of taxes as possible. Many business-owners live through their business by expensing many personal items through the business. In addition to the "perqs," there are noncash expenses, nonrecurrent expenses, and existing expenses that will not continue after you sell the business. There are also interest payments or lease payments you are making that may not necessarily be assumed by the buyer. All these elements must be identified to show the buyer how much money your business really generates. How they choose to spend the money is up to them (expensed through the business or not). I am not talking about "skim" or undisclosed income. This is dealing with what is on record. There are examples of how to show these adjustments to the P&Ls in the sample packages included with this outline).

The financial information should include the most recent balance sheet (if you have one), the most recent year-to-date financial profit or loss statement, and the adjustments to the most recent year-to-date P&L.

Next, put the P&L for the most recent year-end. It should be the December statement which shows not only the month of December, but the whole year-to-date ending 12/31/XX. If your business reports on a fiscal year and not a calendar year, then it will be the month of your year-end (June 30 or whatever month). Follow each P&L with an adjustment summary so the buyer understands how much money you really made.

Marketing and Promo Section

In this section, you should include copies of any Yellow Pages ads, promotional flyers, and brochures about your business or its products. You can put in any additional articles that you have that will be informative and supportive for your business and its industry.

On the very last page, you should include contact information (see the example package).

You can say: For Further Information: and include your name and a telephone number where you can be reached (voice mail). It is a good idea to mention that the information contained in the business presentation package is confidential and should not be discussed with anyone who is not involved in the buying decision.

Exhibits 2.2 and 2.3 are examples for business-owners who do not have the ability to create the financial section on a computer as presented in the example presentation package.

Exhibit 2.2 is a blank adjustment sheet provided for your use. Exhibit 2.3 is an example of what an adjustment sheet would look like when completed. In your presentation package, have the adjustment sheet follow the P&L from which you adjusted the information.

Exhibits 2.1, 2.4, and 2.5 show examples of three completed presentation packages. Each one is a variation of the outline. These examples are provided as guides so you can create your own presentation package. If you follow the form as laid out in these samples and in the outline, you will create presentation materials for your business that will be of great help in selling your business, and will be tremendous time-savers when it comes to informing buyers about your business.

For business-owners who do have the ability to create the financial section on a computer spreadsheet program, you will see in these sample packages a very-easy-to-understand way of presenting the financial information of your business.

Cover Page

PERFECT PRESS
OF
HILLSIDE

1240 MISSION RD.
YOUR TOWN, USA 92121

Exhibit 2.1 Sample of Actual Presentation Package

EXHIBIT 2.1 SAMPLE OF ACTUAL PRESENTATION PACKAGE

You can include a page or two of photos of the business' outside and inside.

Exhibit 2.1 *(Continued)*

113

Table of Contents

Exhibit 2.1 *(Continued)*

EXHIBIT 2.1 SAMPLE OF ACTUAL PRESENTATION PACKAGE

OFFERED FOR

PRICE	$275,000.00
Plus Inventory of approx.	$7,000.00
TOTAL PRICE	$282,000.00
CASH DOWN REQUIRED	$100,000.00
(Plus Inventory of approx. $7,000.00)	
ASSUME BALANCE DUE ON EQUIP. LEASES**	$7,000.00 (approx.)
BALANCE: SUBJECT TO NEW FINANCING	$168,000.00

FINANCING AVAILABLE

LENDER: SELLER	$168,000.00
INTEREST (ANNUAL PERCENTAGE RATE)	10.00%
TERM: (FULLY AMORTIZED)	4 YEARS
PAYMENTS: MONTHLY	$4,260.91
ANNUAL DEBT SERVICE	$51,130.97

Security on loan amount: The note shall be secured by a security agreement and UCC-1 filing on all securable assets of the business and shall be personally guaranteed by the buyer. Seller reserves the right to qualify and approve the buyer for seller financing.

**ASSUMPTION OF EQUIPMENT LEASES TO OWN:
Power Mac (computer) orig. 48 months as of 10-24-91, monthly pmts. $247.83
Bentongraphics 1655 press w/T-51 swing away head orig. 72 month as of 8-17-93
Monthly payments $561.36

There are lease/rental agreements to be assumed on Cannon Copiers and the Credit Card machine.
(It is recommended to continue renting these pieces of equipment and release new equip. when the leases are up)

TOTAL PRICE INCLUDES:

Customer list	Goodwill
Equipment on Lease/Rental is not	Inventory and supplies
included in the asking price	Lease for building
Franchise	Leasehold Improvements
Furniture, Fixtures, and Equipment	Noncompete Agreement
(owned and leased to own)	Training/Consulting

Exhibit 2.1 *(Continued)*

NOTE: Section divider (used a tabbed section divider here). If you do not want to use tabbed dividers then prepare a colored sheet of paper with the title of the section printed out as shown below.

BUSINESS SUMMARY SECTION

Exhibit 2.1 *(Continued)*

EXHIBIT 2.1 SAMPLE OF ACTUAL PRESENTATION PACKAGE

PERFECT PRESS
1240 Mission Rd.
Your Town, USA 92121

Business Summary

Type of Business
Quick Offset Printing 1&2 Color, Graphic Design, and Typesetting
Photo Copying and Duplication Services
SIC Code Classification: 2752-99

Location
Located in the Hillside Community of Your Town in the Hillside Colonnade
Shopping Center, at 1240 Mission Rd.

Organization
General Partnership

Franchise Information
Perfect Press is a franchise business. The franchise fee is 6% of Gross Billings
up to $20,000 in monthly billings. There is no additional advertising fee. (This
franchise does participate in co-op Yellow Page advertising). The term of the
Franchise Agreement is 35 years and is renewable for an additional 35-year
term. Franchisees must attend a two (2) week training program. The Franchisor has a 60-day right to purchase this business at the same terms and conditions that are acceptable to a bona fide prospective assignee. (A copy of the
Franchise Agreement is available to you after an Agreement to Purchase has
been accepted.)

Key Points of Interest
1) Established Reputation for Excellent Service   4) Good Lease and Location
2) History of Dependable Profits   5) Expansion Potential
3) Up-to-Date Equipment   6) Owner will provide training

Exhibit 2.1 *(Continued)*

Reason for Selling
Partners Desire to Pursue Other Business Interests

Business Established
In January 1988 (original owners)

Business Hours
7:30 A.M.–5:00 P.M. Monday through Friday (Closed Saturday and Sunday)

Location, Lease, and Facilities
Perfect Press occupies approximately 1,375 square feet of leased retail shopping center space in the Hillside Colonnade. It is located in the Your Town community of Hillside, which is east of Mission Valley, just off of Freeway 8, at 1240 Mission Rd. The current lease became effective May 1, 1993, and expires April 30, 1998. The base rent is $2,555.84 plus CAM fees of $657.00 per month. There is a security deposit requirement of $1,993.75. It is possible that the landlord could ask for an increase in the deposit since the amount currently held is equal to the original base rent and the current rent is higher. The base rent is subject to annual increases of no less that 4% and no greater than 7%. A full copy of the lease will be made available during the buyer's due diligence phase. The location has proven to be very good. There is plenty of parking, the clients can access the shopping center easily, Freeway 8 is very close which puts the shop within a 20 minute drive of most of the largest commercial/retail business and residential areas of Your Town. The average daily traffic count going past the shopping center is 23.9 thousand cars. The Hillside community is made up of a fairly dense mix of residential and business properties, which provides opportunity for a lot of retail business clients in a close proximity.

Business' History
Perfect Press was established in January 1988 as a sole proprietorship, by July of that same year Ms. Betty Evens joined with Ms. Elmira Kissinger to form a partnership. The business has received the Perfect Press Top Quality Award, The 10-Star Achievement Award and was placed in the Women Business Owner's Grant Competition in 1990. The business continues to receive excellent ratings from the Perfect Press Regional Vice President. *Perfect Press* has shown stability in its business performance and growth since its first year. By 1990 the gross revenue reached $452,802 and $511,000 by the end of 1994.

Exhibit 2.1 *(Continued)*

EXHIBIT 2.1 SAMPLE OF ACTUAL PRESENTATION PACKAGE

Description of Business' Services

Perfect Press is a franchise Offset Printing 1&2 Color, Graphic Design, & Typesetting Photo Copying & Duplication Services business. Perfect Press fills the gap between the "quick print" shop and the commercial printing businesses.

The services offered include Letterheads, Envelopes, Carbonless Business Forms, Color Printing, Typesetting & Design, Bindery & Finishing, Newsletters, High-Speed Copies, Announcements, Invitations, Die-Cutting, Embossing, Index Tabs, Brochures, Flyers, Booklets, Presentation Folders, Engraved Badges & Nameplates, Rubber Stamps, Fax Service, Resumes, Raised-Letter & Engraved Printing, as well as Pick-Up & Delivery.

Business' Operations

The printing job begins with client contact which may include a price quote using a pricing computer or price list, planning and/or preparation of the artwork, and scheduling for a due date.

Once the order is placed, a four-part invoice is completed and the order is processed for in-house printing or sub-contracted (outside) printing. All in-house orders are placed in a numbered job box that follows the order through to completion.

All pre-press work is proofed both in-house and by the client for accuracy. *Perfect Press* maintains a close to error free record. When the client has approved the "final," the order is prepared for the press. The plates are prepared and the order is printed as specified. Any final finishing is competed such as folding, cutting, and so on, and the order receives its final quality check by the manager or owner only before packaging, the order is then packaged.

The client is notified when the order is completed and the project is shipped via a delivery service (Interconnect), a staff member, or picked up by the client.

Regular sub-contracted printing orders, which include business cards, labels, rubber stamps, and so on are completed on forms provided by the companies and are picked up, faxed, or mailed for processing. A hard copy of each order sent out remains on file. When received, the order is carefully checked for accuracy before notifying the client of its completion and that it's ready for pick-up.

Large sub-contracted orders are handled by one of the Partners or Assistant Manager working with trade printers. *Perfect Press* has and maintains very congenial and professional relationships with several top quality trade printers in the area.

Exhibit 2.1 *(Continued)*

The printing operation is divided into three major production stages; pre-press, press production, and finishing (bindery) production. The pre-press operation involves preparation of the artwork for printing which may include graphic layouts, typesetting, and camera work which includes halftones, negatives, and color stripping. The Offset press operation includes the actual printing process of transferring ink to paper. The finishing or bindery operation may include folding, collating, stapling, trimming, cutting, packaging, and a final quality check.

Employees
Perfect Press has four (4) full-time employees including one of the partners, plus the other partner who works part-time. The people and their positions are as follows:

Lisa Fira: **Assistant Manager,** has been on staff since August 1990, and is compensated (salary) $1,750.00 per month.

Edward (Mike) McVain: **Press Operator.** He has been with *Perfect Press* since October 1990 and is paid $14.00 per hour plus Medical Benefits for himself and his son. He is also paid a Christmas bonus of $1,000.000.

John Robins: **Customer Service** (50%) and **Typesetting & Graphics** (50%) He started in early October of 1995 and is compensated at $6.50 per hour.

Elmira Kissinger (Partner): She works in the business full-time and provides the overall daily **General Management** as well as financial management. As managing partner Elmira does what ever tasks are necessary to help the business function smoothly with exception of performing pre-press operations.

Betty Evens (Partner): She currently works part-time and is in charge of the **pre-press operations** (design, typesetting, graphics, photos, etc.)

The Market
Perfect Press has focused on developing a diversified client base which includes larger businesses who have frequent and large volume printing needs, accounts which have the potential of repeat orders of basics such as business cards, letterhead, envelopes, invoices, and brochures, small businesses and individuals who have occasional printing needs, and local as well as national organizations which require Monthly Newsletters and meeting materials. *Perfect Press* has good stable clients from a wide variety of geographic areas of San Diego County, but focuses its marketing efforts on the surrounding three to five mile radius that includes the zip code areas of 92101, 92103, 92104, 92108, and 92116.

Exhibit 2.1 *(Continued)*

EXHIBIT 2.1 SAMPLE OF ACTUAL PRESENTATION PACKAGE

Marketing

The location of *Perfect Press* is a marketing tool in itself. Within its market area, many people who know that *Perfect Press* is the "place to go" for their quality printing needs. Word of mouth through satisfied customers a is very successful way the business continues to grow.

Perfect Press has found much success in a bi-monthly direct mail marketing program (see the sample newsletter). The areas of concentration are on the 7,200 businesses found in the zip codes of 92101, 92103, 92104, 92108, and 92116. *Perfect Press* participates in collective Yellow Page advertising with other *Perfect Press* franchises in the Your Town area.

Perfect Press has plenty of room for improvement, too, such as reestablishing a successful *Perfect Press* marketing program which used students from local colleges who are majoring in Business and Marketing for representing *Perfect Press* to local businesses, or offering free quotes on current printing needs.

There are sample marketing pieces located in the rear of this package.

Competition

The competition in the Hillside area includes POP Printing at 4101 Flanders Street, QuickPrint located at 5302 Fifth Street, and Crown Printing at 1452 Mission Rd. Since *Perfect Press* does not contain itself to just Hillside for its clientele, it is in competition with any printer in the Greater Your Town area.

Perfect Press is competitive in pricing and stresses quality and fast turn-around. The success and margins the business enjoys are maintained by the high level of customer service and satisfaction that far exceeds the competition.

Located in the same shopping center (Hillside Colonnade) for the past 8 years was a competitor in the copy business, Hillside Copy, who just moved about 1½ miles away on November 1, 1995. *Perfect Press* has felt a significant increase in copy business and is making plans to capitalize on the opportunity.

Future Expectations

The number of potential customers within the business's market are still growing and will continue to add revenues to this business. Due to a competitors relocation this business should increase its photo copy business. With continuing changes in technology the business will be able to grow by offering faster turn-around times on projects, Internet marketing, and communication between customers and the business, as well as offering improved quality.

Exhibit 2.1 *(Continued)*

Why you should buy this business

Printing needs are growing and the demand for fast, quality work is always present. This is not a trendy business, it is a mainline manufacturing/service business that is always in demand. *Perfect Press* is a very profitable business and for its volume of gross revenues, has an excellent net profit. The crew of employees assembled are very good and are happy working at *Perfect Press.* It took a long time and a lot of effort to assemble the present crew of employees, a real asset. The price this business if offered for creates a very good return on your investment in the business. The location of this business is very good. Due to the location, less can be spent on advertising than many of our competitors.

List of Furniture, Fixtures, and Equipment

Equipment

Qty	Description
2	Bentongraphics 1650 Offset Press with T-Head
1	Duplo 8-Bin Table Top Collator
1	MBM model 1000 Booklet Maker
1	Challenge Drill (single hole)
complete	Telephone System
1	GBC Binding Cart
Misc.	Drying Racks and Storage Shelves
1	Vacuum
Misc.	Floor Mats
1	Powder Sprayer (for 1650 press)
1	Neon Window Sign
1	600 dpi Hewlett Packard Laserjet Printer
1	Color Scanner
1	Bernouli Drive
1	Apple 14″ Monitor and Keyboard
1	Compaq Computer for Pricing
1	Velo Binding System
1	Extra Blade for Cutter
1	Shrink Wrap Machine
1	Phone Mate Answering Machine
1	Air Purifier
1	Computer Desk

Exhibit 2.1 *(Continued)*

EXHIBIT 2.1 SAMPLE OF ACTUAL PRESENTATION PACKAGE

1	Front Service Counter and Extensions
Misc.	Bookcases—Lobby
Misc.	Computer Furniture
1	Stapler—Electric
1	GBC Electric Binder
1	Large Capacity Stapler
1	Client File System
1	Power Mac 8100
1	Baum Airfeed 714 Folder
1	Ink Mixing Kit
1	Murata 30 Fax Machine
1	1250 Offset Press
1	3M Dual Platemaking System
1	Metal Platemaker
1	Plate Punch
1	Padder
1	Light Table
1	Electric Outdoor Sign
1	Interior Signs
1	Front Service Counter
2	Folding Tables
3	Work Benches
1	18″ Electric Cutter
1	Plate Fuser
1	Friction Feed Folder
5	Chairs
	Lobby Furniture
2	Desks
1	Color Cell Display Message Unit (window)
1	Welbilt Refrigerator
1	Toshiba Microwave Oven
1	Coffee Pot 10 cup
4	4-Drawer Filing Cabinets
2	Under-Desk 2-Drawer Filing Cabinets
2	Equipment Carts: For Folders
1	GBC Manual Binding Machine
1	3 Hole Punch
1	2 Hole Punch

Exhibit 2.1 *(Continued)*

1	Canon P26-D Calculator
1	Perfect Press Clock
4	Sample Display Boards, in Lobby
5	Large Trash Cans
7	Small Trash Cans
2	Fire extinguishers
1	Drafting Chair, behind Counter
1	White Board for Messages
5	Small Hand Staplers
2	Small Hand-Held Calculators
Misc.	Drafting Tools for Light Table
1	Dolly

Lease Hold Improvements

Description

220 Electrical Line (for 1650 Presses)
New Front Window
220 Electrical Line (for Copier)
Hot Water Heater
Alarm System

Exhibit 2.1 *(Continued)*

EXHIBIT 2.1 SAMPLE OF ACTUAL PRESENTATION PACKAGE

NOTE: Section divider (used a tabbed section divider here). If you do not want to use tabbed dividers then prepare a colored sheet of paper with the title of the section printed out as shown below.

FINANCIAL
SECTION

Exhibit 2.1 *(Continued)*

Financial Information Section Organization Tips

You can organize this section in any order you prefer. I start with the most recent balance sheet, followed by the most recent Year-To-Date financial statement, followed by the adjustment page. Next I put the last year's Year-End financial statement followed by the adjustment page. I put the next oldest year's financial statement followed by the adjustment page. You can continue in this method for as many years as you want to include (usually no more than 5 years).

If you have the ability to create a graph or chart of the main financial information, such as the annual gross sales, gross profit, total expenses, and adjusted net profit, then I would put the graph as the page following the balance sheet.

Exhibit 2.1 *(Continued)*

EXHIBIT 2.1 SAMPLE OF ACTUAL PRESENTATION PACKAGE

Perfect Press of Hillside
1240 Mission Rd.   Your Town, USA 92121
Adjusted Balance Sheet

10/31/95

	Reported
CURRENT ASSETS	
CASH	8,000.00
ACCOUNTS RECEIVABLES	75,000.00
INVENTORY	12,500.00
TOTAL CURRENT ASSETS	**95,500.00**
FIXED ASSETS	
FURNITURE, FIXTURES, & EQUIPMENT	85,000.00
DEPOSIT: RENT	2,200.00
TOTAL FIXED ASSETS	**91,932.37**
OTHER ASSETS	
TOTAL OTHER ASSETS	**0.00**
TOTAL ASSETS	**187,432.37**

Liabilities and Stockholder's Equity

CURRENT LIABILITIES	
ACCOUNTS PAYABLE	51,000.00
PAYROLL TAXES	3,500.00
SALES TAX PAYABLE	2,300.00
TOTAL CURRENT LIABILITIES	**56,800.00**
LONG-TERM LIABILITIES	
NOTE PAYABLE	15,000.00
TOTAL LONG-TERM LIABILITIES	**15,000.00**
TOTAL LIABILITIES	**71,800.00**
TOTAL STOCKHOLDERS EQUITY	**115,632.37**
TOTAL LIABILITIES AND STOCKHOLDERS EQUITY	**187,432.37**

Exhibit 2.1 *(Continued)*

Perfect Press of Hillside
1240 Mission Rd.   Your Town, USA 92121

**Statement of Revenue and Income
Reported vs. Adjusted**

SALES	Reported 31-Oct-95	Adjusted 31-Oct-95	%
Sales: B&W Copying	193,254.00	193,254.00	28.00%
Sales: Printing	178,654.00	178,654.00	25.89%
Sales: Binding	52,147.07	52,147.07	7.56%
Sales: Graphic Designs	47,998.00	47,998.00	6.95%
Sales: Color Copy	37,241.00	37,241.00	5.40%
Sales: Subcontract	168,683.21	168,683.21	24.44%
Sales: Self-Serve	15,421.00	15,421.00	2.23%
Sales: Returns (Credits)	(2,918.86)	(2,918.86)	−0.42%
Sales: Discounts	(348.76)	(348.76)	−0.05%
TOTAL SALES	**690,130.66**	**690,130.66**	100.00%
COST OF SALES			
Labor	132,321.00	132,321.00	19.17%
Production Supplies	42,561.00	42,561.00	6.17%
Paper Supplies	61,325.00	61,325.00	8.89%
Equipment Depreciation	10,203.00 [1]	0.00	0.00%
Equipment Maintenance	1,800.00	1,800.00	0.26%
Equipment Interest Charges	750.00 [2]	0.00	0.00%
Equipment Rental	22,416.67	22,416.67	3.25%
Sub-Contract Expense	110,000.00	110,000.00	15.94%
TOTAL COST OF SALES	**381,376.67**	**370,423.67**	53.67%
GROSS PROFIT	**308,753.99**	**319,706.99**	46.33%

Exhibit 2.1 *(Continued)*

EXHIBIT 2.1 SAMPLE OF ACTUAL PRESENTATION PACKAGE

EXPENSES

Accounting	11,500.00	11,500.00	1.67%
Advertising	4,666.67	4,666.67	0.68%
Bad Debt Expense	685.00	685.00	0.10%
Bank Charges	1,878.33	1,878.33	0.27%
Cash Over/Short	25.00	25.00	0.00%
Depreciation Expense	5,250.00 [3]	0.00	0.00%
Entertainment	166.00 [4]	0.00	0.00%
Franchise Royalty Fee	41,407.80	41,407.80	6.00%
Fuel	2,183.00	2,183.00	0.32%
Gas & Electric	2,215.00	2,215.00	0.32%
Insurance: Employees	3,625.00 [5]	2,600.00	0.38%
Insurance: Vehicle	1,916.67	1,916.67	0.28%
Insurance: Workman's Comp	4,200.00	4,200.00	0.61%
Interest	5,500.00 [6]	0.00	0.00%
Leases/Rentals	2,080.00	2,080.00	0.30%
Licenses & Permits	150.00	150.00	0.02%
Maintenance & Repair	3,152.07	3,152.07	0.46%
Office Supplies	1,523.00	1,523.00	0.22%
Payroll Tax Expense	9,333.33	9,333.33	1.35%
Postage & Freight	2,350.00	2,350.00	0.34%
Property Tax Expense	685.00	685.00	0.10%
Rent	22,050.00	22,050.00	3.20%
Salaries: Sales	22,708.33	22,708.33	3.29%
Salaries	60,000.00	60,000.00	8.69%
Security	500.00	500.00	0.07%
Subscriptions	125.00	125.00	0.02%
Telephone	8,708.33	8,708.33	1.26%
Vehicle Expenses	3,800.00 [7]	1,850.00	0.27%
Water & Trash	1,553.00	1,553.00	0.23%
Yellow Pages	6,600.00	6,600.00	0.96%
TOTAL EXPENSES	**230,536.53**	**216,645.53**	31.39%
NET PROFIT / LOSS	**78,217.46**	**103,061.46**	14.93%

Exhibit 2.1 *(Continued)*

129

Notes Explaining Adjustments to Financial Statements

The following notes explaining the adjustments to the financial reports are presented for the purpose of assisting a potential buyer in reaching an understanding of the monetary benefits associated with the ownership of this business

The adjusted net income represents the available cash earnings generated through *Perfect Press.* This proprietary cash flow is that which the business produces prior to the owner's compensation, nonessential expenses, owner's perquisites, noncash expenses, nonrecurrent expenses, and any other expenses which are not mandatory or regular expenses of the business

Adjustments as of Year to Date October 31, 1995

NOTES

[1] **Equipment Depreciation:** This is a noncash expense.

[2] **Equipment Interest:** This is adjusted because the equipment will be paid off therefore the new owner will not have this expense.

[3] **Depreciation Expense:** This is noncash expense.

[4] **Entertainment:** This was a perq. for the owner.

[5] **Insurance, Employees:** The portion adjusted is a perq. for the owner.

[6] **Interest Expense:** The interest expense of the current owner will not continue for a new owner, this also aids in showing the business' earnings power prior to any debt.

[7] **Vehicle Expense:** This is for the owner's personal auto.

Exhibit 2.1 *(Continued)*

EXHIBIT 2.1 SAMPLE OF ACTUAL PRESENTATION PACKAGE

Perfect Press of Hillside
1240 Mission Rd. Your Town, USA 92121

Statement of Revenue and Income
Reported vs. Adjusted

SALES	Reported 1994	Adjusted 1994	%
Sales: B&W Copying	207,321.00	207,321.00	27.33%
Sales: Printing	213,256.00	213,256.00	28.11%
Sales: Binding	45,632.00	45,632.00	6.01%
Sales: Graphic Designs	42,578.00	42,578.00	5.61%
Sales: Color Copy	36,874.00	36,874.00	4.86%
Sales: Subcontract	262,456.00	262,456.00	34.59%
Sales: Self-Serve	17,452.00	17,452.00	2.30%
Sales: Returns (Credits)	(1,589.00)	(1,589.00)	–0.21%
Sales: Discounts	(2,345.00)	(2,345.00)	–0.31%
TOTAL SALES	**821,635.00**	**821,635.00**	100.00%
COST OF SALES			
Labor	139,779.78	139,779.78	17.01%
Production Supplies	45,632.00	45,632.00	5.55%
Paper Supplies	76,142.00	76,142.00	9.27%
Equipment Depreciation	10,206.22 [1]	0.00	0.00%
Equipment Maintenance	3,800.00	3,800.00	0.46%
Equipment Interest Charges	618.00 [2]	0.00	0.00%
Equipment Rental	26,900.00	26,900.00	3.27%
Sub-Contract Expense	132,000.00	132,000.00	16.07%
TOTAL COST OF SALES	**435,078.00**	**424,253.78**	51.64%
GROSS PROFIT	**386,557.00**	**397,381.22**	48.36%

Exhibit 2.1 *(Continued)*

EXPENSES

Accounting	13,800.00	13,800.00	1.68%
Advertising	5,200.00	5,200.00	0.63%
Bad Debt Expense	585.00	585.00	0.07%
Bank Charges	2,254.00	2,254.00	0.27%
Cash Over/Short	0.00	0.00	0.00%
Depreciation Expense	6,300.00 [3]	0.00	0.00%
Entertainment	163.00 [4]	0.00	0.00%
Franchise Royalty Fee	49,298.10	49,298.10	6.00%
Fuel	2,620.00	2,620.00	0.32%
Gas & Electric	2,658.00	2,658.00	0.32%
Insurance: Employees	4,350.00 [5]	1,482.12	0.18%
Insurance: Vehicle	2,265.00 [6]	925.00	0.11%
Insurance: Workman's Comp	4,950.00	4,950.00	0.60%
Interest	6,003.10 [7]	0.00	0.00%
Leases/Rentals	2,496.00	2,496.00	0.30%
Licenses & Permits	365.00	365.00	0.04%
Maintenance & Repair	5,674.00	5,674.00	0.69%
Office Supplies	3,200.00 [8]	2,750.00	0.33%
Payroll Tax Expense	11,200.00	11,200.00	1.36%
Postage & Freight	2,850.00	2,850.00	0.35%
Property Tax Expense	780.00	780.00	0.09%
Rent	26,460.00	26,460.00	3.22%
Salaries: Sales	27,250.00	27,250.00	3.32%
Salaries	61,082.80	61,082.80	7.43%
Security	685.00	685.00	0.08%
Subscriptions	85.00	85.00	0.01%
Telephone	9,200.00	9,200.00	1.12%
Travel	654.00 [9]	0.00	0.00%
Vehicle Expenses	4,018.00 [10]	2,100.00	0.26%
Water & Trash	1,658.00	1,658.00	0.20%
Yellow Pages	7,000.00	7,000.00	0.85%
TOTAL EXPENSES	**265,104.00**	**245,408.02**	29.87%
NET PROFIT / LOSS	**121,453.00**	**151,973.20**	18.50%

Exhibit 2.1 *(Continued)*

132

EXHIBIT 2.1 SAMPLE OF ACTUAL PRESENTATION PACKAGE

Notes Explaining Adjustments to Financial Statements

The following notes explaining the adjustments to the financial reports are presented for the purpose of assisting a potential buyer in reaching an understanding of the monetary benefits associated with the ownership of this business

The adjusted net income represents the available cash earnings generated through *Perfect Press*. This proprietary cash flow is that which the business produces prior to the owner's compensation, nonessential expenses, owner's perquisites, noncash expenses, nonrecurrent expenses, and any other expenses which are not mandatory or regular expenses of the business

Adjustments for Year Ending 12/31/94

NOTES

[1] **Equipment Depreciation:** This is a noncash expense.

[2] **Equipment Interest:** This is adjusted because the equipment will be paid off therefore the new owner will not have this expense.

[3] **Depreciation Expense:** This expense was for the nonproduction equipment and was added back since it is not a cash expense.

[4] **Entertainment:** This is a perquisite of the owner and not a business expense.

[5] **Insurance, Employees:** The portion adjusted is a perq. for the owner.

[6] **Insurance, Vehicle:** This amount adjusted was for the owner's auto.

[7] **Interest Expense:** The interest expense of the current owner will not continue for a new owner; this also aids in showing the business' earnings power prior to any debt.

[8] **Office Supplies:** The amount deducted was from a personal project and not normal overhead.

[9] **Travel:** This expense was a perquisite of the owner, non–business-related expense.

[10] **Vehicle Expense:** The owner expensed his personal vehicle as a perq. The amount is $9,439.88.

Exhibit 2.1 *(Continued)*

Perfect Press of Hillside
1240 Mission Rd.   Your Town, USA 92121

Statement of Revenue and Income
Reported vs. Adjusted

SALES	Reported 1993		Adjusted 1993	%
Sales: B&W Copying	213,851.00		213,851.00	31.34%
Sales: Printing	183,954.00		183,954.00	26.96%
Sales: Binding	49,824.00		49,824.00	7.30%
Sales: Graphic Designs	32,660.00		32,660.00	4.79%
Sales: Color Copy	28,562.73		28,562.73	4.19%
Sales: Subcontract	234,578.32		234,578.32	34.37%
Sales: Self-Serve	16,542.00		16,542.00	2.42%
Sales: Returns (Credits)	(354.00)		(354.00)	−0.05%
Sales: Discounts	(954.00)		(954.00)	−0.14%
TOTAL SALES	**758,664.05**		**758,664.05**	100.00%
COST OF SALES				
Labor	133,811.18		133,811.18	17.64%
Production Supplies	36,215.36		36,215.36	4.77%
Paper Supplies	73,698.00		73,698.00	9.71%
Equipment Depreciation	9,785.00	[1]	0.00	0.00%
Equipment Maintenance	3,600.00		3,600.00	0.47%
Equipment Interest Charges	618.00	[2]	0.00	0.00%
Equipment Rental	24,154.00		24,154.00	3.18%
Sub-Contract Expense	120,145.00		120,145.00	15.84%
TOTAL COST OF SALES	**402,026.54**		**391,623.54**	51.62%
GROSS PROFIT	**356,637.51**		**367,040.51**	48.38%

Exhibit 2.1 *(Continued)*

134

EXHIBIT 2.1 SAMPLE OF ACTUAL PRESENTATION PACKAGE

EXPENSES

Accounting	13,700.00	13,700.00	1.81%
Advertising	4,875.00	4,875.00	0.64%
Bad Debt Expense	1,200.00	1,200.00	0.16%
Bank Charges	2,365.00	2,365.00	0.31%
Cash Over/Short	96.00	96.00	0.01%
Depreciation Expense	6,500.00 [3]	0.00	0.00%
Entertainment	350.00 [4]	0.00	0.00%
Franchise Royalty Fee	45,600.00	45,600.00	6.01%
Fuel	2,540.00	2,540.00	0.33%
Gas & Electric	2,700.00	2,700.00	0.36%
Insurance: Employees	4,200.00 [5]	1,478.00	0.19%
Insurance: Vehicle	2,265.00 [6]	925.00	0.12%
Insurance: Workman's Comp	4,800.00	4,800.00	0.63%
Interest	6,003.10 [7]	0.00	0.00%
Leases/Rentals	2,496.00	2,496.00	0.33%
Licenses & Permits	350.00	350.00	0.05%
Maintenance & Repair	5,421.00	5,421.00	0.71%
Office Supplies	2,800.00	2,800.00	0.37%
Payroll Tax Expense	9,875.00	9,875.00	1.30%
Postage & Freight	3,013.00	3,013.00	0.40%
Property Tax Expense	632.00	632.00	0.08%
Rent	25,200.00	25,200.00	3.32%
Salaries: Sales	26,325.00	26,325.00	3.47%
Salaries	60,324.85	60,324.85	7.95%
Security	685.00	685.00	0.09%
Subscriptions	245.00	245.00	0.03%
Telephone	8,100.00	8,100.00	1.07%
Travel	3,500.00 [8]	0.00	0.00%
Vehicle Expenses	4,325.00 [9]	1,850.00	0.24%
Water & Trash	1,654.00	1,654.00	0.22%
Yellow Pages	5,600.00	5,600.00	0.74%
TOTAL EXPENSES	**257,739.95**	**234,849.85**	30.96%
NET PROFIT / LOSS	**98,897.56**	**132,190.66**	17.42%

Exhibit 2.1 (Continued)

Notes Explaining Adjustments to Financial Statements

The following notes explaining the adjustments to the financial reports are presented for the purpose of assisting a potential buyer in reaching an understanding of the complete monetary benefits associated with the ownership of this business.

The adjusted net income represents the available cash earnings generated through *Perfect Press.* This proprietary cash flow is that which the business produces prior to the owner's compensation, nonessential expenses, owner's perquisites, noncash expenses, nonrecurrent expenses, and any other expenses which are not mandatory or regular expenses of the business. As well, any income that is nonoperational has been eliminated.

Adjustments for Year Ending 12/31/93

NOTES
[1] **Equipment Depreciation:** This is a noncash expense.
[2] **Equipment Interest:** This is adjusted because the equipment will be paid off therefore the new owner will not have this expense.
[3] **Depreciation Expense:** This is noncash expense.
[4] **Entertainment:** This was a perq. for the owner.
[5] **Insurance, Employees:** The portion adjusted is a perq. for the owner.
[6] **Insurance: Vehicle:** This amount adjusted was for the owner's auto.
[7] **Interest Expense:** The interest expense of the current owner will not continue for a new owner; this also aids in showing the business's earnings power prior to any debt.
[8] **Travel:** This expense was a perquisite of the owner, a non–business-related expense.
[9] **Vehicle Expense:** This is for the owner's personal auto.

Exhibit 2.1 *(Continued)*

EXHIBIT 2.1 SAMPLE OF ACTUAL PRESENTATION PACKAGE

Perfect Press of Hillside
1240 Mission Rd.   Your Town, USA 92121

Statement of Revenue and Income
Reported vs. Adjusted

SALES	Reported 1992		Adjusted 1992	%
Sales: B&W Copying	199,538.68		199,538.68	33.16%
Sales: Printing	169,512.80		169,512.80	28.17%
Sales: Binding	37,926.37		37,926.37	6.30%
Sales: Graphic Designs	37,582.30		37,582.30	6.25%
Sales: Color Copy	32,000.00		32,000.00	5.32%
Sales: Subcontract	192,521.96		192,521.96	32.00%
Sales: Self-Serve	14,569.00		14,569.00	2.42%
Sales: Returns (Credits)	(875.00)		(875.00)	−0.15%
Sales: Discounts	(336.00)		(336.00)	−0.06%
TOTAL SALES	**682,440.11**		**682,440.11**	100.00%
COST OF SALES				
Labor	113,354.00		113,354.00	16.61%
Production Supplies	28,541.00		28,541.00	4.18%
Paper Supplies	63,541.00		63,541.00	9.31%
Equipment Depreciation	9,861.25	[1]	0.00	0.00%
Equipment Maintenance	4,800.00		4,800.00	0.70%
Equipment Interest Charges	614.81	[2]	0.00	0.00%
Equipment Rental	23,245.00		23,245.00	3.41%
Sub-Contract Expense	112,000.00		112,000.00	16.41%
TOTAL COST OF SALES	**355,957.06**		**345,481.00**	50.62%
GROSS PROFIT	**326,483.05**		**336,959.11**	49.38%

Exhibit 2.1 *(Continued)*

EXPENSES

Accounting	13,200.00	13,200.00	1.93%
Advertising	4,125.00	4,125.00	0.60%
Bad Debt Expense	125.00	125.00	0.02%
Bank Charges	2,241.00	2,241.00	0.33%
Cash Over/Short	86.00	86.00	0.01%
Depreciation Expense	6,500.00 [3]	0.00	0.00%
Entertainment	540.00 [4]	0.00	0.00%
Franchise Royalty Fee	41,000.00	41,000.00	6.01%
Fuel	2,300.00	2,300.00	0.34%
Gas & Electric	2,631.00	2,631.00	0.39%
Insurance: Employees	3,365.00 [5]	1,235.00	0.18%
Insurance: Vehicle	2,135.00 [6]	850.00	0.12%
Insurance: Workman's Comp	4,200.00	4,200.00	0.62%
Interest	6,834.22 [7]	0.00	0.00%
Leases/Rentals	2,365.00	2,365.00	0.35%
Licenses & Permits	250.00	250.00	0.04%
Maintenance & Repair	425.00	425.00	0.06%
Office Supplies	1,563.00	1,563.00	0.23%
Payroll Tax Expense	8,254.00	8,254.00	1.21%
Postage & Freight	1,845.00	1,845.00	0.27%
Property Tax Expense	524.00	524.00	0.08%
Rent	24,000.00	24,000.00	3.52%
Salaries: Sales	22,315.00	22,315.00	3.27%
Salaries	42,802.09	42,802.09	6.27%
Security	300.00	300.00	0.04%
Subscriptions	150.00	150.00	0.02%
Telephone	7,200.00	7,200.00	1.06%
Travel	585.00 [8]	0.00	0.00%
Vehicle Expenses	3,895.00 [9]	1,700.00	0.25%
Water & Trash	1,142.00	1,142.00	0.17%
Yellow Pages	4,578.00	4,578.00	0.67%
TOTAL EXPENSES	**211,475.31**	**191,406.09**	28.05%
NET PROFIT / LOSS	**115,007.74**	**145,553.02**	21.33%

Exhibit 2.1 *(Continued)*

EXHIBIT 2.1 SAMPLE OF ACTUAL PRESENTATION PACKAGE

Notes Explaining Adjustments to Financial Statements

The following notes explaining the adjustments to the financial reports are presented for the purpose of assisting a potential buyer in reaching an understanding of the complete monetary benefits associated with the ownership of this business.

The adjusted net income represents the available cash earnings generated through **Perfect Press.** This proprietary cash flow is that which the business produces prior to the owner's compensation, nonessential expenses, owner's perquisites, noncash expenses, nonrecurrent expenses, and any other expenses which are not mandatory or regular expenses of the business. As well, any income that is nonoperational has been eliminated.

Adjustments for Year Ending 12/31/92

NOTES

[1] **Equipment Depreciation:** This is a noncash expense.

[2] **Equipment Interest:** This is adjusted because the equipment will be paid off; therefore, the new owner will not have this expense.

[3] **Depreciation Expense:** This is noncash expense.

[4] **Entertainment:** This is a perquisite of the owners. It is not overhead expense.

[5] **Insurance, Employees:** The portion adjusted is a perq. for the owner.

[6] **Insurance: Vehicle:** This amount adjusted was for the owner's auto.

[7] **Interest Expense:** The interest expense of the current owner will not continue for a new owner, this also aids in showing the business's earnings power prior to any debt.

[8] **Travel:** This expense was a perquisite of the owner, non–business-related expense.

[9] **Vehicle Expense:** This is for the owner's personal auto.

Exhibit 2.1 *(Continued)*

Perfect Press of Hillside
1240 Mission Rd.   Your Town, USA 92121

Statement of Revenue and Income
Reported vs. Adjusted

SALES	Reported 1991	Adjusted 1991	%
Sales: B&W Copying	185,237.00	185,237.00	30.79%
Sales: Printing	133,254.00	133,254.00	22.15%
Sales: Binding	31,336.00	31,336.00	5.21%
Sales: Graphic Designs	53,247.00	53,247.00	8.85%
Sales: Color Copy	28,754.00	28,754.00	4.78%
Sales: Subcontract	155,321.00	155,321.00	25.81%
Sales: Self-Serve	16,325.00	16,325.00	2.71%
Sales: Returns (Credits)	(1,254.00)	(1,254.00)	–0.21%
Sales: Discounts	(536.00)	(536.00)	–0.09%
TOTAL SALES	**601,684.00**	**601,684.00**	100.00%
COST OF SALES			
Labor	110,236.00	110,236.00	18.32%
Production Supplies	19,356.00	19,356.00	3.22%
Paper Supplies	62,354.00	62,354.00	10.36%
Equipment Depreciation	10,110.00 [1]	10,110.00	1.68%
Equipment Maintenance	5,200.00	5,200.00	0.86%
Equipment Interest Charges	500.00 [2]	500.00	0.08%
Equipment Rental	26,000.00	26,000.00	4.32%
Sub-Contract Expense	108,000.00	108,000.00	17.95%
TOTAL COST OF SALES	**341,756.00**	**341,756.00**	56.80%
GROSS PROFIT	**259,928.00**	**259,928.00**	43.20%

Exhibit 2.1 *(Continued)*

EXHIBIT 2.1 SAMPLE OF ACTUAL PRESENTATION PACKAGE

EXPENSES

Accounting	12,000.00	12,000.00	1.99%
Advertising	3,654.00	3,654.00	0.61%
Bad Debt Expense	250.00	250.00	0.04%
Bank Charges	2,085.74	2,085.74	0.35%
Cash Over/Short	40.00	40.00	0.01%
Depreciation Expense	6,500.00 [3]	0.00	0.00%
Entertainment	150.00 [4]	0.00	0.00%
Franchise Royalty Fee	36,000.00	36,000.00	5.98%
Fuel	2,100.00	2,100.00	0.35%
Gas & Electric	2,521.00	2,521.00	0.42%
Insurance: Employees	3,625.00 [5]	1,100.00	0.18%
Insurance: Vehicle	1,950.00 [6]	850.00	0.14%
Insurance: Workman's Comp	3,954.00	3,954.00	0.66%
Interest	6,925.70 [7]	0.00	0.00%
Leases/Rentals	2,365.00	2,365.00	0.39%
Licenses & Permits	250.00	250.00	0.04%
Maintenance & Repair	385.00	385.00	0.06%
Office Supplies	369.58	369.58	0.06%
Payroll Tax Expense	6,897.00	6,897.00	1.15%
Postage & Freight	1,465.62	1,465.62	0.24%
Property Tax Expense	654.00	654.00	0.11%
Rent	24,000.00	24,000.00	3.99%
Salaries: Sales	18,987.00	18,987.00	3.16%
Salaries	0.00	0.00	0.00%
Security	300.00	300.00	0.05%
Subscriptions	352.00	352.00	0.06%
Telephone	7,500.00	7,500.00	1.25%
Travel	1,500.00 [8]	0.00	0.00%
Vehicle Expenses	3,500.00 [9]	1,500.00	0.25%
Water & Trash	985.00	985.00	0.16%
Yellow Pages	4,290.69	4,290.69	0.71%
TOTAL EXPENSES	**155,556.33**	**134,855.63**	22.41%
NET PROFIT / LOSS	**104,371.67**	**125,072.37**	20.79%

Exhibit 2.1 *(Continued)*

Notes Explaining Adjustments to Financial Statements

The following notes explaining the adjustments to the financial reports are presented for the purpose of assisting a potential buyer in reaching an understanding of the complete monetary benefits associated with the ownership of this business.

The adjusted net income represents the available cash earnings generated through *Perfect Press.* This proprietary cash flow is that which the business produces prior to the owner's compensation, nonessential expenses, owner's perquisites, noncash expenses, nonrecurrent expenses, and any other expenses which are not mandatory or regular expenses of the business. As well, any income that is nonoperational has been eliminated.

Adjustments for Year Ending 12/31/91

NOTES

[1] **Equipment Depreciation:** This is a noncash expense.
[2] **Equipment Interest:** This is adjusted because the equipment will be paid off therefore the new owner will not have this expense.
[3] **Depreciation Expense:** This is noncash expense.
[4] **Entertainment:** This is a perquisite of the owners. It is not overhead expense.
[5] **Insurance, Employees:** The portion adjusted is a perq. for the owner.
[6] **Insurance: Vehicle:** This amount adjusted was for the owner's auto.
[7] **Interest Expense:** The interest expense of the current owner will not continue for a new owner, this also aids in showing the business's earning power prior to any debt.
[8] **Travel:** This expense was a perquisite of the owner, a non–business-related expense.
[9] **Vehicle Expense:** This is for the owner's personal auto.

Exhibit 2.1 *(Continued)*

EXHIBIT 2.1 SAMPLE OF ACTUAL PRESENTATION PACKAGE

NOTE: Section divider (used a tabbed section divider here). If you do not want to use tabbed dividers then prepare a colored sheet of paper with the title of the section printed out as shown below.

Marketing Materials
&
Promotional Examples
Section

Exhibit 2.1 *(Continued)*

What to Include in This Section

In this marketing materials and promotional examples section you should include copies of any promotional flyers you have used, handouts, mailers, promotional letters, photo copy of your yellow page ad, any articles that were written about your business, and the like.

Exhibit 2.1 *(Continued)*

EXHIBIT 2.1 SAMPLE OF ACTUAL PRESENTATION PACKAGE

For any further information about this business

Contact

Fred B. Seller
Voice MailBox (619) 271-4048

The Information Contained In This Presentation Package Is Confidential

Exhibit 2.1 *(Continued)*

For the Period Ending: _____

Net Operating Income <Loss> $ _____
(per Profit & Loss Statement)

Perquisites, nonrecurrent, and noncash expenses

_____ $ _____

_____   _____

_____   _____

_____   _____

_____   _____

_____   _____

_____   _____

_____   _____

_____   _____

_____   _____

Total Adjustments $ _____

Proprietary Net Income* $ _____

*Proprietary Net Income reflects the true earnings of the business for the reporting period shown. Expenses such as owner's salary, depreciation, amortization, personal perquisites, for example, entertainment, travel, owner's health, auto or life insurance, also one-time unusual expenses, and nonrecurrent expenses have been identified and added back to the profit to show the true earnings to an owner operator.

Exhibit 2.2 Blank Form: Adjustments to Financial Statements

EXHIBIT 2.3 A COMPLETED ADJUSTMENTS TO FINANCIAL STATEMENT FORM

For the Period Ending: 6/30/XX

Net Operating Income <Loss> (per Profit & Loss Statement)	$10,000.00

Perquisites, nonrecurrent, and noncash expenses

Marketing Meals	$ 1,500.00
Health Insurance	3,850.00
Parking	375.00
Contributions	1,000.00
Store Computer	3,495.00
State Income Tax	800.00
Food & Supplies (personal use)	1,200.00

Total Adjustments	**$11,950.00**
Proprietary Net Income*	**$21,950.00**

*Proprietary Net Income reflects the true earnings of the business for the reporting period shown. Expenses such as owner's salary, depreciation, amortization, personal perquisites, for example, entertainment, travel, owner's health, auto or life insurance, also one-time unusual expenses, and nonrecurrent expenses have been identified and added back to the profit to show the true earnings to an owner operator.

Exhibit 2.3 Example of Completed Adjustments to Financial Statement Form

Betty's Flowers
2302 Market Street
San Francisco, CA 92304

Exhibit 2.4 Sample of Very Small Retail Business' Presentation Package

EXHIBIT 2.4 VERY SMALL RETAIL BUSINESS' PRESENTATION PACKAGE

Betty's Flowers
Table of Contents

INFORMATION PACKAGE #_____

Exhibit 2.4 *(Continued)*

149

Betty's Flowers

2302 Market Street
San Francisco, CA. 92304

Offered For:	*$185,000.00 plus Inventory (approx. $1,500.00)*
Down Payment	*$85,000.00 Plus inventory*
Balance	*$100,000.00*

Financing Available
Lender:	Seller
Interest rate:	10% (annually)
Term:	10 years
Payments monthly:	$1,321.51
Annual debt service:	$15,858.09

Security
The note shall be secured by assets acceptable to Seller and personally guaranteed by Buyer.

Total Price Includes
Fixture & Equipment (see list included in this package)
Noncompete agreement
Lease
Customer list
Goodwill
Operating supplies (normal operating amount)
Trade Name

Exhibit 2.4 *(Continued)*

EXHIBIT 2.4 VERY SMALL RETAIL BUSINESS' PRESENTATION PACKAGE

Map Page

On this page a map of the local area was shown. Betty's location was identified. This enables potential buyers, at a quick glance, to see where the business is located in relationship to the whole town.

Exhibit 2.4 *(Continued)*

PREPARING THE PRESENTATION OF YOUR BUSINESS

Business Summary

Type of Business
Betty's Flowers is a retail flower shop specializing in *fresh* cut flowers, bouquets, basket arrangements, arrangements in vases, plants, and helium filled balloons.

Organization
Betty's Flowers is a sole proprietorship owned and operated by Betty Flanders.

Location
Betty's Flowers is located at 2302 Market Street. *This is an excellent site* for such a business because it sits on a corner and is *very visible* to all the passing auto traffic as well as walking traffic. The business is located next to a freeway exit and entrance and the property where the business is located is *very easy to get into and out of.* The traffic going past Betty's Flowers on Market Street is *15,800* cars daily.

One very important factor effecting the success of this business is the location. *Many regular* customers stop on their way to visit one of the several cemeteries located very near Betty's Flowers. Greenbrier Cemetery, Cypress ViewCemetery, and Mount Hope Cemetery are located just south of Betty's Flowers with Holy Cross Cemetery just north on the east side of the freeway. There are more cemeteries concentrated in this area, than anywhere else in the county.

Business Established
Betty's Flowers was originally established in 1979 and was located across the street in a small flower stand. Observing that the (future) site across the street was an ideal site to sell flowers, Betty in 1989 bought the property across the street and developed the lot and built the building which all contributed to the success Betty's Flowers is today.

Reason for Selling
Betty would like to change the pace of her life and slow down a little, perhaps pursue other business interests.

Business Hours
Betty's Flowers is open to serve her customers 7 days a week from 8:00–5:00. During the summer, the shop is kept open later.

Exhibit 2.4 *(Continued)*

EXHIBIT 2.4 VERY SMALL RETAIL BUSINESS' PRESENTATION PACKAGE

Employees

Betty's Flowers employs two plus Betty. Judy is compensated @ $7.00 per hour plus 10% of the gross sales generated during her hours. Annie is compensated $6.00 per hour. There are some part-time people that are called on if needed.

The work shifts are manned as follows; **Sundays,** Betty works from 8:00–5:30 along with Annie who works 9–5 P.M.; **Mondays & Tuesdays** the shop is run by one person, Judy; **Wednesday & Thursdays** are run by Betty alone; **Fridays,** Judy works the full day and Annie for about 4 hours. **Saturdays,** Betty works the whole day assisted by Annie, usually from 10:00 A.M.–5:00 P.M.

Business Description

Betty's Flowers is engaged in the retail sale of Fresh cut flowers, bouquets, basket arrangements, arrangements in vases, living plants, and helium filled balloons. The busiest day of the week is Sunday with Friday and Saturday a close second. The business has seven main suppliers, five for flowers and two for plants. Betty currently picks up flowers at the suppliers once per week. Plans are in place to make two pick ups per week. North Coast, the largest supplier, delivers the wholesale orders.

Eighty percent (80%) of Betty's customers are repeat customers and they tell their friends that this is *the* place to get Fresh quality flowers at fair prices. The location and very visible sign help to advertise the business and bring in new customers.

There are a few restrictions which are part of the Deed of the property and a new owner must understand them and abide by them. The business **cannot** *sell casket sprays, deliver flowers,* or *offer* any *Floral Wire Service.* These restrictions are in force until January 19, 1999.

Marketing & Competition

The best and most effective marketing which benefits Betty's Flowers are the customers themselves, they spread the word about Betty's Flowers. The business is located on a street with a lot of traffic and excellent visibility. People traveling north bound on Interstate 15 can see the large sign and can easily get off and back on the freeway after making their purchases at Betty's. The owner does not advertise the business except via the signs at the business and word of mouth.

There have been over the past years, some people come and open a flower stand down the street from Betty's, yet they never last too long. There are no shortages of florists, yet due to Betty's location, length of time in business, and excellent reputation for quality flowers at fair prices, the business can with-

Exhibit 2.4 (Continued)

stand even severe competitive forces. Today Betty's *IS* the competition. Someone that would consider opening a competing stand in the same market area as Betty's must weight very carefully the risks of lost investment capital.

Lease & Facilities
Betty's Flowers is located on approximately 6,967 square feet of specially designed commercial real estate. The building was built to be a Flower Shop and is approximately 900 square feet plus a loft area. There is plenty of parking and the customers appreciate the drive-up access.

The landlord will consider a 5-year lease plus an option to renew the lease for an additional 5 years. The rent will be $1,500.00 per month flat. The lease will have a cost of living increase annually, which will be tied to the Consumer Price Index. Further details of the lease will be set out in a formal lease, which shall be approved by the Landlord's legal counsel.

Future Expectations
Betty is not aware of any conditions or changes that could have a negative impact on the business. In fact, there is much more that a new owner could do with the business, such as adding additional items for sale, adding corporate or business accounts, taking credit cards, offering arrangements for weddings and church-alter sprays, making wrist corsages, or wire service to name a few.

Betty's Flowers is a good business and the profits are expected to remain strong with a excellent possibility to greatly increase them.

Betty's Flowers has an excellent location with years of profits as evidence that it is a superior location.

The owner/seller is the landlord and therefore understands how not to burden the business with rents too high.

A long favorable lease will be worked out with a new owner.

There is a shed located on the property, very near the front of the business and would be very suitable for placing another business inside it. You could either rent the space out to a complimentary business or operate it yourself. Some ideas for use are; a fruit and vegetable stand, key shop, fresh fish stand, and so on.

There are many businesses that can be started up with less cost than buying an existing business. The risks of spending money on an undeveloped, unproven site are very high. Typically, a person starting up a new business *cannot* draw a decent salary (or any money) out of the business for quite a while, especially when any profits are used for establishing the business.

In this case, a new owner can begin taking profits out TODAY and count on the earnings to continue.

Exhibit 2.4 *(Continued)*

EXHIBIT 2.4 VERY SMALL RETAIL BUSINESS' PRESENTATION PACKAGE

Contact

For Any Questions Regarding Betty's Flowers

Please Call:

(619) 273-4141

Exhibit 2.4 *(Continued)*

Notice

Upon an acceptable offer being made, the original books and records of the business will be made available.

Exhibit 2.4 *(Continued)*

EXHIBIT 2.4 VERY SMALL RETAIL BUSINESS' PRESENTATION PACKAGE

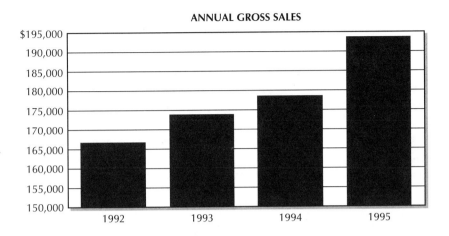

ANNUAL GROSS SALES

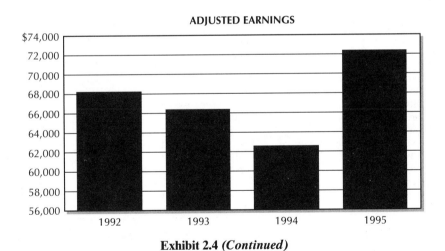

ADJUSTED EARNINGS

Exhibit 2.4 *(Continued)*

Betty's Flowers
2302 Market Street, San Francisco, CA 92304
Recast Financial Statements

SALES	As of Dec. 31 1992	As of Dec. 31 1993	As of Dec. 31 1994	As of Dec. 31 1995
Sales—Product	167,014.00	174,035.00	178,609.00	193,799.00
	0.00	0.00	0.00	0.00
TOTAL SALES	**$167,014.00**	**$174,035.00**	**$178,609.00**	**$193,799.00**
COST OF SALES				
Flowers	42,078.00	43,406.00	45,402.00	49,839.00
Plants	0.00	1,514.00	2,175.00	2,691.00
Direct Supplies	7,800.00	8,073.00	10,000.00	7,246.00
Subcontract	0.00	0.00	0.00	1,514.50
Freight In	0.00	0.00	0.00	0.00
TOTAL COST OF SALES	**49,878.00**	**52,993.00**	**57,577.00**	**61,290.50**
GROSS PROFIT	**117,136.00**	**121,042.00**	**121,032.00**	**132,508.50**
EXPENSES				
Auto	2,500.00	2,500.00	2,780.72	2,588.81
Bad debt	0.00	0.00	0.00	108.00
Bank Charges	100.00	98.60	136.40	160.45
Insurance	300.00	300.00	463.00	336.00
Insurance—Workman's Comp.	1,143.20	1,143.20	1,214.85	709.32
Legal and Accounting	990.00	990.00	990.00	1,080.00
Licenses, Permits, & Testing	135.00	135.00	135.00	120.00
Office Supplies	100.00	100.00	93.00	237.90
Payroll Taxes	1,438.00	1,438.00	1,276.62	1,165.36
Rent	15,300.00	15,800.00	16,300.00	16,800.00
Repairs & Maintenance	50.00	50.00	50.00	50.00
Security	240.00	240.00	264.00	405.00
Salaries & Wages	24,465.00	29,627.00	31,884.00	33,004.00
Taxes	613.00	613.02	1,241.62	1,269.20
Telephone	680.00	683.00	680.43	948.81
Utilities	900.00	903.58	960.34	1,059.15
TOTAL EXPENSES	**48,954.20**	**54,621.40**	**58,469.98**	**60,042.00**
NET PROFIT / LOSS	**68,181.80**	**66,420.60**	**62,562.02**	**72,466.50**

EXHIBIT 2.4 VERY SMALL RETAIL BUSINESS' PRESENTATION PACKAGE

Betty's Flowers
Sample Retail Price List

The following are basic prices.

Flowers
$2.50 Bouquet, includes 3 flowers, filler, and green
$5.00 Bouquet, includes 7 carnations or equivalent
$5.00 Arrangement in plastic cup
$7.00 Arrangement in small basket
$12.00–$15.00 up to $22.00 for 1 dozen carnations, fillers, and greens in a large basket
$28.00 1 dozen carnations in a large ceramic vase
$36.00 1 dozen roses in a large ceramic vase

Helium Balloons, filled
Large—$3.25
Medium (9″)—$1.50
Small (4″)—$1.00

Plants
$6.00 for 6″ Kalanchoe plants with pot cover
$3.50 for 4″ Kalanchoe plants with pot cover
$6.00–$15.00 Hanging Plants

Exhibit 2.4 *(Continued)*

Betty's Flowers
Equipment & Supply List

Equipment

Quantity	Description
1	Walk-in refrigerator 4′ × 6′ × 8′
1	VCR
2	Telephones, 1 AT&T remote, 1 w/answering machine
1	Video camera
3	Flower cutters
1	Alarm system (Protection One)
3	Panic buttons
2	Cash register
1	Coffee maker
1	Toaster oven
1	Microwave oven
1	Floor Safe
2	Fans
Misc.	Misc. items:
	Tools
	Coffee mugs

Supplies

The following are included with the business. A normal operating amount will be on hand for the new owner.

Rubber bands	flower sleeves
cellophane	buckets
spray paint	tissue paper
baskets	oasis
card sticks	plastic bags
vases	balloon sticks
erecto cups	paper mache
trash bags	preservatives
disinfectant	ribbons
plastic cups (for arrangements)	bowl tape
corsage stem wrap	corsage bags
corsage pins	plant pot covers
ground containers	enclosure cards

Exhibit 2.4 (Continued)

EXHIBIT 2.5 SERVICE/RETAIL BUSINESS' PRESENTATION PACKAGE

10344 Scranton Trail, Suite 2
Duluth, MN 92304

Exhibit 2.5 Sample of Service/Retail Business' Presentation Package

Table of Contents

Samples of Promotional & Marketing Materials

Exhibit 2.5 *(Continued)*

EXHIBIT 2.5 SERVICE/RETAIL BUSINESS' PRESENTATION PACKAGE

Postal Station #62

10344 Scranton Trail Suite 2
Duluth, MN 92304

Offered for

Offering Price:	$89,000.00
Includes Inventory	$5,000.00
Total Selling Price:	$89,000.00
Cash Down Required:	$39,000.00
Balance of Total Price:	$50,000.00

Financing Available

Lender: Seller	$50,000.00
Annual Percentage Rate (Interest)	10.00%
Fully Amortized Over (Term)	7 Years
Principal & Interest Payments	$830.06 (monthly)
	$9,960.71 (annually)

Security of Loan: The note shall be secured by a security agreement and UCC-1 filing on all securable assets of the business and shall be personally guaranteed by the buyer. Seller reserves the right to qualify and approve buyer for seller financing.

Assumption of Equipment Lease: One (1) Xerox Copier Model 1065 @ $426.16/Mo. Final payment is in October of 1997.

Point of Sale Upgrade (one time expense): To comply with new UFOC requirements, the present Point of Sale equipment requires an upgrade. Costs would be $2925.00. This includes a new cash register.

Fully Refundable Training Deposit: $2,500.00 to Franchisor which is refunded upon close of escrow and successful completion of entire training program which is 3 weeks long, with one week in store.

Total Price Includes:

100% of the assets as set forth below.
  Franchise
  Lease
  Leasehold Improvements

Franchise Information:

Transfer Fee: $2000.00
Option to Renew: Every 10 Yr.
Royalty: 5% of Monthly Gross
Advertising: 2% of Monthly Gross

Exhibit 2.5 *(Continued)*

Non-Compete Agreement
Training/Consulting (by Seller)
Furniture, Fixtures, & Equipment
Goodwill
Inventory

Note: *The purchase of Postal Station+ #62 is subject to a right of first refusal held by Postal Station-Franchisor*
Training is 3 Weeks, w/one week in-store.

Exhibit 2.5 *(Continued)*

164

EXHIBIT 2.5 SERVICE/RETAIL BUSINESS' PRESENTATION PACKAGE

Business Summary

Type of Business
Copying, mailing and business related services and supplies
SIC Code Classification: 7389 and 4822

Organization
Sole Proprietorship

Location
In the Duluth community of Black Hawk, at 10344 Scranton Trail, Suite 2
Duluth, MN 92304

Key Points of Interest
1) Great Location: This business is in the middle of an upper income residential area that is mixed with many home-based businesses and professional service businesses.
2) Four (4) Year Growth Trend in Gross Revenue and Profits
3) Profitable
4) Excellent Work Environment
5) Good Lease

Reason for Selling
Owners are moving out of state

Business Established
March 1990 by present owners

Business Hours
Postal Station #62 is open from 8:30 A.M.–6:00 P.M. Monday through Friday, and from 9:00 A.M.–2:00 P.M. on Saturday. The store is closed on Sunday.

Location, Lease, and Facilities
Postal Station #62 occupies approximately 610 square feet in a strip center known as Scranton Trail Center at 10344 Scranton Trail, Suite 2. Located in the heart of Black Hawk, its central location is accessible to the community at large. Traffic counts on the frontage business street, Scranton Trail, are between 3,500 to 4,200 vehicles on an average weekday.

Exhibit 2.5 *(Continued)*

The original lease was entered into February of 1990. It was for a term of five (5) years. On March 10, 1995, a 5-year option was exercised which became effective May 1, 1995, and expires April 30, 2000. There was also granted another 5-year option. As of the effective date of this option, the fixed minimum rent has been reduced and under the newly agreed on terms, the first six (6) months will be $854.00 per month plus additional rent charges (refer to Section #20 of the Lease Agreement) including CAM (Common Area Maintenance) fees of $148.00 per month. On November 1, 1995, the fixed minimum rent will increase to $903.00 plus CAM fees. CAM fees are adjustable on a yearly basis. There is a Cost of Living increase of five (5) percent of the fixed minimum monthly rent, which takes affect the first month of each successive lease year. (Refer to Section #22 of the Commercial Lease Agreement) The tenant is responsible for the payment of utilities. The landlord is responsible for maintaining the roof and exterior walls of premises excluding glass, doors, and door operators. *A copy of the lease is available upon an acceptable offer being approved by all parties.*

Company History
Postal & Business Services businesses got their start in the late 1970s in Southern California. The early operators primarily offered private mailboxes for rent and served as outlets for U.S. Mail services and parcel shipping. With changes in the U.S. Postal Service, increased competition in the parcel shipping arena, and changes in how and where people perform work, the Postal & Business Services industry has become characterized by a truly diversified portfolio of products and services.

There are estimated to be over 7,000 such business throughout the United States, as well as outlets being established internationally. The industry has experienced steady growth, and is expected to continue growing for at least the next 10 years. Most stores are owner operated single locations. There are several active franchising companies in the industry, the most notable being Postal Station, Mail Boxes Etc., and Pak-Mail.

Postal Station was begun as a single independent retail outlet in San Diego. The franchising of Postal Station units began in 1986. There are approximately 220 Postal Station stores throughout the United States. In the Duluth county area there are 48 independently owned Postal Station stores. The present owners established postal Station #62 in Black Hawk in March 1990.

Exhibit 2.5 *(Continued)*

EXHIBIT 2.5 SERVICE/RETAIL BUSINESS' PRESENTATION PACKAGE

Products & Services

Postal Station #62 offers a carefully designed mix of products and services targeted to the small business, professional, and residential market in the area. The store's success is built on convenience, high quality, and friendliness. The total number of mail boxes available are 148. Currently, 80 are occupied. While other products and services may be added from time to time, the current offerings include:

Services Offered

- Parcel Shipping (UPS, U.S. Mail, Federal Express)
- Overnight Express Delivery
- International Shipping
- Boxes & Packaging Supplies
- Custom Packaging Service
- High Speed & Self-Serve Copies
- Notary Public
- Key Duplication
- Postal Services (Certified, Return Receipt, Insured)
- Engraving
- Office Supplies
- Greeting Cards
- Postage Stamps
- Private Mailbox Rental
- Rubber Stamps
- Public FAX Sending & Receiving

Customers

The customer base for Postal Station #62 is representative of that for the postal and business services industry, and can be broadly divided between the residential, small business, and professional markets. The average monthly customer count is 2,250. The average transaction price is $7.42 based on an average over the last 12 months.

The residential market resides within a three to five mile radius of the store. This customer is typically in the middle to upper income range, and is principally interested in convenience, quality, and friendly service. Among the services that appeal to this customer segment are mailbox rental, parcel packaging and shipping, postal services, copies, notary services, greeting cards, and office supplies. Promotions that seem to reach this market segment include mail, door hangers, flyers, and some media advertising.

Exhibit 2.5 (Continued)

The small business and professional market segment also is typically located within a three to five mile radius of the store. In addition to those business customers operating out of retail or office sites, there is a significant segment of business and professional people who work out of their homes in this area. Among the services that appeal to business customers are mailbox rentals, parcel packaging and shipping, overnight express deliveries, copies, and office supplies. This market segment has best been reached through direct mail. Business people who work out of their home are typically reached through targeted direct mail and community involvement.

As is generally the case in this industry, customers are repeat-oriented. Most sales are conducted on a cash or check basis. It is noteworthy that Postal Station #62 has encouraged the establishment of "house accounts," whereby frequent customers can "charge" their purchases and receive a monthly invoice. There are approximately 80 house accounts which represent a markedly loyal customer base who often patronize the store on a weekly or even daily basis. In addition to these accounts, there are 84 active mailbox customers, all of whom have paid in advance. The mailboxes can only be accessed during regular business hours.

Marketing & Competition

Advertising has included the yellow pages, banners and posters, door hangers, flyer, coupon books, direct mail, frequent shipper cards, and community sponsorship and involvement.

Promotions have included special services during the tax season, Mother's day, copy month, back-to-school, and the Christmas holidays.

Competition to Postal Station can be categorized into three areas: the U.S. Postal Service, United Parcel Service, and other postal and business service retailers. The U.S. Postal Service is, in fact, both a competitor and supplier to Postal Station and similar businesses. Postage stamps and meter postage can be purchased only from the Post Office, and all mail received or sent by Postal Station is handled through the Post Office. The owners of Postal Station #62 have maintained an exceptionally cooperative relationship with the management and employees of the Duluth Post Office. The Duluth Post Office is located approximately 8 miles from Postal Station #62. The Twin-Cities Post Office is located approximately 4 miles from Postal Station #62.

During the past year approximately 32% of Postal Station #62's revenue was from postage stamp sales. This is indicative of the fact that many customers prefer the convenience with less regard for the surcharges added to

Exhibit 2.5 (Continued)

168

EXHIBIT 2.5 SERVICE/RETAIL BUSINESS' PRESENTATION PACKAGE

postal services. Although postal services are often low profit margins for retailers, Postal Station #62 has maintained the same pricing for parcel post shipping
as for other shippers. Additionally, a 10% surcharge is added to the cost of
postage stamps. Thus, postal services are a profitable area of business.

United Parcel Service, like the U.S. Postal Service, is both a competitor and
supplier. The majority of packages are handled through UPS. The nearest UPS
terminal is located approximately 10 miles away in Strausburg. With respect to
competition from other postal and business service retailers, Mail Boxes Etc. is
located in the Lucky's Shopping Center, approximately 2 miles from Postal
Station #62, and Black Hawk Copy and Mailstop is located in the old Mar-
shall's Center, approximately 2½ miles from Postal Station #62. (Refer to map
for location of competitors in relation to Postal Station #62.)

Exhibit 2.5 *(Continued)*

Mapped View of Competitors

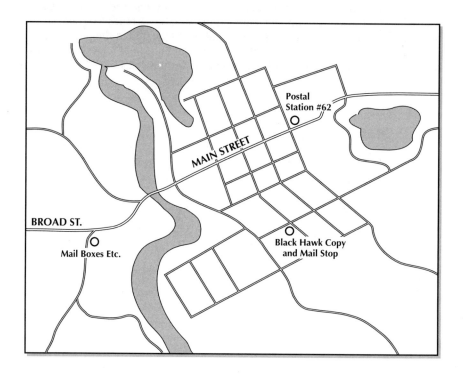

Exhibit 2.5 *(Continued)*

170

EXHIBIT 2.5 SERVICE/RETAIL BUSINESS' PRESENTATION PACKAGE

Future Expectations

Addition copy machines could be added since the copy business is continually growing and is about at capacity. A color copier should also be considered as more customers are requesting color copies.

Jumbo Shipping will be the next major profit center to be unveiled. This new program will give us the ability to ship any size item to any destination in the world through a well-developed network of freight companies. Jumbo Shipping is part of a $100 billion industry. According to Ryder Systems Inc., the nation's largest truck rental company, more than 42 million Americans will move this year, the largest number since 1990. There is a significant niche for us between the option of high priced moving companies and the do-it-yourself movers. Jumbo Shipping fills this niche perfectly. The margins on Jumbo Shipping are excellent and it's a perfect extension to our current shipping services.

Employees

Currently the business is managed and operated by its two owners, Tom and Diane Cruthers. Although part-time employees have been tried in the past, for the most part the owners have preferred to operate the store without any additional employees.

Why You Should Buy This Business

Buying a business can be risky and has been likened to walking through an uncharted minefield. Here we have a well-established business with a proven track record of providing an owner operator with many benefits. This business has an historic upward trend in growth of sales and profits. This business is located within in a good, safe, community spirited neighborhood. With the continued strong growth in Home-based businesses, this franchise has a future you can be confident in. The franchisor provides helpful support and marketing. Being a franchise operation, the owner of this business can call on the wealth of knowledge of the franchisor and fellow franchisees, which can accelerate the achievement of profits.

When you purchase this business, you can start receiving your investment back, the very first day you take over. No waiting for the business to "develop."

Postal Station #62 is an experience in successful entrepreneurship we are sure you will enjoy not only as a self employed, master of your own destiny but as an investment you too can sell or pass along to a family member in the future.

Exhibit 2.5 *(Continued)*

List of Furniture, Fixtures, & Equipment
Xerox 1065 Copier
(2) Xerox 5018 Copiers
Credit Card Terminal and Printer
Two (2) Panasonic Telephones, KX-T3155
Desk Chair
Desk
486sx/33 Computer System & Color Monitor
Panasonic Dot Matrix Printer, KX-PII24
Hoover Elite Vacuum Cleaner
Xerox 7009 Fax Machine
Postal Scale—Detecto MS-8
Manual Utility Scale, 250 lb.
Manual Utility Scale, 5 lb.
Pitney Bowes Rebuilt 5460 Meter Base
Sharp 3210 Cash Register
Pelaspan Dispenser
Premier Rotary Drive Trimmer
Swingline Model #13 Heavy Duty Stapler
GBC Surebind 2000 Binding Machine
Postalmate Software System
Toledo 100# Bench Scale
Mailbox Units
Shelves & Hooks
Ibico Comb Binding Machine

Exhibit 2.5 *(Continued)*

EXHIBIT 2.5 SERVICE/RETAIL BUSINESS' PRESENTATION PACKAGE

Price List for Xerox Copies

Self Service Copies

1–99	.06
100–249	.05
250–499	.04
500–999	.03
1000+	.025

High Speed Copies

	Single Sided	Double Sided
1–19	.08	.14
20–49	.07	.12
50–99	.06	.10
100–249	.05	.08
250–499	.04	.06
500–999	.03	.05
1,000+	.025	.05

Additional Copy Products

White 60#	Add .01
Pastel	Add .01
Astrobright	Add .02
Astroparche	Add .02
Card Stock	Add .04
Linen	Add .04
White 8½ × 14	Add .01
Pastel 8½ × 14	Add .02
White 11 × 17	Add .06
Pastel 11 × 17	Add .06
Astrobright 11 × 17	Add .07
Reduction/ Enlargement	.25
Label Sheet	.35
Transparency	.65

Postal Station   10344 Scranton Trail Suite 2   Duluth, MN 92304

Exhibit 2.5 *(Continued)*

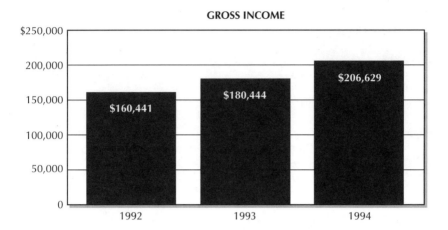

Exhibit 2.5 *(Continued)*

EXHIBIT 2.5 SERVICE/RETAIL BUSINESS' PRESENTATION PACKAGE

Postal Station #62
10344 Scranton Trails, Suite 2   Duluth, MN 92304

Balance Sheet

CURRENT ASSETS	12/31/94
CASH	198.00
ACCOUNTS RECEIVABLES	6,179.00
INVENTORY	4,973.00
TOTAL CURRENT ASSETS	**11,350.00**
OTHER ASSETS	
Rent Deposit	824.00
Start-Up Costs	17,500.00
TOTAL OTHER ASSETS	**18,324.00**
TOTAL ASSETS	**29,674.00**

Liabilities and Stockholder's Equity

CURRENT LIABILITIES	
ACCOUNTS PAYABLE	14,799.00
DEPOSITS	915.00
SALES TAX PAYABLE	437.00
TOTAL CURRENT LIABILITIES	**16,151.00**
LONG-TERM LIABILITIES	
TOTAL LONG-TERM LIABILITIES	**0.00**
TOTAL LIABILITIES	**16,151.00**
OWNER'S EQUITY	13,523.00
TOTAL STOCKHOLDERS EQUITY	**13,523.00**
TOTAL LIABILITIES AND STOCKHOLDERS EQUITY	**29,674.00**

Exhibit 2.5 *(Continued)*

Reported vs. Adjusted Financial Statements

	1994 Reported	**Notes**	**1994 Adjusted**
INCOME			
Binding Sales	2,249.00		2,249.00
Card Sales	2,799.00		2,799.00
Copy Sales	59,066.00		59,066.00
Fax Sales	8,888.00		8,888.00
Key Sales	1,669.00		1,669.00
Labor Sales	395.00		395.00
Mail Box Sales	4,732.00		4,732.00
Notery Sales	2,901.00		2,901.00
Office Supply Sales	3,693.00		3,693.00
Other Shipper Sales	2,899.00		2,899.00
Outside Service Sales	1,621.00		1,621.00
Packaging Supply Sales	6,134.00		6,134.00
Postage Sales	65,023.00		65,023.00
UPS Sales	44,560.00		44,560.00
Total Income	**206,629.00**		**206,629.00**
EXPENSES			
Advertising & Promotion	$4,135.00		$4,135.00
Amortization	$897.00	[1]	$0.00
Bank Charges	$585.00		$585.00
Binding Costs	$576.00		$576.00
Building Maint. & Repairs	$0.00		$0.00
Card Costs	$831.00		$831.00
Copy Costs	$17,696.00		$17,696.00
Depreciation	$4,148.00	[2]	$0.00
Equipment Leases	$6,288.00	[3]	$5,115.60
Equipment Maint. & Repair	$13,094.00		$13,094.00
Fax Costs	$564.00		$564.00
Insurance	$978.00		$978.00
Interest	$1,646.00	[4]	$0.00
Key Costs	$285.00		$285.00
Licenses, Permits, & Dues	$475.00		$475.00

Exhibit 2.5 *(Continued)*

EXHIBIT 2.5 SERVICE/RETAIL BUSINESS' PRESENTATION PACKAGE

Office Supply Costs	$1,398.00		$1,398.00
Other Shipper Costs	$1,956.00		$1,956.00
Outside Service Costs	$849.00		$849.00
Packaging Supply Costs	$2,628.00		$2,628.00
Payroll Contributions—Company	$489.00	[5]	$0.00
Payroll	$2,105.00	[6]	$0.00
Postage Costs	$56,429.00		$56,429.00
Rent	$13,788.00		$13,788.00
Royalties	$10,574.00		$10,574.00
Supplies	$480.00		$480.00
Telephone	$883.00		$883.00
Travel	$170.00		$170.00
UPS Costs	$26,830.00		$26,830.00
Utilities	$1,366.00		$1,366.00
Vehicle	$1,440.00		$1,440.00
Total Expenses	**$173,583.00**		**$163,125.60**
Net Income	**$33,046.00**		**$43,503.40**

Exhibit 2.5 *(Continued)*

Notes Explaining Adjustments to Financial Statements

The following notes explaining the adjustments to the financial reports are presented for the purpose of assisting a potential buyer in reaching an understanding of the monetary benefits associated with the ownership of this business.

The adjusted net income represents the available cash earnings generated through *Postal Station #62.* This proprietary cash flow is that which the business produces prior to the owners compensation, nonessential expenses, owners perquisites, noncash expenses, nonrecurrent expenses, and any other expenses which are not mandatory expenses of the business.

Adjustments for Reporting Period of 1/1/94–12/31/94

NOTES

[1] **Amortization:** This is a noncash expense.

[2] **Depreciation:** This is a noncash expense.

[3] **Equipment Lease:** The amount of this expense has been reduced because two of the copiers on lease will be paid off, and therefore not a continuing expense.

[4] **Interest:** This expensed amount will not continue for a new owner.

[5] **Payroll Contributions—Company:** This is the payroll taxes and was adjusted because the present owners only experimented with having employees and discontinued the practice. This then shows how the business's cash flow looks for a husband/wife ownership/management.

[6] **Payroll:** This was adjusted because the present owners only experimented with having employees and discontinued the practice. This then shows how the business's cash flow looks for a husband/wife ownership/management.

Exhibit 2.5 *(Continued)*

EXHIBIT 2.5 SERVICE/RETAIL BUSINESS' PRESENTATION PACKAGE

Reported vs. Adjusted Financial Statements

	1993 Reported	Notes	1993 Adjusted
INCOME			
Binding Sales	2,245.00		2,245.00
Card Sales	3,117.00		3,117.00
Copy Sales	50,137.00		50,137.00
Fax Sales	9,841.00		9,841.00
Interest Income	0.00		0.00
Key Sales	1,409.00		1,409.00
Labor Sales	268.00		268.00
Money Order Sales	26,976.00	[1]	0.00
Mail Box Sales	3,807.00		3,807.00
Notary Sales	2,209.00		2,209.00
Office Supply Sales	4,575.00		4,575.00
Other Shipper Sales	311.00		311.00
Outside Service Sales	1,864.00		1,864.00
Packaging Supply Sales	4,824.00		4,824.00
Postage Sales	61,140.00		61,140.00
Promo	0.00		0.00
UPS Sales	34,697.00		34,697.00
Income—Other	0.00		0.00
Total Income	**207,420.00**		**180,444.00**
EXPENSES			
Advertising & Promotion	$2,893.00		$2,893.00
Amortization	$897.00	[2]	$0.00
Bank Charges	$409.00		$409.00
Binding Costs	$610.00		$610.00
Building Maint. & Repairs	$97.00		$97.00
Card Costs	$1,923.00		$1,923.00
Copy Costs	$13,043.00		$13,043.00
Depreciation	$6,090.00	[3]	$0.00
Equipment Leases	$5,726.00		$5,726.00
Equipment Maint. & Repair	$14,399.00		$14,399.00
Fax Costs	$1,123.00		$1,123.00

Exhibit 2.5 (Continued)

Insurance	$1,424.00		$1,424.00
Interest	$1,397.00	[4]	$0.00
Key Costs	$264.00		$264.00
Licenses, Permits, & Dues	$408.00		$408.00
Money Order Costs	$26,746.00	[5]	$0.00
Office Supply Costs	$1,617.00		$1,617.00
Other Shipper Costs	$206.00		$206.00
Outside Service Costs	$1,055.00		$1,055.00
Packaging Supply Costs	$2,156.00		$2,156.00
Payroll Contributions—Company	$154.00	[6]	$0.00
Payroll	$694.00	[7]	$0.00
Postage Costs	$52,759.00		$52,759.00
Rent	$13,077.00		$13,077.00
Royalties	$8,989.00		$8,989.00
Supplies	$670.00		$670.00
Telephone	$860.00		$860.00
Travel	$0.00		$0.00
UPS Costs	$20,913.00		$20,913.00
Utilities	$988.00		$988.00
Vehicle	$1,005.00		$1,005.00
Total Expenses	**$182,592.00**		**$146,614.00**
Net Income	**$24,828.00**		**$33,830.00**

Exhibit 2.5 *(Continued)*

EXHIBIT 2.5 SERVICE/RETAIL BUSINESS' PRESENTATION PACKAGE

Notes Explaining Adjustments to Financial Statements

The following notes explaining the adjustments to the financial reports are presented for the purpose of assisting a potential buyer in reaching an understanding of the monetary benefits associated with the ownership of this business.

The adjusted net income represents the available cash earnings generated through *Postal Station #62*. This proprietary cash flow is that which the business produces prior to the owners compensation, nonessential expenses, owners perquisites, noncash expenses, nonrecurrent expenses, and any other expenses which are not mandatory expenses of the business.

Adjustments for Reporting Period of 1/1/93–12/31/93

NOTES

[1] **Money Order Sales:** Sales of money orders was discontinued due to the almost nonexistence profit margin and therefore we removed it from the income to show the business without this discontinued revenue source.

[2] **Amortization:** This is a noncash expense.

[3] **Depreciation:** This is a noncash expense.

[4] **Interest:** This expensed amount will not continue for a new owner.

[5] **Money Order Costs:** This expense was eliminated because the income has also been eliminated (as mentioned above) to show the business as it is without money orders being offered.

[6] **Payroll Contributions—Company:** This is the payroll taxes and was adjusted because the present owners only experimented with having employees and discontinued the practice. This then shows how the business's cash flow looks for a husband/wife ownership/management.

[7] **Payroll:** This was adjusted because the present owners only experimented with having employees and discontinued the practice. This then shows how the business's cash flow looks for a husband/wife ownership/management.

Exhibit 2.5 *(Continued)*

Reported vs. Adjusted Financial Statements

	1992 Reported	Notes	1992 Adjusted
INCOME			
Binding Sales	2,157.00		2,157.00
Card Sales	3,021.00		3,021.00
Copy Sales	43,763.00		43,763.00
Fax Sales	8,660.00		8,660.00
Interest Income	7.00		7.00
Key Sales	1,629.00		1,629.00
Labor Sales	115.00		115.00
Mail Box Sales	2,116.00		2,116.00
Money Order Sales	15,457.00	[1]	0.00
Notary Sales	1,740.00		1,740.00
Office Supply Sales	4,625.00		4,625.00
Other Shipper Sales	549.00		549.00
Outside Service Sales	1,205.00		1,205.00
Packaging Supply Sales	4,855.00		4,855.00
Postage Sales	54,149.00		54,149.00
Promo	0.00		0.00
UPS Sales	31,850.00		31,850.00
Income—Other	1,513.00	[2]	0.00
Total Income	**177,411.00**		**160,441.00**
EXPENSES			
Advertising & Promotion	$2,310.00		$2,310.00
Amortization	$897.00	[3]	$0.00
Bank Charges	$291.00		$291.00
Binding Costs	$710.00		$710.00
Building Maint. & Repairs	$28.00		$28.00
Card Costs	$2,561.00		$2,561.00
Copy Costs	$12,387.00		$12,387.00
Depreciation	$6,090.00	[4]	$0.00
Equipment Leases	$10,983.00		$10,983.00
Equipment Maint. & Repair	$10,493.00		$10,493.00
Fax Costs	$996.00		$996.00

Exhibit 2.5 *(Continued)*

EXHIBIT 2.5 SERVICE/RETAIL BUSINESS' PRESENTATION PACKAGE

Insurance	$737.00		$737.00
Key Costs	$241.00		$241.00
Licenses, Permits, & Dues	$413.00		$413.00
Money Order Costs	$15,272.00	[5]	$0.00
Office Supply Costs	$1,997.00		$1,997.00
Other Shipper Costs	$386.00		$386.00
Outside Service Costs	$651.00		$651.00
Packaging Supply Costs	$2,057.00		$2,057.00
Company Payroll Contributions	$0.00		$0.00
Payroll	$0.00		$0.00
Total Payroll & Contrib.	$0.00		$0.00
Postage Costs	$48,195.00		$48,195.00
Rent	$12,543.00		$12,543.00
Royalties	$8,050.00		$8,050.00
Supplies	$675.00		$675.00
Telephone	$801.00		$801.00
Travel	$524.00		$524.00
UPS Costs	$20,684.00		$20,684.00
Utilities	$893.00		$893.00
Vehicle	$1,004.00		$1,004.00
Expenses Other	$1,442.00	[6]	$0.00
Total Expenses	**$164,311.00**		**$140,610.00**
Net Income	**$13,100.00**		**$19,831.00**

Exhibit 2.5 *(Continued)*

Notes Explaining Adjustments to Financial Statements

The following notes explaining the adjustments to the financial reports are presented for the purpose of assisting a potential buyer in reaching an understanding of the monetary benefits associated with the ownership of this business

The adjusted net income represents the available cash earnings generated through *Postal Station #62*. This proprietary cash flow is that which the business produces prior to the owners compensation, nonessential expenses, owners perquisites, noncash expenses, nonrecurrent expenses, and any other expenses which are not mandatory expenses of the business.

Adjustments for Reporting Period of 1/1/92–12/31/92

NOTES

[1] **Money Order Sales:** Sales of money orders was discontinued due to the almost nonexistence profit margin and therefore we removed it from the income to show the business without this discontinued revenue source.

[2] **Income—Other:** This was for Money Grams (wiring money). It was not a very profitable revenue source and was discontinued.

[3] **Amortization:** This is a noncash expense.

[4] **Depreciation:** This is a noncash expense.

[5] **Money Order Costs:** This expense was eliminated because the income has also been eliminated (as mentioned above) to show the business as it is without money orders being offered.

[6] **Expenses Other:** This was the expense related to the income of Money Grams, which was discontinued and therefore was eliminated to normalize the P&L.

Exhibit 2.5 *(Continued)*

EXHIBIT 2.5 SERVICE/RETAIL BUSINESS' PRESENTATION PACKAGE

Three Year Comparison of Income, Expenses and Profits

	1992	1993	1994
INCOME			
Binding Sales	$2,157.00	$2,245.00	$2,249.00
Card Sales	3,021.00	3,117.00	2,799.00
Copy Sales	43,763.00	50,137.00	59,066.00
Fax Sales	8,660.00	9,841.00	8,888.00
Interest Income	7.00	0.00	0.00
Key Sales	1,629.00	1,409.00	1,669.00
Labor Sales	115.00	268.00	395.00
Mail Box Sales	2,116.00	3,807.00	4,732.00
Notary Sales	1,740.00	2,209.00	2,901.00
Office Supply Sales	4,625.00	4,575.00	3,693.00
Other Shipper Sales	549.00	311.00	2,899.00
Outside Service Sales	1,205.00	1,864.00	1,621.00
Packaging Supply Sales	4,855.00	4,824.00	6,134.00
Postage Sales	54,149.00	61,140.00	65,023.00
UPS Sales	31,850.00	34,697.00	44,560.00
Total Income	**$160,441.00**	**$180,444.00**	**$206,629.00**
EXPENSES			
Advertising & Promotion	$2,310.00	$2,893.00	$4,135.00
Bank Charges	291.00	409.00	585.00
Binding Costs	710.00	610.00	576.00
Building Maint. & Repairs	28.00	97.00	0.00
Card Costs	2,561.00	1,923.00	831.00
Copy Costs	12,387.00	13,043.00	17,696.00
Equipment Leases	10,983.00	5,726.00	5,115.60
Equipment Maint. & Repair	10,493.00	14,399.00	13,094.00
Fax Costs	996.00	1,123.00	564.00
Insurance	737.00	1,424.00	978.00
Key Costs	241.00	264.00	285.00
Licenses, Permits, & Dues	413.00	408.00	475.00
Office Supply Costs	1,997.00	1,617.00	1,398.00
Other Shipper Costs	386.00	206.00	1,956.00
Outside Service Costs	651.00	1,055.00	849.00

Exhibit 2.5 *(Continued)*

Packaging Supply Costs	2,057.00	2,156.00	2,628.00
Postage Costs	48,195.00	52,759.00	56,429.00
Rent	12,543.00	13,077.00	13,788.00
Royalties	8,050.00	8,989.00	10,574.00
Supplies	675.00	670.00	480.00
Telephone	801.00	860.00	883.00
Travel	524.00	0.00	170.00
UPS Costs	20,684.00	20,913.00	26,830.00
Utilities	893.00	988.00	1,366.00
Vehicle	1,004.00	1,005.00	1,440.00
Total Expenses	**$140,610.00**	**$146,614.00**	**$163,125.60**
Proprietary Income	**$19,831.00**	**$33,830.00**	**$43,503.40**

Exhibit 2.5 *(Continued)*

186

EXHIBIT 2.5 SERVICE/RETAIL BUSINESS' PRESENTATION PACKAGE

Samples of Promotional & Marketing Materials

(The next several pages is where we put various promotional flyers that the business had used.)

Exhibit 2.5 *(Continued)*

3

MARKETING THE BUSINESS

CRITICAL QUESTIONS TO KNOW WHEN SELLING OR BUYING A BUSINESS

A potential buyer may ask the following questions of you. These questions are not specific to any particular industry, but do cover many topics that will or can be asked of you. Review them and make sure that as many as are applicable are answered in your presentation package.

General Questions

- Why do you want to sell your business?
- How much do you want for the business?
- Are you willing to accept terms; if so, what would they be?

- How did you arrive at the price?
- When was the business established?
- How long has the business been under present ownership?
- In what form is the business owned: corporation (C or S), sole proprietorship, or a partnership?
- If the business is a corporation, how many stockholders are there and how are the shares divided? Are all stockholders or partners in favor of a sale?
- If incorporated, when was it incorporated?
- What calendar is your financial information reported on, fiscal or calendar year? If fiscal, when is the year ending?
- What are the operating hours of the business?
- Are you aware of anything that could be construed as detrimental to the future of the business?
- Are there any new competitors opening or planning to open within your market?
- Are there any new local, state, or federal laws being considered or enacted which would adversely affect this business?
- Are there any historical, pending, existing, or anticipated law suites? If so, give details.
- How is the business regarded by its customers?
- How is the business regarded by its competitors?
- How is the business regarded by its suppliers?
- How is the business regarded by its employees?
- How is the business regarded by its banks?
- Are there any contractual obligations which will continue after the sale, such as advertising/Yellow Pages, employment, leases, rental agreements, warranties on products or services, trade agreements, outstanding or prepaid coupons, layaways, and so on?
- How many direct competitors do you have? What are their sales volumes? Where does your business fit in the standings? How

strong are they? How do they operate (tactics)? Are your customers or markets being encroached on by anyone other than direct competitors?

- How many competitors are there?
- Who are your competitors, where are they located, what is the size of their companies, and how long have they been in business?
- Does anyone working in the business know it's for sale?
- Is there anyone employed here who has given notice to leave, or do you suspect anyone may leave, especially if a sale takes place?
- Are you prepared to sign a noncompete agreement?
- Will you provide training for a new owner; if so, how long and how often? (Daily, a few days per week, eight hours per day, two hours per day, five days, seven days per week?)
- Are you aware of any other business like yours for sale or that has been sold in the last two years?

Products and Services

- What are the products or services of the business? Any proprietary products? If so, may I have a line card, price sheet, or product catalog?
- How long have you been selling, making, or distributing each product or line?
- Do you represent any products or lines exclusively or have territorial rights?
- What is the percent to overall income of each product or line or service?
- Do you have any backlog?
- Do any of the products or services carry a warranty or guarantee?
- What added product or service do you perform to the products bought from others to increase the finished value of your products?

- What is the nature of the agreements with your suppliers?
- How often, if at all, do you shop around for competitive rates from your suppliers?
- Why do you buy from your existing suppliers and do they offer any exchange or warranty to you?
- If relationships with suppliers is important to the entity, find out all you can about what holds the relationship intact: are the relationships contractual or not, will any of the key supplier relationships be in jeopardy if the business changes hands?
- Are there any new or different products or sources becoming available in the next few years?
- Where in the business cycle do you feel your products are (collectively or individually)?
- How much inventory do you generally keep on hand (finished goods, work in progress, raw material)?
- To what extent does the business rely on the services and/or products of outside vendors or subcontractors?
- What other products or services should be or could be produced or furnished by your company with the existing personnel and facilities?
- How do your competitors market their products or services?
- Are there any major potential customers or demographic segments who have not been secured as actual customers?
- Why do your customers buy from you? What can you, or do you, offer that is different from your competitors' products?
- Are there any new trends developing within your markets?
- Do you attend trade shows? As a spectator or participant?
- Do you or anyone on staff belong to networking organizations?
- Has the business's past sales growth generally followed the industry trend or has it been ahead or behind this trend?
- What is the forecast of future industry-wide sales for each product or service?

- Who keeps up with market information? How?
- If your business uses distributors or sales reps, what is the nature of the relationship? What is their track record with you? How long have you used each?

Employees

- Are you a working owner; if so, how many hours per week?
- Do you employ any family members; if so, how long have they worked with you? Will they stay after the sale? What functions or positions do the family members occupy?
- Please describe your duties or routines at work.
- How many people do you employ full-time, part-time? What are the positions covered? What pay rate do you start paying?
- Who are the key employees or managers, if any? If there are key personnel then assess their expertise and the customer relationships they have, and determine if it would take some time to transfer the employees to new management and transfer the expertise to other employees. Is the key employee under a contractor noncompete agreement?
- How much is each employee paid?
- Who figures the payroll?
- What benefits, if any, do you offer your employees? Does the company pay for them or do the employees contribute part?
- Do you or your partners draw a salary?
- Do you get medical or insurance benefits?
- What is your policy covering vacations?
- Have you had workers' compensation claims?
- Any past or current problems with the labor board or employment development department?
- Typically how long has it taken you to locate an employee when needed?

- Does the nature of the work performed by the employees indicate a skilled workforce; if so, how technical and how large is the resource pool?
- Do you offer any training programs?
- What has your experience been with employee turnover?
- Do you have written personnel policies or procedures?
- Do you have an organization chart available?
- If there is management in the organization, ask the following: what is the background of key members of management? Is any management under contract? Give details. Will anyone in management leave if the business is sold? How capable is the present management? Are they progress-minded and willing to take risks? Are there any problems between management personnel? Do all departments cooperate willingly and effectively? Does the success of the business depend to a greater degree on the capabilities, performance, or contacts of one or more of your staff or yourself?

Financial Information

- What was last year's sales volume?
- Is your financial information reported by cash or accrual method?
- Can you furnish the last three to five years' income/expense statements, balance sheets, and tax returns?
- How much is your average monthly accounts receivable?
- Can you provide an aging report? If not, how many accounts are over 30, 60, or 90 days?
- What is your normal inventory level? What is it at present? Is any of the inventory on consignment? If so, please give details.
- How much is the current level of accounts payable?
- Are there any assumable loans; if so, what are the current terms?

- Are all state and federal taxes including employee-withholding taxes current?
- What is the business's depreciation policy for fixed assets?
- How much is your monthly/yearly payroll?
- Would you make a list of perquisites (personal expenses) which you expense through the business, such as personal insurance, autos, travel, entertainment, and household purchases?
- *Note:* After seeing the financial statements, you'll be able to ask specific questions regarding the line items.
- Please provide a complete list of all machinery, equipment, furniture, fixtures, leasehold improvements, office equipment, and vehicles that will go with the sale.
- Are there any personal items that won't go with the sale?
- Do you have an appraisal of the equipment or of the total business?
- Please provide any available brochures or other printed information about your company.

Market

- What are the principal markets for your product or services?
- To what extent has the market been reached, and how much and what areas do you feel still can or should be developed?
- By what means do you sell or market your products or services?
- Do you advertise? Who creates the advertising? Are there any other marketing avenues you feel would benefit the company which are not being done currently?

Physical Facilities

- Is the business property leased?
- Is it owned by the business or its principals?

- If leased, how long was original term? How long left? Any options? If there are options, are the terms identified, or will they be renegotiated at the time the option is exercised?
- What is the current rent?
- Are there common area charges or NNN charges? (N, maintenance; N, real property insurance; N, real property taxes)
- Does the rent increase annually; if so, by what calculation?
- How much is your lease deposit?
- Are there any restrictions on the use of the premises? If retail, are the products you sell identified in your lease for non-competitive reasons?
- Who is your landlord? Does the landlord handle the property management, or is it handled by a property management company?
- How has the landlord or property management company been to work with?
- Are there any associations in connection with the premises?
- How many locations are involved in your business?
- Are they all leased or owned?
- Do you rent or own any storage facility used by your business?
- Is the present location optimum?
- Is the space too big?
- Have you ever moved the business; if so, when? What was the effect on sales? How were your sales compared to now? Can you recall the cost of the move?
- Is there any center or facility to be built within your market area where a competitor may locate?
- Are there any Occupational Safety and Health Administration (OSHA) or Environmental Protection Agency (EPA) or other compliance requirements for the business?

General Industry Information

- Are there any licenses or permits required beyond a regular business license?
- What are the expectations with regard to future growth or lack of growth in the whole industry?
- What company's activities, if any, exert a major influence on your industry as a whole?
- Are there any likely changes from existing marketing methods within your industry?
- What insight or information can you supply regarding sources of materials used by companies within the industry, including any predictable future changes in the material supply situation?
- Are there any recent or anticipated future technological developments likely to have a significant effect on the future of the industry and of individual companies within it?
- Are there any probable future changes in the industry due to federal, state, or local regulatory activities?

Future Aspects

- Please tell me what, if any, industry changes are occurring and how they will effect things?
- How can the business be expanded? What improvements should be made?
- Knowing the market, how far can this business grow?

BE PROPERLY PREPARED BEFORE A BUYER CALLS

Business-owners think this is the hardest or most mysterious element involved in selling a business. Follow the instructions in this chapter and you will succeed easily.

Now that you have determined a value for the business and pre-pared a presentation package, you are ready to begin the process of finding a suitable buyer for the business. It only takes one person to be that right buyer. Initially, you never know which person will be the one. You want to sell the business as quickly as is practical. That is why it is so important to have priced the business correctly and have taken the time to create an informative presentation package. You do not want to be unprepared and miss a golden opportunity to sell your business. If you are not properly prepared you can, unbe-knownst to you, turn off a valid, qualified, prospective buyer. You do not want to lose a good buyer because you over-priced the business or just threw together some bare essentials about your business.

I cannot stress enough the importance of providing everything to the potential buyer honestly. From all the material in the presenta-tion package to anything you say to the buyer or additionally show them, be consistently straightforward. If you misrepresent anything at one point, you will lose integrity; everything you say and the mate-rials you provide will be taken with suspicion. Everything will be dis-covered, sooner or later. Later could mean a lawsuit.

WHAT ABOUT MULTIPLE-LISTING SERVICES?

There are several different means you can use to locate potential buyers. There are no multiple-listing services for businesses (at this writing). I have seen many gallant attempts to create and succeed at a multiple-listing source for the sale of businesses. I have not seen one succeed over a long period. There are many reasons why they have not been successful. I will only mention a few here. Selling a business is usually considered a confidential matter. If a business is put into a multiple listing (like a home or condo is) then any agent or broker anywhere in town can tell anyone (qualified or not) about the fact that your business is for sale. Most business-owners do not like the idea that all their customers and employees will know that the business is being sold before a proper buyer is found. The business-owners especially do not want their competitors to know (there are many competitors that can and will use that knowledge against you).

When it comes to business-brokers and sales agents, unfortunately there is a fairly high level of technical incompetence. This comment is based on over 16 years in the field of business-brokerage, business-appraisal, and buy/sell consulting. I have been told by hundreds of buyers how incompetent the business-brokers were that they met. This is a serious problem within the business-brokerage industry. Many business-brokers know that what I am saying here is true and therefore do not submit their listings into a multiple-listing service. They especially keep out any quality business they have for sale. They do not want some incompetent or inexperienced broker or agent working on the sale of a business with them. Lawsuits are too expensive to tangle with because of a sales agent who knows little about properly selling a business or doesn't care enough to find out.

Most business-brokers know that if they can list a desirable business for sale, they can and will sell it without any help from a multiple-listing service. In addition, many business-brokerages do not want to split fees with another agency. They will not tell you that, but it is true nonetheless.

After spending over 16 years in the business-brokerage industry, having worked for five years in what was probably the largest single-location business-brokerage company in the United States, I have seen most ways that a business offered for sale can be promoted. There are only so many ways that marketing a business takes place.

The following information is correct. There are many business-brokers and agents that will not tell you the following because it is one of the biggest roles they play.

CONFIDENTIALITY, A VERY IMPORTANT ISSUE

To begin with, most business-owners want the fact that their business is for sale to be kept very confidential. There is a good reason for this. As I mentioned earlier, it is not good that competitors know the business is for sale. Competitors have been known to spread rumors about a sale, and do it with a negative slant, hoping to attract customers to them by making your business sound unstable, with a questionable future. Some competitors have solicited employees who either gave notice immediately or did so right after the sale was finished. In some cases, employees get very nervous just hearing from the owner that the business is for sale and begin looking for another job.

Potential buyers become very nervous when they perceive that the business they are looking at is unstable, or may become that way.

Most business-owners do not want customers knowing the business is for sale. It is also not a good idea that vendors or subcontractors know the business is for sale. Sometimes a vendor's delivery person is the worst to find out. Many route delivery drivers want to appear friendly, caring, and helpful (it promotes goodwill for the vendor); therefore, they will inform many other business-owners or managers along their route. Of course, if you are sure that you do not care that everyone knows your business is for sale, then you should be sure to mention the fact to the vendors and their drivers. In fact, give them a promotional flyer about the sale of your business. I will explain more about the use of promotional flyers later. There are some samples for you to look over and one that I received from an owner, along with a critique of it.

I did meet an owner once, on the advice of a real-estate broker, who put a "Business for Sale" sign in the front window of the business. The business was a successful business. It was not as though the owner was under any particular compulsion to sell. The window sign did not help the business sell at all. All that happened was that a lot of people wondered why the business was actually for sale; maybe even thought it was not doing too well. I have a piece of experience to share before we get into the actual marketing aspects. This is especially for those of you who have interviewed or will interview a business-broker regarding a listing of your business. No matter how large a business-brokerage office there may be, they market businesses in the same way I will explain here.

HOW TO HANDLE A BROKER'S INQUIRY

In fact, many owners think that because they list their business with a business-broker, the business-broker has buyers for their business. Many business-owners have, at some point, received a letter or a telephone call stating how some broker in their area has a potential buyer for their business. In 90 percent of the cases, this is not so. If you are told this on the telephone, it is most likely not true. They want a listing contract. With the contract in hand, they can begin to search for a buyer.

You can test this the next time you are solicited. All you need do is ask who the buyer is. Listen carefully for their reaction. The brokers will not answer the question. Of course, in an effort to protect their commissions, they may decline to tell you who the buyer is. The odds are that you would not know the buyer anyway. If you do, you should not pay brokers to bring over a buyer to whom you have already exposed your business. Tell them that if they in fact have a potential buyer for the business, they should bring the prospect, as soon as possible, to a confidential meeting to discuss the matter. If they say they cannot do that, then ask them to provide you with a *One-Party Show Agreement* or a *One-Party Sales Commission Agreement.* In other words, if they have a real potential buyer, have them produce him or her. If you refuse to sign a regular listing agreement and insist on a one-party agreement for the specific, proposed buyer, their charade will be up. If they do happen to have a real buyer, there will be no reluctance on their part to provide a one-party sales commission agreement. After all, they would be turning down an opportunity to make a quick commission. If you are solicited in this manner and the broker or sales agent does not have or know about a one-party show agreement, then for your use at such times a one-party show agreement is provided in Exhibit 3.1 at the end of this chapter.

Some brokers or sales agents get quite deceptive here. I have known some who had a fellow broker or sales agent act as though they were the potential buyer. In this way, the agent could show sincerity; when the buyer (of course) did not proceed, the agent now had a great opportunity to speak with the owners about their desire to sell—and why not just list the business with them?

There are sales agents who respond to *For Sale by Owner* newspaper ads as if they were buyers themselves, even changing their names. When they learn enough about the business (posing as a buyer, over the telephone) to decide that they like it and want to sell it, they disclose that they are really agents. It can take more than one telephone conversation to play out the entire deception. Believe me, if that is the way a business-broker or sales agent will act in the beginning, do not expect any greater amount of integrity from there. There are many ways that dishonest agents compromise business-owners and sellers. If you carefully follow my instructions in this section, you will succeed in selling your business and save thousands of dollars on commissions. In addition, you will be better protected against deception.

WHAT GOES ON INSIDE THE BROKERAGE THAT YOU SHOULD KNOW

Most business-brokers and brokerages do not have a buyer for your business, specifically. The typical scenario is that a broker will blindly solicit listings, calling or writing to businesses they know nothing in particular about. When they get the listing contract signed, they begin a marketing campaign shortly thereafter. They can usually generate some initial interest in a week or two. The exception to this is when the brokerage already has some businesses for sale in the same industry as the one they are soliciting for a listing. Because they have businesses in the same industry already for sale, they have marketing underway for buyers interested in such businesses.

You can and will be able to do exactly what most brokers or agents do: start a marketing program. I know that some of you may think that just because a business-brokerage office is in the business of selling businesses, they have a lot of buyers for your business already on hand. That is not generally the case. As I mentioned previously, once the agent secures a listing, they begin to search for a buyer. Most buyers working through a business-brokerage have responded to some marketing effort regarding a specific business that is or was for sale. For example, the brokerage may have been marketing a retail business or a manufacturing business, and your business is a service business. The buyers for a manufacturing business do not usually want a service business. It might even get more specific than this example. The broker may have buyers who respond to a certain type of retail business, such as a bookstore, but have no interest in a retail shoe or toy store.

THE FIRST STEP IN THE MARKETING PROCESS

So if confidentiality is so important, how does one go about marketing the business while maintaining the confidentiality? To begin with, having a confidential way for potential buyers to contact you is essential. In addition to confidentiality, convenience is an important factor. Most of my clients in the past have preferred to not discuss the sale of their business during business hours unless they have to. I have set up a procedure so that you do not have to, at least not until your potential buyer is interested enough to have a tour of the business.

An important key is to set up a voice mailbox. These are quite common today and you should have no trouble finding a company that will rent you a voice mailbox for the next few months. The advantages are substantial and the cost is minimal, perhaps $15 to $18 per month. Look in the Yellow Pages directory under Voice Mail or Answering Services. What you should get is a telephone number, an outgoing message lasting a minute or more (no longer than two minutes), and mailbox room for 10 or more messages.

THE IMPORTANCE OF A VOICE MAILBOX

What does a voice mailbox do for you? You can receive phone calls from potential buyers without them calling your business and disturbing you, your employees, or hearing the name of your business. You won't need to use your private home telephone or home answering machine. You will have access to all the messages left and you will be able to retrieve the messages at any time, 24 hours a day. The voice mailbox also acts as a way to eliminate none serious lookeloos. Those people who will not leave a message are not interested enough in buying a business to even worry about. Advertising space in the newspaper is expensive, especially when compared to the cost of what you can say about your business in two minutes in an outgoing message on the voice mailbox. In this way, you can use the newspaper ad and some other advertising methods to excite potential buyers to call the telephone number, not to explain the business.

The outgoing message on the voice mailbox also serves as a qualifier. You can say more about your business (nothing that will let the caller know which business it is exactly) which will allow the buyer to make an initial decision: "Do I like what I hear enough to leave my name and telephone number and proceed further?" Remember, they will make that decision without knowing who you are or the exact name of your business. Another important aspect of the voice mailbox is that you are in charge. You decide when you are up to speaking with a potential buyer. We all have bad days or afternoons. Isn't it better to respond to the callers when you are ready, when you are comfortable and prepared to deal with the issues of selling the business?

All you will have to do is take down the messages on the Buyer's Response to Marketing Log provided in Exhibit 3.2, and return the calls when you are ready. I have provided special instructions for handling the telephone interview; by following them you will be prepared to handle the calls. I have also provided some examples of what to say for the outgoing message.

THE MOST WIDELY USED FORM OF ADVERTISING

When it comes to advertising and getting those inquiry calls coming in, the following are the choices you have. The most popular and widely used form of advertising in the entire country for selling a business is the use of an ad in the business opportunity section of your local newspaper. I know that this seems a bit too common, but it is the mainstay of marketing a business. What you say in the ad is important. Some people, especially in Southern California, think that if they place an ad in the Chicago papers or some newspapers on the East Coast or in the Midwest, they will be getting right to those who want to get away from the bad weather and move to sunny climates through buying a business. This does not work and is a waste of money. People desiring to move to Southern California or Arizona do not look in their local New Jersey newspaper to read about a business for sale in San Diego. They subscribe to a newspaper in the area where they want to move. Today, you can find classified ads for many major newspapers on the Internet.

WHEN BEST TO ADVERTISE THE SALE

Newspaper ads are best received on Sundays and weekdays. Many times, it is better to run the ad Sunday and Monday. Saturday ads usually do not get much response. Try to avoid running an ad on a holiday weekend, or on Super Bowl Sunday. Run the ad in the largest newspaper in town. It does not hurt to run an ad in a smaller community paper, but many times there is little or no response.

HOW TO COMPOSE A PROPER ADVERTISEMENT

When you compose the ad *do not* use the name of your business or any words that will allow anyone to recognize that it is your business in the ad. I have provided some examples at the end of this chapter, in Exhibit 3.3, of ads and how they should be typeset within the ad. You want to use enough words to get a buyer to call on the ad, no more than that. It is wise to identify what type of business you are selling. For example: dry cleaner, toy store, deli, pizza restaurant, steak house, auto parts—wholesale, plastics manufacturing, metal fabrication, florist. In this way, potential buyers know what industry the business is in without knowing it is "Daisy Fresh Dry Cleaners," "Patsy's Florist," or "Aztec Plastic Manufacturing, Inc."

You can either say something about your gross sales volume, your adjusted net profit, the years your business has been around, how wonderful the expected growth is, that the business is management-run (if it is), the asking price, the down payment required, or that it is *For Sale by Owner.* The idea is to limit what you say to a few attractive features without disclosing which specific business in town this is. Do not be shy about stating the gross sales or the adjusted net profit; remember, they do not know who you are or specifically which business it is. As long as there are more than two other businesses in your town in the same industry, you will be okay.

You should plan to run an ad in the newspaper every week. Whether you change what the ad says, or how often you place the ad, depends on the response level. If you are getting 5 to 10 calls per ad placement, then only run the ad every two weeks. If you get one or two calls, run the ad each week and rotate what is said in the ad with one or two versions. You can effectively handle only a certain number of buyers' inquires. You should not try to build up a big backlog of buyer inquiries that you cannot answer.

For those of you who understand fishing, the process is something like fishing. The ads are the bait or lure. If you are attracting or catching fish, you do not change bait. If what you are doing is not working, you switch things around until you get a bite. The presentation package is used to net the fish.

MORE WAYS TO MARKET THE BUSINESS

Another way to market the business is to mention your interest in selling the business to your certified public accountant (CPA) and banker. Of course, you should stress to them that even the idea that your business is for sale is confidential. Have them refer any interested party to the voice mailbox telephone. By providing your CPA or banker with a copy of your presentation package, you will impress them and possibly generate a more sincere effort on their part.

You can fax or mail a flyer to all the local business-brokers or real estate brokers in your area. Exhibit 3.4 is an actual flyer I received from an owner that was doing just that. In the next section, I have provided comments and a critique of another flyer for your education in what not to write. If you choose to send flyers out to brokerages you should be prepared to pay a half-commission. *Do not pay more than half.* There are examples of some other types of flyers in Exhibits 3.5 and 3.6. The flyer in Exhibit 3.5 is one that could be used to fax to owners of businesses that are the same. They very well may want a second location, or a store in your part of town. Those who know your type of business very well can appreciate what they get if they were to consider purchasing an established business such as yours. We all know how much work and risk is involved in starting from scratch, even if you know what you are doing.

The flyer in Exhibit 3.6 was written to an owner of a business that may be a synergistic match for the business for sale. There are businesses that have similarities to yours or that would profit much more if they owned a business such as yours and either made your business a division of theirs or vice versa. As an example, if you were the owner of a small food-processing plant or you manufactured some specialty food product such as a type of candy, you should contact owners who are in similar businesses that may want to add your particular type of product to theirs. Sometimes you may even find a retailer who sells products that you produce, or who sell products that are produced by someone else and they may want to become more vertical in their market and therefore are interested in the purchase. These types of prospective buyers can be very good. There is much for them to gain in acquiring a business that will enhance their own business.

CRITIQUE OF A PROMOTIONAL FLYER

Exhibit 3.7 is a copy of an actual flyer that was faxed to my office. An owner who was selling his business himself sent it to me via the fax machine. I do applaud the owner for taking the initiative to create the flyer and fax it to brokerage/consulting offices.

I wrote some comments on the flyer but to be clear, I will discuss them here. First of all and most glaringly wrong is the fact that the owner has exposed to the world the specific business that is for sale. I have seen this mistake before and in almost all cases the owner just did not know any better. Some owners have so much pride in their business that they think exposing the name alone will bring a buyer. I have personally sold many very well-known or you could even say famous businesses, at least regionally famous. It was the performance of the business that created the desire, not the name. I have seen businesses with very well-known names hit down periods and have such marginal profit performances that they were difficult to sell. As I mentioned before, employees and customers get questionable if they know too prematurely that the business is for sale. It is almost like looking for trouble.

The owner not only put his business telephone number in the flyer, he put his personal home telephone number there, too. I hope he is planning on getting a new residence telephone number. There are some very strange people in this world and letting everyone know your name, your telephone number, and that you are the owner of a restaurant and nightclub is risky. He should have used a voice mailbox.

Listing the attributes of the business is fine. I would have mentioned the down payment I wanted. There are some people who may or may not be qualified to even discuss the prospects of buying the business. I would not want to expose my business to someone who could not afford to buy the business.

The owner seems as though he were inviting people to patronize his club. He not only provided the address, he gives directions on how to get to his business. As I mentioned previously, he should have said something like, located near Mission Valley. That is plenty of geographical information for a buyer to decide if that area is too far to drive to work or not. In addition, a prospective buyer can get an idea of the demographics of the area by saying that the business is near San Diego State University. The address and directions did not need to be mentioned.

Finally, the mention of the finder's fee for a broker is almost a joke. I have doubts that any respectable broker will call this owner. A broker will want no less than half a full commission. As I mentioned previously, if a broker had a potential buyer, the broker would try his hardest to convince a "For Sale by Owner" that he should pay him a full commission. In this case, the owner should have offered at least to co-op and pay a half-fee.

NO NEED TO PAY MORE THAN HALF A COMMISSION

There are two sides to every transaction. One is the seller's side and the other is the buyer's side. With the information in this package, you can handle the seller's side. You do not need to pay a broker to represent you. You are the one marketing and selling your own business. If a broker can bring you a buyer without advertising your business (that is what you are doing) then he is entitled to half of the usual commission, or whatever lower figure you can get them to agree to. The broker is aware of your business because you marketed the business to him or her. The broker or sales agent will try his hardest to convince you to pay a full commission. You tell them "this is a co-op transaction; are you interested in making some money?"

You see, a co-op transaction is the most common type found in residential real estate transactions. One broker works for the seller by listing the home and marketing it; he is known as the "listing broker." The other broker brings the buyer and is known as the "selling broker." They split the commission in half. That is standard practice.

There is less of this type of activity in the business-brokerage side of real estate, at least as far as a co-op between different brokerages is concerned. Within a business brokerage company, the agents or brokers co-op between themselves.

One agent lists a business (the listing agent) and if another agent interests a buyer working with that agent, then the agent become the selling agent and the two agents or brokers split the commission. I mention this because when you are selling your own business, you are the listing agent. You should not pay the selling broker both sides of the commission, only half. You may want to see how successful you are in locating a buyer yourself before you open the possibilities to a co-op with a broker.

A GOOD SOURCE OF QUALIFIED BUYERS

There are, many times, other business owners who operate a business the same or similar to the one you desire to sell, who would be interested in having a second location or merging the two businesses into one location. You can find this out without too much risk. Speaking to a competitor is always risky, though. This can be a very effective method of finding a buyer, but be cautious. If you can find someone in the same business that is interested in a merger of the two businesses, you can sell him your business for more than you can to anyone else. They will benefit monetarily more than anyone else, too.

All you have to do to figure out how much more the business is worth if you sell it to a merger candidate, is to eliminate all expenses that realistically will be duplicated if the two businesses became one. Do this after you have determined the adjusted net profit spoken about in the valuation section. You can eliminate such expenses as the rent, utilities, insurance, dues and subscriptions, payroll and payroll taxes, and so on. I have seen some business's adjusted net go from $65,000 per year to over $185,000 for a merger candidate. If they would make that much more profit from buying your business, shouldn't they pay more, too? Remember this is only for merger candidates. If you explore this avenue of selling, be sure to create two different offering pages for your presentation package. That is the page that tells the buyer what you want for the business. In addition, make a different financial representation based on the additional adjust-ment due to the merger.

IS THE INTERNET A VIABLE PLACE
TO MARKET THE BUSINESS?

If you have access to the Internet, then look up the words *business, business for sale, business appraisal,* and *business brokerage.* You should find several sources through which you can advertise your business on the Internet. This is the newest way to advertise a busi-ness. I am unsure of the results. I did have my own homepage and I advertised some of the businesses I was offering for sale. The results were disappointing, but the Internet was much newer then. I am sure that you will hear more hype than worthwhile fact, but do check out using the Internet. One key thing to keep in mind is that you should do your best to have a way to monitor the rate of success that comes from the money spent on advertising, especially on the Internet. The Internet would be the closest thing to a multiple-listing service for businesses. Anyone who has access to the Internet, worldwide, can see the businesses for sale. There are a few publications that special-ize in advertising businesses for sale. One is called *Businesses for Sale;* they also have an Internet site.

TRADE PUBLICATIONS AND FRANCHISORS

Many trade associations publish magazines. You can place an ad in the classified section; they usually have a business for sale section or business opportunity section. If your business is a franchise, you can ask the franchisor if they will spread the word about the sale of your business. Be sure that the franchisor does not try to get a commis-sion. Some of them try, but are not licensed in some states to receive commissions from the resale of a franchise. Some franchisors have been helpful in locating a buyer. Many just get in the way.

IF YOU HAVE AN INTERESTED BUYER, WHAT THEN?

Once you have returned the voice mailbox messages, made contact with the potential buyer, prequalified the buyer enough to set up a meeting with them, follow the instructions found later in this chapter titled Interview In Person with Prospective Buyer. You should arrange a meeting at some neutral place, not your business. Perhaps you can use a restaurant far enough from your business that the buyer will not figure out that your business is close by. Have the buyer sign a confidentiality agreement. (There are two versions provided in Exhibits 3.8 and 3.9 in this chapter.). Provide them with a presentation package and you are done with the meeting. There is no need to have a long meeting. Just explain to the buyers that all their questions will be answered in the package. Tell them to take it home and read it. Tell them that if after reading the package they are interested further, they should make a list of any questions and call you to set up a meeting which will include a tour of the business. That's all you need to do in the first face to face meeting.

WHAT TO DO AFTER YOUR INITIAL MEETING WITH A BUYER

After your initial meeting and when the buyer calls you again, set a meeting to answer any further questions and to show them the business. Some owners prefer to make the first tour or meeting at the business after regular business hours. If having the buyer see the business during operating hours would make a good impression and be a motivational factor for them, then by all means do so. The main caution is confidentiality.

You will not want the meeting to look or sound like a meeting in which you are selling your business—to the employees and customers, that is. When the tour is over and you have answered all the prospective buyer's questions, it is time to ask him to make an offer. The next chapter picks up the progression from here.

WATCH OUT FOR THE MENTION
OF OUTSIDE FINANCING

If the buyers mention verbally or in an offer they make that they are going to seek outside financing, be very careful. The optimum situation is with a buyer who has all the down payment, closing costs, working capital, and some reserves. These are most of the elements that constitute a really qualified buyer. If the buyer speaks of getting the down payment or any portion of it from anywhere, you need to investigate that issue right away. Many buyers who talk of needing to do such things are never able to accomplish them. If they can actually get a commitment for the funds, then whoever loans or gives the money to them will have a vested interest in how the money is being spent. The person or financial institute will need to be sold on the proposition of buying your business, too. If the lender is an individual, you will need to sell the business to that person as much as you need to sell the business to the potential owner-operator. The odds on a sale taking place under these circumstances are poor. That does not mean they do not occur. There are essential steps to follow if you are faced with this circumstance.

When you ask a buyer about financial capability to buy your business, or if a buyer tells you that he will be seeking money from an another source, find out if he needs to borrow the money for the down payment.

If the buyer does, he will need enough money to cover closing cost, possible attorney and CPA fees, business license fees, deposits for rent or possibly utilities and the State Board of Equalization, working capital, and any other items particular to your business. Ask him if he is aware of how much money he will really need. You may be surprised how many people do not have a clue about what they need—a very scary thing. A buyer who needs to borrow the down payment is a high-risk buyer. Unless you are *really* motivated, I would suggest finding someone else.

If the buyer says that he can get the money, ask him to provide you with some evidence of this ability. Ask him to get a letter of commitment from the person for at least the total amount needed. Many times, the selling process will come to a halt right there or shortly thereafter. You should also inquire about a personal financial statement, if you have not done so already. I would insist on seeing one (there is a blank form provided in Exhibit 3.10). Look over the statement and see how much equity the buyer has. If he has little or none, he will most likely not qualify for a loan from any institution.

If the buyer has the down payment and desires to borrow the rest of the purchase price from a bank instead of asking you to carry a note for the balance, you must address this issue specifically in your counteroffer. If there is no other issue to be settled between the two parties, then this alone should constitute the contents of a counteroffer. Please read what I have written about this in Chapter Four, Negotiating the Sale.

As you begin to receive responses from potential buyers, take note of their comments. You should be especially alert to comments made by those who take a deeper look into your business. If you have potential buyers who decline to proceed after having checked the business over, find out why they declined to go further.

It is worth the call to them. Sometimes you will find out that they just could not afford the business. You may find out that the type of business was after all not their forte. The feedback which concerns elements of your business that you cannot change is of little use. The feedback concerning elements within your control is very important. If you get a statistically significant number of comments about a particular aspect of the business offering, you might take it under advisement to consider altering the element that is getting in the way of selling your business.

A REVIEW OF THE WAYS TO MARKET YOUR BUSINESS

Let's review the list of ways to market your business.

- Newspaper ads
- Notify your CPA and banker, especially those who offer Small Business Administration (SBA) financing

- Check the Internet for advertising sources
- Place an ad in a *Business for Sale* specialty publication
- Classified ad in your industry's trade magazine
- Direct mail or fax a flyer to other owners in the same business
- Tell your vendor's delivery driver (give him a flyer)
- Co-op with the business brokers in your area (send a flyer to them)
- Contact your franchisor

You can contact the publishers of *Business For Sale* at (510) 831-9225. Their Internet address is: www.biz-exchange.com. Their address is: 480 San Ramon Valley Boulevard, Suite A, Danville, CA 94526.

EXAMPLE OF A VOICE MAILBOX OUTGOING MESSAGE

"Thank you for calling about the wholesale distribution business we are selling. Our business has been established for 17 years and is a very stable source of income. There are several ways of expanding the business. The business is located in North San Diego County. Our gross sales last year were $1.5 million. We have a net profit of approximately $145,000. We are going to retire after we sell the business. We have an entire business information package available for qualified buyers. We are asking $285,000 plus inventory of approximately $140,000 for the business. The down payment is $120,000 plus the inventory. If you would like further information, please leave your name and telephone number and I will return your call as soon as possible."

Comments: What I have done in the preceding voice mailbox outgoing message is to provide some basic yet important information. Many items were mentioned to not only inform the buyer, but equally important, to qualify the buyer to the business. Mentioning that the business is in a particular area lets the buyer consider if they are willing to drive that far to work, without being specific about your location. The gross sales and net profit are also there so the buyer will know if your business is too large or too small for them. As well, the down payment information lets them know if they can afford to buy the business. I also answered a common question: why are you selling?

TELEPHONE INTERVIEW WITH A PROSPECTIVE BUYER

I. OBJECTIVE: Preliminary qualifying of the prospect and if qualified, set the first meeting. Do not say the name of the business, address or specific location, business telephone number, or your full name. Set the initial meeting at a neutral location (coffee shop, restaurant) far enough away that the buyer will not figure out where the business is located. The reason for the meeting is to further qualify them and then answer more detailed questions and give a presentation package to them. Inform the prospective buyer that if you proceed beyond the initial meeting, they will need to provide a personal financial statement and/or a credit report.

II. QUESTIONS AND ANSWERS

On the telephone, tell the prospect that what you tell them is to be held confidential along with the fact that your business is for sale. You can ask the following questions in a casual conversation style of questioning or just tell them that there is a little preliminary information you need and could you ask them some questions. (Some people like mixing, asking a question and then answering some, alternating questions and answers.)

A. Find out where they live; what part of the city or county. If they live quite far, ask them how they feel about driving XX minutes or relocating. (Some people want something close to home.)

B. Have they ever owned their own business? If yes, then what industry or type of business. If not, you should question them about their business experience and evaluate what they say.

C. Do they plan to manage the business themselves, with a spouse, partner, or relative?

D. Do they have at least $XX dollars to use to purchase the business or would they please tell you about their financial capabilities. Don't let them evade the answer.

Some will say they have enough, or give a vague answer. If they do say that, then ask if it is within their means to pay $750,000 to $1 million down to purchase the business. Sometimes they'll say "Oh no, not that much!" Then you say, "How much *do* you have to invest?" Again, they may say "Enough to buy this business." So you restate the question again and keep at it, so you get, *at the very least,* a small range of figures like $250,000 to 500,000 or whatever range you may be in. You can tell them that you are not trying to get too personal but you must get an idea if they can afford to buy your business.

If the buyer objects to the price by saying something like "Your asking price is quite high" or any such comment, respond by telling them that after they have had an opportunity to become familiar with the particulars of the business, they will understand that the price actually represents a good value.

E. You can ask them a question that relates to their expectations of a business they want to buy. Example: In the first year, what is the minimum profit you need to take out of the business you buy?

If there is a certain amount they answer with that is an absolute minimum and your business does not meet the requirement, save yourself wasted time and politely end the conversation and go on to the next prospect.

Or, do you have any preference about the number of days the business is open? If your business hours and days cannot or should not be changed from its present schedule and the prospective buyer has a preference in opposition to it, then end the telephone call as soon as possible.

III. ANSWERS TO THEIR QUESTIONS

Keep your answers to the following:

A. Very general location information (i.e., beach area, North County, downtown San Diego, east suburban area, National City, Oceanside, etc.). If your business would be difficult for them to locate due to many similar businesses in the area, you can narrow the geographic parameters when you answer the question of location. If your business is a beauty salon and you say it's in Carlsbad, the buyer will hopefully have a difficult time figuring out which one is yours. On the other hand, if you have the only plastic manufacturing company in Del Mar, I would say that the business is located in the North County.

B. How long you have owned the business?

C. How long it has been established?

D. Last full year's gross sales, net income.

E. Reason for selling.

F. Number of employees.

G. Hours the business is open; hours you put in.

Tell them (if they are preliminary-qualified) that you have a complete presentation package to give them which should completely inform them about your business and you would like to set up a personal meeting. Make arrangements to meet with them at a neutral location (if possible).

If they are not qualified, thank them for their interest but tell them that at this time you are going to pursue other prospects. If you need to tell them why you don't feel they are the right buyer, then do so.

INTERVIEW IN PERSON WITH A PROSPECTIVE BUYER

I. OBJECTIVE: Further qualify the buyer and give them information about your business.

II. Introduction

   A. Proceed with usual customs of introduction.

   B. Have them sign the confidentiality agreement and tell them verbally that everything to be discussed and given to them is to remain confidential. If you are meeting in the business, instruct them to not openly discuss anything in hearing range of employees. You can answer any reasonable questions after they have signed the confidentiality agreement.

III. Interview

   Explain to the prospects that in order for you to gain a better understanding of their background and qualifications to buy your business you need to ask them some questions.

   Ask if they brought their personal financial statement with them; if so, ask to look at it. If not, tell them you need to see one as soon as possible. *You now need to decide whether to allow them at this meeting to have access to your presentation package.* If you feel from what they have said on the telephone and how they present themselves at this meeting that you could take the risk of them not being qualified, don't go ahead with this meeting. You could request to postpone the meeting until they present a personal financial statement, especially in light of the fact that you asked them to bring it and they were not prepared for the meeting or did not care enough to prepare it. Don't accept too many excuses. You can always meet tomorrow or another time, but once you give out your information, that's it! And perhaps you will have exposed your business to an unqualified person.

   Ask the following questions about them. You can make it a pleasant social conversation with the questions mixed with casual conversation. (Conversation-style questioning is more comfortable for a lot of people.)

   Note: If you like, you may answer a few of their less confidential questions about your business (prior to qualifying them), in a give-and-take format of questioning or just go through this list as set out.

IV. Questions

These do not have to be in any particular order.

A. What line of work were they in before? Are they currently employed?

B. Have they ever owned a business before? If so, what and when? Also inquire why they got out of it. (Did they bankrupt the business?)

C. Depending on the circumstances, ask them if they have a formal education (college). If so, what?

D. Ask if they plan to manage the business themselves or hire management.

E. Ask how long they have been looking for a business to buy.

F. Ask why they are interested in your type of business.

G. Do they have any experience in your type of business?

H. If your business entails a process or product that could cause an allergic reaction to someone with a particular sensitivity or known allergy, ask them if they are affected by that condition. (Your particular business may require a lot of eye strain, exposure to cold, contact with chemicals, long hours on your feet, etc.) *The point is that if you waste a lot of time with someone who will not buy your business for such a reason or may not run it well due to an aversion, you are wasting your time or exposing yourself to additional risk if you are offering to carry a note.*

I. Ask them about the availability of their funds. Is the money they plan to use for the down payment readily available? Is it in some CD or investment that may take some time to liquidate? You may see via the financial statement where the down payment is coming from.

1. If you cannot plainly ascertain the source of the down payment money, inquire about how they plan to obtain the necessary funds for the down payment or total price.

If they mention any third-party source for the funding, inquire about the following:

2. Are they going to be looking for bank financing, SBA financing, or financing from a friend or relative?

3. If they are looking to a bank or SBA, ask what collateral they are planning to offer the lender. Also inform them that third-party funding to purchase a business, especially from a bank, is very difficult to achieve.

4. If they are going to have a friend, partner, relative, or spouse finance the purchase or the down payment, ask them to have that person prepare a letter of commitment to them which you can see. It might be best to have them attend any future meetings between you.

Note: If the funding is coming from one of the sources mentioned above, usually that person will have influence on your buyer prospect with respect to the analysis of your business and whether your business is the right business to buy or some other value considerations. In other words, in many instances you must sell *this other person* on the idea that your business is the right one and the asking price is correct also. In essence, you have two parties to educate and persuade. This is very difficult because the true people with the influence are usually the ones putting up their money and if they are not one and the same as the buyer and future operator of the business, then the job can be tough and many times fatal to a successful sale.

V. Close

When you have gotten the answer to these questions and others which you may ask as a result of the information these questions reveal, and you feel the buyers meet your approval so far, give them the presentation package and let them know that it will answer most of their questions. Tell them that it may be better for them to thoroughly read it and get together with you again to answer any questions they may have. (They will be better informed and have more intelligent questions after a study of the package.) You can then adjourn the meeting. Tell them that if they find that they are not interested after reading the information, you would prefer them to return the package as you do not want it left for the garbage man or anyone else to see.

VI. Business Tour

If the buyer asks for a tour of your business or asks when they can have a tour, tell them it could be done in conjunction with your next meeting. Don't be too flexible on this issue. There is no reason to further expose your business or risk having your employees find out too soon until you are sure the prospect is coming from informed judgment and you both want to proceed further. If you feel comfortable enough to give them a tour before they have time to read the information, then do so. I caution you that it may be premature.

Note: If they are true prospects and have a sincere interest, they will not be turned off by these procedures; the procedures are tried and true.

EXHIBIT 3.1 AUTHORIZATION FOR A ONE-PARTY SHOWING

Authorization For a One-Party Showing and Agreement to Pay Commission

In consideration of obtaining _____ or assignee as a buyer for my business located at _____, California, known as _____ , I hereby agree to pay _____, a sales commission in the sum of _____ percent (_%) of the selling price* or _____ dollars ($_____) whichever is greater, at close of escrow.

_____   _____
Seller   Date

Accepted

_____   _____
Sales Agent/Broker   Date

*Total selling price shall mean and includes but is not limited to goodwill, fixtures, equipment, noncompete agreements, consulting and employment agreements, leases, leasehold improvements, real property, franchise, inventory, options, cash, notes, assumption of notes, liabilities, or stocks whether the foregoing are personal in nature or corporate.

Exhibit 3.1 Authorization for a One-Party Showing and Agreement to Pay Commission

Marketing Response Log

Business Name: _____

Buyer Response From: *N*ewspaper / *F*lyer / *D*irect *M*ail /*R*eferral / *W*ord of *M*outh / *T*rade *M*agazine

#1 NAME	TELE#
ADDRESS	DATE
COMMENTS	
#2 NAME	TELE#
ADDRESS	DATE
COMMENTS	
#3 NAME	TELE#
ADDRESS	DATE
COMMENTS	
#4 NAME	TELE#
ADDRESS	DATE
COMMENTS	
#5 NAME	TELE#
ADDRESS	DATE
COMMENTS	

Exhibit 3.2 Marketing Response Log

EXHIBIT 3.3 EXAMPLES OF HOW TO WRITE A CLASSIFIED ADVERTISEMENT

Newspaper Ad Templates and Samples

PLASTICS MFG. COMPANY
$2 Million Gross Sales   Net $185K
Asking $485K plus Inv. Owner 111-1111

PACKAGE-POSTAL BUSINESS
Busy Location, EST 10 yrs
Dwn pmt $50K Owner 111-1111

POOL SERVICE COMPANY
Lrg Repeat Customer Base, Net $80K
Asking $165K Owner 111-1111

*Check with your local newspaper for
their particulars on the following:*

---

*NOTE:

*ALL LINES CAN ONLY BE 30
CHARACTERS MAXIMUM*

LINE 1: **ALL CAPS AND BOLD AND
Left Aligned**
LINE 2: Title Case, No Bold and
Centered
LINE 3: Title Case, No Bold and
Justified

If you are going to advertise
one day a week, we recommend
Sunday.

If you are going to advertise
two days a week, we recommend
Sunday and Monday.

Ad should be placed in the
business opportunities section.

Three lines on Sunday and Monday.

Exhibit 3.3 Example of How to Write a Classified Advertisement

SPREAD THE NEWS

DO YOU KNOW OF ANYONE THAT COULD BE
INTERESTED IN OWNING/OPERATING THEIR OWN
PRINTING BUSINESS?

AVAILABLE

A FULL-SERVICE COMMERCIAL AND RETAIL PRINTER, WELL
ESTABLISHED AND PROFITABLE. THE PROFITS ARE ON A
CONTINUING TREND OF GROWTH. TRAINING IS
OFFERED BY THE SELLER.

FROM CURRENT CASH FLOW, ALL THE INITIAL
INVESTMENT SHOULD BE RETURNED TO THE BUYER IN
APPROXIMATELY 26 MONTHS!! AT THE SAME TIME
RETIRING THE DEBT, BOTH PRINCIPAL AND INTEREST.

YOU COULD NOT ASK FOR MORE COOPERATIVE
SELLERS THAN THE OWNER OF THIS BUSINESS.
(YOU KNOW WHAT THAT'S WORTH.)

THE GROSS SALES ARE $698,000 WITH AN ADJUSTED
NET PROFIT OF $150,000.

THIS BUSINESS SALE IS VERY CONFIDENTIAL. PLEASE CALL
THE FOLLOWING TELEPHONE NUMBER IF YOU KNOW OF
ANYONE WHO WANTS TO OWN AN ESTABLISHED PRINTING
BUSINESS.

TO THE SELLING AGENT, WE ARE OFFERING 5% OF THE
PURCHASE PRICE AS A COMMISSION OR A MINIMUM OF
$5,000, WHICHEVER IS GREATER. PAID UPON CLOSE OF
ESCROW OR UPON CONSUMMATION OF THE SALE.

CALL 269-2345

Exhibit 3.4 Example of a Flyer to a Brokerage

EXHIBIT 3.5 A SAMPLE FLYER TO AN OWNER OF A SAME BUSINESS

For Sale

AN ESTABLISHED, PROFITABLE, GROWING POSTAL ANNEX AND FRANCHISE

NO GROWING PAINS • NO TRYING TO FIGURE OUT WHAT PRODUCTS AND SERVICES ARE BEST TO OFFER

IT'S DONE AND TIME FOR YOU TO ENJOY THE BENEFITS OF OWNING AN ESTABLISHED, SUCCESSFUL FRANCHISE. OWNING A SECOND FRANCHISE COULD BE EASIER THAN YOU THOUGHT.

SOME KEY POINTS OF INTEREST

- RENT IS LESS THAN $1,000 PER MONTH (including CAM charges)
- SAFE AND ENJOYABLE LOCATION
- GROSS OVER $200,000. PLENTY OF ROOM LEFT TO GROW
- REVENUE SOURCES HAVE BEEN SELECTED FOR MAXIMUM PROFITS

The owner will carry a note or obtaining an SBA loan for the purchase of a second franchise may be much easier than you thought.

THE SALE OF A BUSINESS IS VERY CONFIDENTIAL AND THEREFORE WE CANNOT DISCLOSE THE LOCATION OR UNIT# UNTIL THE BUYER HAS BEEN PREQUALIFIED AND HAS SIGNED A CONFIDENTIALITY AGREEMENT.

IF YOU OR ANYONE YOU KNOW MIGHT HAVE AN INTEREST IN PURCHASING THIS EXISTING FRANCHISE, PLEASE GIVE US A CALL. WE HAVE AN ENTIRE PRESENTATION PACKAGE EXPLAINING EVERYTHING YOU WANT TO KNOW.

For further information call:
(619) 234-8778

Exhibit 3.5 A Sample Flyer to an Owner of a Same Business

AVAILABLE

*GROWING A BUSINESS ONE CUSTOMER AT A TIME IS COSTLY AND
CONSUMES A LOT OF TIME.*

* *GREATLY EXPAND YOUR BUSINESS'S GROSS REVENUES IN 30 DAYS*
* *GREATLY EXPAND YOUR CUSTOMER BASE IN 30 DAYS*
* *DRAMATICALLY INCREASE YOUR NET PROFIT IN 30 DAYS*

ALL THIS IS ACTUALLY POSSIBLE!

*WE ARE OFFERING OUR BUSINESS FOR SALE AND WE FEEL OUR BUSINESS
IS A GREAT MATCH WITH YOURS.*

* *MERGING THE TWO BUSINESSES HAS VERY REWARDING POSSIBILITIES.*

OR

* *HAVING A SECOND LOCATION RUNNING SMOOTHLY AND PROFITABLY
  CAN PROVIDE MANY BENEFITS FOR YOU AND YOUR CURRENT OPERATION.*

* *SELLER FINANCING OR SBA FUNDING ARE AVAILABLE.*

IF YOU WANT TO EXPLORE THE POSSIBILITIES, JUST GIVE US A CALL AT
(619) 543-0978

Exhibit 3.6 A Sample Flyer to a Similar Business, a Merger Candidate

EXHIBIT 3.7 AN EXAMPLE OF WHAT NOT TO DO WHEN CREATING A FLYER

FOR SALE BY OWNER

Bar-Restaurant-Night Club
Music and Dancing

> By using the name of the business, you have lost confidentiality.

Patch Work Sports Bar & Grill
7215 Adobe Brick Road
San Diego, CA 92129

> Should not use such personal information!

Owner Joe Paccaginelli
Home (619) 462-8306
Fax (619) 256-4255

Price: $175,000 with terms

Sublease: 23 years at $3,800 per month, no increases, no NNN, no percentage (approx. $.33 per square foot)

Liquor licence: (Old 47—unrestricted)

Building size: 6,500 sq. ft., plus 4,500 sq. ft. patio area (all licensed for drinking)

Parking: 80 cars

Kitchen: Fully equipped with large walk-in refrigerator and freezer

Large banquet room: With dance floor and big-screen TV and satellite

Bar: Modern cocktail lounge, stools, tables and chairs, and dart room

Gross: Approximately $200,000 per year +plus

> Should not say any of this.

> This information is okay.

Patch Work Sports Bar & Grill is located at Interstate 15 and Willow Road, one mile from the university and the stadium, next to the Sleep Tight Inn.

> No respectable broker would respond to this.

Commission to Brokers: Finder's fee for qualifed buyer. *Please do not contact any employees or phone place of business. Your discretion is greatly appreciated.*

BY APPOINTMENT ONLY!!!!

Exhibit 3.7 An Example of What Not to Do When Creating a Flyer

Confidentiality Agreement &
Receipt for Information Package

This is a Confidentiality and Receipt for Information Package Agreement, dated

_____ by and between _____ (hereinafter called

"Seller"), and _____ (hereinafter called "Buyer").

1. Seller has provided to Buyer directly, information of a confidential and proprietary nature concerning financial, technical, and management information
   ("Information") for the purpose of allowing Buyer to determine whether Buyer
   wishes to acquire the Seller's business operation by purchase of all or some of
   its assets through any means, including but not limited to merger, acquisition, or
   otherwise taking over Seller's operation.

Seller advises buyer to read the Information Package in its entirety.

2. For and in consideration of Seller providing this and any further Information to
   the Buyer, as may be required by Buyer to better enable Buyer to evaluate the
   Seller's business operation. Buyer agrees that the Information will be maintained as Confidential and Proprietary and Buyer shall not disclose such Information (including but not limited to the fact that the Seller's business is for sale,
   except the release of Information as may be authorized in writing by Seller) or
   any notes, summaries, analysis, or other material derived from such evaluation
   or discussion of the Information to others.

3. Buyer acknowledges and agrees that disclosure of Information to anyone other
   than as set forth in this agreement could be detrimental to the business and
   profits of the Seller as well as the retention of the Seller's employees and Buyer
   could be held financially responsible for any damages sustained by the Seller or
   its business if such Information were disclosed or used to compete with Seller.

4. Buyer agrees to return to Seller any and all Information provided in a physical
   form after a decision has been made by Buyer to not pursue acquisition of
   Seller's business or within ten (10) days of demand for same by Seller, and
   Buyer further agrees to not retain photocopies or other reproductions of any
   kind of said Information.

Acceptance and receipt acknowledged   Information Package #_____

_____

Buyer (signature)   Date

_____

Print Name

Exhibit 3.8 Confidentiality Agreement and Receipt for Information Package

EXHIBIT 3.9 CONFIDENTIALITY AGREEMENT

Confidentiality Agreement

This is a Confidentiality Agreement dated _____

by and between _____ (Hereinafter called "Seller")

and _____ (Hereinafter called "Buyer").

1. Seller will provide to Buyer directly, information of a confidential and proprietary nature concerning financial, technical, and management information ("Information") for the purpose of allowing Buyer to determine whether Buyer wishes to acquire the Seller's business operation by purchase of all or some of its assets through any means, including but not limited to merger, acquisition, or otherwise taking over Seller's operation.

2. For and in consideration of Seller providing Information to the Buyer, as may be required by Buyer to better enable Buyer to evaluate the Seller's business operation, Buyer agrees that the Information will be maintained as Confidential and Proprietary and Buyer shall not disclose such Information (including but not limited to the fact that the Seller's business is for sale, except the release of Information as may be authorized in writing by Seller) or any notes, summaries, analysis or other material derived from such evaluation or discussion of the Information to others.

3. Buyer acknowledges and agrees that disclosure of Information to anyone other than as set forth in this agreement could be detrimental to the business and profits of the Seller as well as the retention of the Seller's employees and Buyer could be held financially responsible for any damages sustained by the Seller or its business if such Information were disclosed or used to compete with Seller.

4. Buyer agrees to return to Seller any and all Information provided in a physical form after decision has been made by Buyer to not pursue acquisition of Seller's business or within ten (10) days of demand for same by Seller and Buyer further agrees to not retain photocopies or other reproductions of any kind of said Information.

ACCEPTED BY BUYER

_____

Buyer (Signature)   Date

Exhibit 3.9 Confidentiality Agreement

MARKETING THE BUSINESS

The information supplied on this form is joint if you are married. If you are being considered for credit as a partnership then each General Partner must complete a separate form.

As of: _____
DATE

☐ Married   ☐ Unmarried   ☐ Separated

NAME _____ DATE OF BIRTH _____

HOME TELEPHONE # _____ WORK TELEPHONE # _____

ADDRESS _____

CITY _____ STATE _____ ZIP _____ SOCIAL SECURITY # _____

BANK _____ BRANCH _____

If needed, please attach any supporting documentation that will enable your current financial condition to be verified. If there is not sufficient room on this form, use a separate piece of paper and attach it to this form. The values used should be current fair market value.

ASSETS	AMOUNT	LIABILITIES	AMOUNT
Cash in bank (checking)		Notes payable to bank	
Cash in savings		Notes payable (others)	
Accounts receivable (schedule C on reverse)		Accounts payable	
Stocks and bonds (schedule B on reverse)		1.	
Notes receivable (schedule C on reverse)		2.	
Cash surrender value: life insurance		3.	
Auto (year and make)		4.	
Auto (year and make)		Taxes payable	
Real estate (schedule A on reverse)		Real estate loans (schedule A on reverse)	
Household goods		Other liabilities (describe)	
Other assets (describe)		1.	
1.		2.	
2.		3.	
3.		4.	
4.		5.	
5.		**Total Liabilities**	$
		Net worth (total assets minus total liabilities)	$
Total Assets	$	**TOTAL LIABILITIES and NET WORTH**	$
ANNUAL INCOME		ANNUAL EXPENDITURES	
Salary (gross)—applicant		Real estate payment(s)	
Salary (gross)—spouse		Rent/lease payment(s)	
Securities income		Income taxes	
Rental income		Insurance premiums (all types)	
Other income (describe)		Property taxes	
1.		Alimony, child support	
2.		Other (describe—include installment payments other than real estate)	
3.		1.	
4.		2.	
TOTAL INCOME	$	3.	
LESS TOTAL EXPENDITURES	$	**TOTAL EXPENDITURES**	$
NET CASH INCOME (exclusive of ordinary living expenses)	$	Contingent liabilities (debts you guaranteed or co-signed for, etc.)	
Is any of this income likely to be reduced within the next year? ☐ Yes ☐ No		**TOTAL**	$

Exhibit 3.10 Personal Financial Statement

EXHIBIT 3.10 PERSONAL FINANCIAL STATEMENT

Schedule A—Real Estate

Property Address and Type of Improvement	Purchase Date	Names of Owner(s) and How Held (Joint Tenants, Tenants in Common, Community Property, Etc.)	Estimated Market Value	Amount Owing	To Whom Payable

Schedule B—Stocks and Bonds

Number of Shares and Amount of Bonds	Description	Names of Owner(s) and How Held (Joint Tenants, Tenants in Common, Community Property, Etc.)	Current Market on Listed or Estimated Value on Unlisted

COMMENTS SECTION – If you are married and there is any property that is held separately, you can include it here.

Schedule C—Accounts/Notes Receivable and Trust Deed (Mortgages) Owned

Name of Debtor	How Paid		Balance Due	Final Maturity Date	Collateral
	$	per	$		
	$	per			
	$	per			
	$	per			
		TOTAL	$		

Schedule D—General Information

Are there any suits or unpaid judgements now pending against you? ☐ Yes ☐ No   If yes, give details on a separate sheet.

Have you ever voluntarily surrendered or had a vehicle, appliance, or any other item repossessed? ☐ Yes ☐ No   If yes, give details on a separate sheet.

Have you or your spouse ever been the subject of bankruptcy proceedings? ☐ Yes ☐ No   If yes, give details on a separate sheet.

Have you ever applied for credit under another name? ☐ Yes ☐ No   If yes, give other name(s):

Are you a U.S. citizen? ☐ Yes ☐ No   If no, give country of citizenship and visa status:

Number of Dependents: Ages:

Life Insurance $ _____   Name of Insured _____   Name of Company _____

Beneficiary's Name _____   Address _____   Relationship _____

Life Insurance $ _____   Name of Insured _____   Name of Company _____

Beneficiary's Name _____   Address _____   Relationship _____

Automobile Insurance—Public Liability ☐ Yes ☐ No   Property Damage ☐ Yes ☐ No
Comprehensive Personal Liability ☐ Yes ☐ No

By signing below, you certify that the statements above and on any attachment(s) are true and complete as of the date given below. You authorize the Business Owner (Seller) to verify or check any of the information given, check your credit references (see Exhibit 3.11), verify employment, and obtain credit reports.

X _____   X _____

Exhibit 3.10 (Continued)

235

Credit Report Authorization

Date: _____

To: _____ (the seller)

From: _____ (the buyer's name)

I hereby authorize _____ to obtain a credit report(s) on the following named person.

Name _____

Address _____

Date of Birth _____

Social Security Number _____

_____

Authorization by (Buyer)

Exhibit 3.11 Credit Report Authorization

4

NEGOTIATING THE SALE

When the buyers have read the presentation package, taken a tour of the business, and asked any follow-up questions, they should be ready to make an offer. The only reason that they would not be ready is if they have some unanswered question or concern about the business or about the information that has been given to them. Many times the questions that the buyer pose have to do with the financial aspects of the business, or the business' financial reports themselves. That is, unless there is some particular weakness they have become aware of and need to get to a point of confidence that they can correct whatever they see is wrong. I cannot overstress the point that if you do a thorough job in presenting your business in the presentation package, you eliminate many difficulties usually encountered in the prenegotiation stage or during the negotiations. Whenever you discuss your business with a potential buyer remember: you are really selling, and the buyer is really buying, all the benefits of the business.

HAVING THE BUYER MAKE AN OFFER

At the conclusion of the meeting with the buyer, where the tour takes place, you should ask something like, "Do you have any more questions at this time?" "If you would like to make an offer to buy the business, I can provide you with a blank Business Purchase Agreement." "Would you like one?" By taking the time to create a complete and detailed presentation package, and having an informative tour which includes an opportunity to answer any follow-up questions the buyer might have, you have set the stage to move successfully into the offer phase of the sale.

Having received a good presentation of the information about the business, the buyers' response can only be one of a very few choices. They will either accept the blank Purchase Agreement and make some comment about filling it out and getting it back to you, or they will say that they will contact their attorney to draft an offer or letter of intent. The buyers may decide to not make an offer or they may say they need to think about it for a while longer. If you are a more assertive person and have presented the business in a thorough manner, then if the buyer says they need time to think more about it (the purchase), ask them what they have to think about. Explain to them that you have gone over all the aspects of the business. Ask them if they have any unanswered questions or concerns. If they say "no, we have no more questions at this time," then you can restate your question about them making an offer or re-offer them a blank Business Purchase Agreement (a Blank Purchase Agreement is provided in Exhibit 4.1). If they in fact do have any further reservations (questions), find out what they are and get them answered. So you will be more familiar with the purchase contract, and if needed to help the buyer, a filled-in Business Purchase Agreement has been provided in Exhibit 4.2. If you are ever in the market to buy a business, the Business Purchase Agreements provided herein will come in very handy.

GET ALL OFFERS IN WRITING

The blank purchase agreement is easy to fill out. If the buyers want to make a verbal offer, decline to orally negotiate the sale. Tell the buyers that there are many things to consider and you want them to put all their intentions down in writing so you can give them careful consideration.

THE GOOD-FAITH DEPOSIT

A buyer should provide a good-faith deposit at the same time the offer is made. The amount of the deposit can be between 5 and 10 percent of the offering price. I would not accept less than $5,000 on any size business sale. The deposit can be made with a personal check, business check, cashier's check, money order, or some other liquid cash means. Sometimes, but rarely, the offer is accompanied by a promise to provide a deposit at some date shortly following. The deposit check should be made out to the escrow company you will be using. If you are not using an escrow company, the check should be made out to the attorney who will perform the closing. The deposit is usually put into a bank after the negotiations are completed successfully.

THE POWER OF A NONREFUNDABLE DEPOSIT

Sometimes a powerful tactic to use is to say in the contract that the deposit is nonrefundable once the due diligence has been completed. If you can get the buyer to agree to this, then the buyer will be much more motivated to see the transaction through to a successful conclusion. In transactions where you can get the buyer to agree to the nonrefundable deposit, it is possible sometimes to actually have the deposit released (cash in your pocket) in whole or a portion at a time.

Sometimes it works in the following manner. The buyers may speak of how you should be confident that they will see the transaction through to the closing. As proof of this commitment, the seller asks that the deposit or a portion of the deposit become nonrefundable when escrow is opened or as soon as due diligence is finished. Then in one or two stages, the deposit is actually released—unconditionally—on certain occurrences.

The occurrences can be the satisfaction of each remaining major contingency. The use of this nonrefundable deposit will not be suited for everyone, nor for many standard transactions; but there will be some of you who will want to seriously consider using this stipulation.

I would be more apt to include this stipulation in a transaction where I was going to have to spend a considerable sum of money to accommodate the requests of the buyer; such as if they asked that the financial records be audited, or I would have to spend a lot on accounting or legal fees (above normal levels for a transaction). If the business is especially vulnerable to negative effects created because the buyer failed to complete the transaction, I would ask for a nonrefundable deposit. Some businesses can have very negative effects if the employees, vendors, and customers are alerted that Mr. X is going to buy the business and he then backs out of the deal for any reason. I believe that you get the point.

MORE TO CONSIDER THAN JUST THE PRICE AND DOWN PAYMENT

I know that the sale price and down payment are very important issues, but your idea about what price you are willing to accept may be swayed by additional information; you should consider everything altogether. Elements such as the terms of a seller carry-back note may influence your decisions. The buyer may want one or more conditions that are unacceptable to you. If you agree to verbally negotiate the price and down payment, you may find yourself unable to effectively get any other conditions in your favor, or at least into a win–win status. In addition, after verbal negotiations have been completed and it comes to getting things into writing, sometimes people get weak memories and do not remember details in the same fashion as the other party does. If the buyer is serious, he will make a written offer. If the buyer is just fishing around to see if they can get a steal of a deal, he will come up with all sorts of excuses for sticking with the idea of making a verbal offer. Believe me, if the buyer is a serious, qualified buyer, he will not walk away from buying the business if you insist on a written offer. When the buyer says he will write an offer, ask when you should expect to hear from him.

I have provided in Exhibit 4.3 a blank Counteroffer form for your use. In Exhibit 4.4 you will also find a list of 106 conditions and contingencies used in various business purchase contracts. Read them over and include any in your counteroffer that are important to you. Most business sales do experience multiple rounds of negotiations. Make copies of the counteroffer forms and use one each time you respond to the buyer.

HOW TO HANDLE THE ISSUE OF OUTSIDE FINANCING

If the buyer desires to seek outside financing such as a Small Business Administration (SBA) loan or a loan through conventional funding, be sure to address the issue specifically in the contract. Even if the buyer does not address the issue as set forth herein, you should address it in a counteroffer. The important factor is that the transaction be conditional on the buyer successfully obtaining the funding. Not only that, but you should also set a deadline for the buyer to be prequalified by the lender. The confirmation of the buyer qualifying for the loan should be made to you directly. In other words, you should speak directly to the loan officer handling the loan. You want some kind of assurance that the buyer is a qualified borrower. In some cases, all the emphasis is put on the business qualifying to have a loan made on it. Do not allow your interest in the buyer being a qualified borrower to be lost in all the goings-on.

I would allow no more than one week to 10 days for the buyer to be prequalified and for you to be able to call and speak with the loan officer. If the buyer is qualified then the loan will usually weigh heavily on the books and records of the business. The lender will want tax returns and profit and loss statements, minimally. I would highly recommend that you provide the lender with your presentation package. Just like it helped sell the buyer on your business, it will also help for the lender to read it. I have been told by clients that the detail and clarity of the presentation package made the difference between getting the loan and not. One of the key areas of the package was the financial section wherein all the adjustments were clearly spelled out.

If the loan process—thus the purchase—is stopped by action or inaction of the buyer, the buyer should be held responsible; he may be in default. You can have a clause (liquidated damages) in the purchase contract (offer or counteroffer) that calls for the buyer to forfeit a predetermined amount of money should he not conclude the purchase for any reason other than the specific contingencies contained in the contract. There are several versions of this in the list of contingencies provided for you in Exhibit 4.4, the Purchase Agreement Conditions and Contingencies List.

Just in case the following experience will be of help to someone, I will convey a case in point. There was a buyer who wanted to get a bank loan to buy my client's business. We had a liquidated damages clause included in our contract. That clause called for a predetermined amount of money to be forfeited if the buyer backed out for any reason not contained in one of the contract's contingencies. We also had the buyer tied to a specific amount of time to be prequalified for the loan. The buyer told us that he had been turned down by the bank and therefore had to discontinue the purchase of the business. We found out by calling the bank that the buyer was approved for the loan but decided to cancel the loan request because he did not like the interest rate. The seller was able to keep $1,000 of the buyer's deposit. No court action or attorneys were needed.

IMPORTANT ISSUES TO CONSIDER WHEN CONTRACTING TO SELL

When you are responding to the buyer's offer and you are asked to carry a note, be sure to add a clause in your counteroffer such as: *The buyer shall provide a current credit report and personal financial statement to seller within three days of an agreement being reached between the parties. The seller herein reserves the right to approve buyer for the requested seller-financing. If the buyer is disapproved for said financing, then seller shall provide written notice of such to the buyer within five days of seller's receipt of the credit report and personal financial statement.*

The note you are asked to carry will, depending on the specific terms, begin to accrue interest from the day possession changes, with the first payment due 30 days from the date of closing.

Do not accept any clause in the buyer's offer where they try to have you guarantee something that is out of your control. Two examples would be: asking you to guarantee that a certain employee will stay with the business, or asking you to guarantee that the lease will be extended or an option for a lease extension be granted. In both cases, you may help in any way possible to see that both occur, but you cannot guarantee that they will happen. Much of the outcome of such things is very dependent on the buyer, not you.

MATTERS CONCERNING THE LEASE AND THE LANDLORD

Some landlords require a fee to administrate the assignment. Either split the cost with the buyer or better yet, have the buyer pay the whole thing. Check the lease to see if any such fee is mentioned.

As long as the buyer has good credit and a positive net worth shown on their personal financial statement, the lease assignment should be approved. There are some occasions where the seller is much more substantial financially than the buyer. The landlord will not want his new tenant to be a greater risk than his present tenant.

This should not be too difficult to overcome since the seller usually remains liable for the performance of the lease if the buyer defaults.

Generally, I would not mention that you are selling the business to the landlord until you have accepted an offer to buy your business. As soon as the books and records of the business have been checked and approved by the buyer, then you should contact the landlord.

If you can avoid a sublease, do so. A lease assignment is better in most cases. A lease assignment will not, depending on the stipulations in the lease, let you off all your liabilities under the lease agreement. The buyer or assignee moves into first position. You will remain liable for the rent and damages if the buyer defaults. Unless a novation is done, there is nothing, in most cases, to change this. A novation in this case is the substitution of a new contract between the landlord and the buyer. In other words, the landlord lets you off the hook completely. Your liability under the lease does not usually extend to any option periods.

Depending on the length remaining on the lease, the buyer may ask for the lease to be extended or an option for more years to be granted by the landlord. If this is the case, make sure that your liability does not extend into any years more than are currently remaining.

When you have considered the various conditions and contingencies and have decided on which to include, and are ready to give the buyer your counteroffer, reemphasize the strong points about your business and why your counteroffer is very fair. Make some points in favor of your business whenever discussing the business with the buyer.

ELEMENTS THAT AFFECT NEGOTIATIONS

A key factor involved in how well you can achieve your price and terms objectives (provided the business is priced correctly to begin with) is the motivation of the buyer. If the buyer is not motivated toward the purchase of your business then any uncomfortable irritation can cause them to back out. If you work with a buyer that seems

246

too distant and unmotivated, you may be better off with someone else. Obviously, do attempt to transact with the less motivated or unmotivated buyer, but do not continually try to accommodate their lack of motivation by giving concession after concession. Unless you are unusually compelled to sell your business, always maintain the attitude that you can walk away from any buyer at any time, and be ready to do that.

Many buyers will attempt to slowly prepare you. They will say things in an effort to "soften the beach head." (A military term meaning to lessen the resistance of the opposition, in advance of the main attack.) Sometimes this occurs right from the start, just after they meet you and learn anything about the business. Each time I spoke to potential buyers, they had some critical comment, but the amazing thing was that they kept right on going down the path of buying the business. They will make comments, either boldly or just in passing that are meant to create a lower opinion of the business. They will point out those weaknesses or nonfatal flaws in the business. All this is usually in an effort to buy the business at a lower price and at more favorable terms. The thing to keep your mind on is: are they truly going to walk away from the prospect of buying your business, or are they continuing on?

I once heard that the negotiating process is like a tennis match in that as long as the ball keeps moving over the net the game is going on. It does not matter that the ball moves at varying speeds or directions—just so long as it keeps moving.

HANDLING A BUYER'S CONSIDERATIONS

Know this; that by reading and following *Sell Your Business Successfully* you are much more informed and prepared than most all the buyers you shall encounter. Many buyers will make comments that have little or no real foundation other than mere opinion. Buyers may make comments about the business's value yet have no real foundation to their opinion. They may have just heard (from a

247

business-broker, uninformed CPA, or mysterious other person) that a business like yours does not sell for such a price. I wish I had all the money my clients received that was higher than the values stoutly purported by uninformed buyers. I have had many uninformed business-brokers try to tell me that the business I was selling was over-priced—just to sell it for *much more* than they said. The wonderful thing was that the final price was a very good value and the buyer was happy to pay the price and own the business. Many business-brokers want to see the business priced on the low side because it makes selling the business, therefore collecting the commission, so much easier. After all, that is why they are there—to collect a commission—not to get you the best price. *Do not be misled; the previous comment is all too true.*

Not only because you own the business, but by having gone through all the work in the valuation chapter of this guide and having taken the time to create a detailed presentation package, you are informed. You know all the good aspects and the weaknesses of the business. You know that any weaknesses are advantages or powerful reasons for a buyer to buy your business. Do not let the buyer lower your opinions due to disparaging remarks. Tell them that the weakness that they are pointing out is *exactly why they should buy the business.* Any correctable (maybe not by you) weakness in the business or in its management is a golden opportunity for the buyer to make more profits, have a smoother running business, better-known business, or whatever. You are not selling the business based on all the weaknesses corrected, but on the business's present value.

A POWERFUL QUESTION TO ASK

A powerful question to ask any buyer who expresses a low opinion of your business's value (either in conversation or in an offer) is: "How did you arrive at your opinion of value or what you think the correct value is?" You can in a nonconfrontational manner ask them to please explain how they arrived at the price they offered. Most buyers and even business-brokers will be hard-pressed to give you an answer that makes a lot of common sense. They may give you some uninformed, generalized rule of thumb—at best!

You can respond by repeating all the reasons why your business is worth what you are asking. Remember all the points you considered when going through the valuation process, why your business is different and better than the competition or average other business in your industry. Remember that trying to place all businesses into a generalized valuation multiple is not giving any attention to the differences of the business, good or bad.

Keep in mind also that many times a buyer will have one or a few elements of the transaction that are more important to them than other elements. For example, the buyer may be limited in ability to provide the down payment you optimally prefer. Therefore, you can keep the total price higher, and/or the payment terms more favorable. Maybe you can ask for greater security than you might normally get.

KEEPING YOUR FOCUS ON WHAT IS IMPORTANT

Try to determine if the buyer has a particular facet that he is leaning toward. To some buyers, having very low monthly payments is of critical importance; therefore, you can get some other aspect in your favor. Some astute buyers purposely draw your attention to some element that is really not too important so they can achieve what they really want in some other area. Beware of having your attention drawn to some facet of the offer or counteroffer that appears to be significant only to forfeit some aspect that you should not have.

Some attorneys and buyers will really overload the offer or counteroffer with many stipulations, all obviously very advantageous to their side. By operating from this tactic, they hope to get your attention focused on what is most important to you while they actually achieve all the rest of the inflated points. If you get faced with this, it is sometimes better to just entirely scrap their proposal and create your own from scratch, in your favor. I have especially seen this when the other side of the negotiations scrapped our offer or counteroffer and completely rewrote it. But this time it was not a compromise on what we had proposed, it was so heavily and so obviously built to benefit the other party that it almost appeared ridiculous.

HOW TO HANDLE MULTIPLE OFFERS

If you have more than one buyer looking at your business, tell the buyers that there are multiple parties investigating the business. If you get more than one buyer who wants to make an offer at the same time (it happens frequently), you can inform them that the first party who gets an acceptance is in first position. If the second party wants to continue, then their offer or negotiated agreement will be a "back-up" agreement—contingent on whether the first party goes all the way to closing.

If you get multiple offers at the same time, say in the counteroffer that you are making multiple counteroffers and that the party achieving a final agreement will be in the first position. Whoever is in first position with you is the party to go forward with into the due diligence phase. The second or back-up party does nothing; they just wait to see if the first party successfully completes the transaction.

WHAT TO DO IF YOU PUSHED THE BUYER TOO HARD

When negotiating the price and terms of the sale, remember that if you push too far you can always withdraw a condition or amount. In other words, so you do not leave any gap in the price and terms that you could have gotten, push a bit higher than feels comfortable. When the buyer is truly ready to walk away, perhaps you have gotten as far as you can. You can point out to the buyer how close you both really are and that perhaps both of you can compromise and meet in the middle. I have hardly ever seen negotiations fail with $5,000 to

$10,000 between the parties. ($10K for a business with an adjusted net of $100,000 or more, and $5K for smaller businesses.)

You must remember that you are not selling a house or car or any consumer product. You are selling the thing (your business) that creates the money the buyer will use in his life. A business does not appreciate or depreciate like most all other forms of property. A business does not automatically get more expensive with age, or automatically become worthless or obsolete. Therefore, when the difference between your position and the buyer's position on the final price is a relatively small amount of money, under $10,000, it makes economic sense for the buyer to go ahead and accept your final price. The buyer will make up the difference by getting into your business as soon as possible because the business creates money. The amount of money the business creates can be increased and enjoyed each day of ownership. When you buy a home, making up such a difference may never happen (the appreciation must exceed the difference paid to make economic sense).

Many buyers' interest in buying your business goes beyond mere price and terms. They develop an interest in owning, operating, and improving your business. Therefore, do not be too timid in pushing the price and terms you feel are a good value.

CONSOLIDATE AFTER SEVERAL ROUNDS OF NEGOTIATIONS

The original offer made by the buyer and all the counteroffers make one agreement. That is, if you did not rewrite each counteroffer like the original offer in its entirety. When making a counteroffer you only need to counter the specific things you do not like in the buyer's offer or subsequent counteroffers, provided you link them as the counteroffer form provided herein states.

When you have reached a point of mutual agreement with the buyer, both parties' signatures should be on the final document. If you have gone several rounds of offers and counteroffers, you may desire to put all the points of agreement into one clean contract. This does not absolutely need to be done. You can use the blank counteroffer form provided in Exhibit 4.3 or have someone—such as an attorney—prepare a final contract with all the points of agreement. If you do have someone consolidate the various offers and counteroffers, be sure that he is instructed to not change the intent of the parties; he should not add or delete items they do not like, yet were already agreed to by you and the buyer. Unfortunately, many times this consolidation allows some people to think they can reopen the negotiations all over again.

BEWARE OF NEGOTIATIONS DISGUISED AS "PROPER CONTRACT STRUCTURE"

In business sales, some brokers or agents work with a very simple contract form. They initially try to keep the contract very simple in order to decrease the possible number of points on which the two parties must agree (they get paid only if the sale goes through). The reasoning goes in manner similar to this: even though it is known that more issues must be covered in the contract and must be agreed between the parties, the contract will be kept simple for now so the transaction is not put in jeopardy. Unfortunately for the clients, when the completed and agreed-to contract is taken to the escrow company or closing agent, the broker, without prior discussion with the seller or buyer, has the escrow company or closing agent (attorney) add many clauses to the contract. The final product is called "the escrow instructions or definitive agreement." There are a few reasons why things are done in that manner. I do not believe that procedure is the best for the clients. In fact, it actually increases the overall risks to the close of the transaction. By following that procedure, you, the seller, and the buyer have negotiated in good faith the sale of the business and have gone through offers and counteroffers until an agreement was reached. The broker or agent then takes your agreement into the escrow company or closing agent (attorney) and when you see it next, the agreement now contains many new points between the parties—points that have not been agreed to previously. Now (one of the top reasons) under pressure of blowing the deal, each party—almost blindly—signs the documents, with the broker or agent convincing them that all is well and normal. There are those sellers and buyers who, with eyes open, do not go for the broker's manipulations and presumptuous additions to the agreement, post negotiations.

It is far better to take the time to put all the points to be considered and agreed to in the contract as you are negotiating the sale. Some people may think this is a great manipulative tool to use (to keep adding new stipulations when the other party feels that the sale points have all been agreed to and included) until the covert tactic is used against them. Believe me when I say there are plenty of buyers out there that will negotiate in an up-front, straightforward manner.

You must at all times maintain the mindset that you can and will walk away from the sale (with that particular party) if they pull underhanded, covert, and/or manipulative tactics.

Beware: There are some people who make a practice out of initially putting together what seems to be a smooth and agreeable transaction, only to keep reopening the negotiations just when you thought you had a complete agreement. If you allow this to happen once, it will happen again and perhaps many more times until the sale is really closed—each time you will lose something. You could and will most likely lose money, but it can be rights that you lose as well. The party that pulls this tactic will do their best to make each change sound reasonable. There are two ways to stop this from being used on you. The first way is to take the time to get all points of the contract discussed, negotiated, and agreed to. The second is to refuse to make changes to the agreement—no matter how demanding the buyer is or how rational the arguments sound. If a correction or clarification is requested which does not decrease your monetary position or diminish your rights under the contract, then it may be appropriate to agree to the changes.

Despite the fact that in some states, brokers or sales agents act only as pure salespeople and do not compose offers or have a hand in what an escrow company or closing agent (attorney) puts into the final contract, you can still create your own letter of intent with the forms and clauses provided in this guide. It may save you some legal costs.

A FEW WORDS OF WISDOM REGARDING ATTORNEYS

Finding an attorney who is active and expert in business transactions and honest is a real blessing. The time it takes to locate a quality attorney is well worth it. A good and honest lawyer can make life that much nicer. Some people may not have thought about it, but the use of an attorney in the sale of a business is not always necessary. Attorneys in advocacy for their profession are the first ones to disagree with this. The legal profession has grown to the point where those who advocate for the profession would like people everywhere to be codependent on the attorneys. Of course, most businesspersons would also like to promote codependency on their services or their products, too. Attorneys have interfered in the process of selling a business to the point of blowing the deal completely. If lawyers were paid based on the outcome being a successful and timely closed transaction, then the incidents would be less. Ask any professional intermediary, broker, or sales agent actively involved in the sale or purchase of small businesses. It is they and their clients who have the tales of ruined transactions. The results when encountered are: they get paid, you get frustrated, they make themselves to be the heroes, and you go away empty-handed, but feeling that it was the other guys' fault, not the lawyer's. I have no axe to grind with attorneys, I only mention this because it is a reality in the world of selling and buying businesses, and this is a guidebook to get you through the maze you are about to enter.

There are many times when their expertise is welcomed, but you have to carefully consider what they are doing or proposing to do. An attorney purposely creating difficulties in the transaction or the relationship between the parties is occasionally a problem. Attorneys have actually admitted that this is true. All I can say about this is, you are the boss. If best, you should instruct your attorney to not change the original intent contained in the purchase agreement or letter of intent you have worked out with the buyer. Ask the attorney to check your agreement for any essential details that you missed. Of course, the attorneys will come up with changes in all cases. It is up to you to control the situation. Likewise, if the buyer has gone to an attorney with your agreement and when you see it next you do not recognize it, you can reject the document right there and send *them* back to the drawing board. In many business sales I have been through, the safest thing to do was to not make any material changes in the agreement once made. Be careful, thoughtful, and as complete as possible the first time around. The best legal work I have seen is where the attorney keeps the contract simple, yet effective, maintains the parties' original intent, and does not try to create conflict that they may resolve later—at someone's expense. There are very good attorneys who practice transaction law and know what they are doing. Look around until you find one you are comfortable with. You will have a very stressful time if you do not. Many attorneys have a specialty; find one who knows business transactions and can provide you with some sort of assurance that they actively handle this sort of legal work.

SOME STANDARD CONTINGENCIES YOU CAN USE

I want to mention a few contingencies that are fairly standard. Each business sale does have its own differences and you should know that you can modify any condition or contingency to fit your particular needs.

Many times it is better to state the price as $XXX,XXX plus the inventory of approximately $XXX,XXX. It is usually better to state it this way because the inventory can fluctuate from hour to hour.

The inventory is usually figured at cost. If you want an inventory company to do the counting, split the cost of the inventory service with the buyer.

HOW LONG DOES THE TRANSFER OF OWNERSHIP USUALLY TAKE?

If escrow companies are used in your state, the escrow time usually takes 30 to 60 days. Most small-business sales take about the same amount of time to close no matter where you are located or whether or not an escrow company or closing attorneys are used.

CHANGING POSSESSION OF THE BUSINESS

Physical possession usually takes place on the day of closing, but is not limited to that. I have been involved in many early possessions. Only one time did I regret it. The early possessions were to take place only after all conditions that would directly cancel the deal had been met and all funds were on deposit with the escrow company or closing attorney. The early possessions I have been involved with were no more than a week early. All the parties felt very good about it and got along extremely well with each other.

A small but important technicality regarding possession before actual closing is that possession should take place just prior to closing in every case. I will explain myself. In order to provide an accurate inventory and accounts receivable amount so you have precise accounting and a precise total purchase price you must cease doing business, take an accounting of the inventory, accounts receivable, and work-in-process, if included, then provide all those final figures to the escrow company or closing attorney so they can calculate the final total purchase price. The seller does not then continue in possession and operation of the business. If the seller did, then another inventory would have to be done. The buyer actually takes over from that point on. In the next chapter I will explain how to do this, and do it properly.

IMPORTANT OCCURRENCES TO BE AWARE OF

Typically, both seller and buyer split the costs of the escrow or cost of the closing attorney, especially if neutral. I explain what an escrow company is and does in the next chapter.

The buyer customarily pays the state sales tax assessed on the value of the furniture, fixtures, and equipment. Depending on the state, the seller is technically charged and the buyer reimburses the seller. If the business is a service-type business and does not have a resale permit, then no tax is assessed on the furniture, fixtures, and equipment.

The due diligence or books and records check is many times an event that takes from a few hours to a couple weeks, depending on the complexity of the business and the desires of each party.

More transactions never close because of a failed due-diligence investigation than any other factor. Why? Because the business's records and operations were misrepresented to the buyer.

Noncompete agreements are a part of practically every sale. The most common stipulations I have seen articulated in the non-compete agreement are: the seller is not to compete with the business being sold for five years and within five miles (in all directions) of the business. Of course, if your business has its customer base spread over a wider area than five miles, the buyer will more than likely stipulate that the range should be over whatever distance makes sense. It is not unusual to see entire counties included. I have seen an entire state and nearby states included.

PARTICULARS ABOUT SELLER-FINANCED NOTES

The down payments typically range from 30 to 50 percent. The SBA and other conventional lenders will allow as low as 20 percent. The note carried by the seller is usually carried over three, five, or seven years. The interest rate is many times around 10 percent. The security is not typically the buyer's home or any real property they own. I hear attorneys tell clients to only accept real estate as collateral. I believe that those attorneys who say such things do not have much experience in selling a business. The market is for notes carried by sellers to be secured by all the business's securable assets. In addition, I do like to insist on a personal guarantee by the buyer. With a personal guarantee, you can file for a judgment against any asset the buyer may have. That means you could attach the car, house, cash, jewelry, or anything allowable under your state law. A second trust deed or second mortgage on a buyer's home or other property is not too exciting unless the buyer has a lot of equity; in other words, comfortably in excess of the note amount.

Remember, the holders of the first trust deed or the first mortgage get their money first if there is a foreclosure. You get what is left. In most cases, the holders of the first trust deed or first mortgage will come in and control the disposition of the property. They will hire the real estate sales company and have the most say in setting the listing price. They will have the majority of influence over the final price that is accepted. In many cases, the other lien-holders have nothing much to say about the proceedings. After commissions are paid and anything else, you get your share. Hopefully, the prices in the area were not declining and therefore eroding the equity and thus the amount you may receive. One way to avoid the bank or whomever is in the first position from getting in on the foreclosure is for the holder of the second trust deed or second mortgage to make the payments due to the bank or whomever, not missing any payments. If you are offered a third trust deed or third mortgage, forget it!

The most optimum situation is to sell the business at a fair price on terms that will not drown the business in too much debt. The buyer will then be able to repay you from the earnings of the business. As the buyer increases their equity and improves the business, he will not want to default on the payments unless he is in very serious trouble. If he is in trouble so serious—get in line.

TRANSITIONAL TRAINING FOR THE BUYER

Most sales of small businesses include some sort of agreement for the seller and/or the manager to provide transitional training/consulting to the buyer. It seems to be quite common for the seller to provide, free of charge, training for a period of 30 days. If your business is more technical or complex, you may be asked to stay longer, up to six months in some cases. If you are asked to stay any longer than four weeks, I would suggest getting paid for the time you spend there. For some businesses and buyers, two weeks of training is adequate. For those of you who are anxious to get away from the business and perhaps the buyer, you might consider starting the buyer's training during the last week or two before the sale is closed. Of course, I would not try this if the transaction's closing is in doubt.

ALLOCATION OF THE PURCHASE PRICE

If you are selling the assets of a corporation, a sole proprietorship, or partnership, you will be faced with what is called the *allocation of the purchase price*. Some people include a clause in the purchase agreement which specifies that an allocation of the purchase price will be agreed to before or as part of the closing. The allocation is the dividing of the entire price of the business, including inventory, accounts receivable, and the like into separate categories and allocating various values to those items.

The allocation has tax consequences and you may want to discuss the allocation with your CPA, tax attorney, or other financial advisor who understands the tax consequences. Each category can be expensed, depreciated, or amortized. The training/consulting can be expensed. Each asset category has its own time frame in which it can be depreciated or amortized. To create the allocation, you list the different asset categories and assign a value to each category. The values assigned to the different categories must then, when totaled, equal the entire purchase price. For example, the business is sold for $290,000, plus the inventory. The accounts receivable are not included in the sale. The liabilities will be paid off so the business transfers free and clear of all encumbrances and liens except the new loan carried by the seller.

An allocation may look like the following:

Lease	$ 15,000
Goodwill	$ 55,000
Inventory	*$ 70,000*
Franchise	$ 25,000
Training/consulting	$ 50,000
Leasehold improvements	$ 10,000
Covenant not to compete	$ 50,000
Furniture, fixtures, and equipment	$ 85,000
Total consideration	$360,000

On occasion, the seller and buyer can have a difference of opinion as to how the total price is to be allocated. In years past, the tax treatment for each side was opposite for many categories. Now the differences that created the opposite effects are negligible. There is a form in Chapter Five, Exhibit 5.4, that is made to be used for writing the allocation. Have all parties sign it, showing their agreement to the allocation.

Once you have achieved an agreement with the buyer, you should begin and complete the due diligence phase of the sale before opening escrow or paying an attorney to draw up any final papers. The next chapter will guide you the rest of the way through closing.

EXHIBIT 4.1 A BLANK BUSINESS PURCHASE AGREEMENT

Business Purchase Agreement

Received From, _____ herein called Buyer, the sum of $_____ (_____ Dollars) by Personal Check payable to _____, to be deposited in escrow or with closing agent after completion of due diligence, as a good-faith deposit on account of and to be applied toward the purchase price of $_____ (_____ Dollars) for the assets set forth herein and for the business situated in the City of _____, County of _____, State of _____, located at _____, known as _____ owned and operated by _____ hereinafter known as Seller, on the following terms and conditions precedent:

1. **CLOSING:** To be held on _____ 19___ or **sooner;** both parties shall deposit with _____, all funds and instruments necessary to complete the sale in accordance with the terms hereof including the balance of the purchase price for the benefit of the Seller, a valid bill of sale of said business, and property together with any lease or assignment thereof of the premises on which the business is located.
2. **CLOSING COSTS:** Any transfer tax—any tax other than Sales tax pursuant to paragraph 15 shall be paid by **Seller, if any.**
3. **COVENANT NOT TO COMPETE:** Seller, individually shall execute, prior to close of escrow, a covenant not to compete wherein Seller shall not operate, invest in, manage, be employed by, or consult for a business which competes with the business sold to the Buyer, within a distance of ___ miles of the business being sold herein, for a period of ___ months from close of escrow, so long as Buyer or his successor in interest are operating the business in said area. Seller recognizes that this agreement not to compete is a material inducement to the Buyer concerning the purchase of their business.
4. **CLOSING AGENT FEES or ESCROW and ASSOCIATED FEES:** Shall be paid by _____. (Typically Buyer 50% and Seller 50%.)
5. **INSPECTIONS:** Seller represents that he knows of no defects in the premises, in the equipment of the business which is being conveyed in connection with this agreement, or in any factors regarding the premises or business which would materially affect the decision of the Buyer to

Exhibit 4.1 Business Purchase Agreement

enter into this agreement. Furthermore, Seller represents that he knows of no defects in the premises or in matters regarding environmental issues or of anything pertaining to the business which would interfere with the lawful operation of the business by Buyer, and agrees that he will advise Buyer in writing of any defects which come to his attention prior to completion of the sale.

6. **LEASE ASSIGNMENT:** This sale is contingent on Buyer's approval of the existing lease, and assignee, assignor, and landlord's consent to the assignment of said lease. Seller shall provide Buyer with a copy of the lease and all modifications and amendments thereto within days of acceptance of offer.

7. **LEGAL NOTICES:** Seller shall obtain any approvals necessary and give any notices required by law or necessary to avoid liens on the property sold.

8. **LICENSES:** This sale is contingent on approval of transfer of any licenses by state or local agencies or on issuance of any new licenses required by Buyer. The Buyer thereof shall pay all costs.

9. **MAINTENANCE:** Until possession has changed, Seller agrees to continue to operate the business in the manner in which it is being operated at the date of the offer, and to maintain the goodwill of the business and all personal property in good working condition.

10. **NAME:** Title to be taken in the name of _____.

11. **PHYSICAL POSSESSION:** Physical possession shall be delivered to Buyer after ____ A.M./P.M. on the closing date, following the completion of a physical inventory of all merchandise held for resale.

12. **PRORATIONS:** Personal property tax, rents, franchise or other taxes, if any, equipment leases, premiums for insurance that is acceptable to Buyer, and other expenses of the property to be prorated as of the date of change of possession of the business. Security deposits or advanced rentals, if any, shall be credited to the Seller and charged to the Buyer of the business through escrow or closing agent.

13. **REVIEW of RECORDS:** Seller shall furnish or cause to be furnished to Buyer or Buyer's representatives all data for the past ____ years and other operational information concerning the business that may reasonably be requested by Buyer, within _____ days of acceptance. Buyer and Buyer's legal counsel, accountants, or other designated representatives shall be given access to Seller's original books, bank records, payroll records, employee records, and business tax returns for the

Exhibit 4.1 *(Continued)*

EXHIBIT 4.1 A BLANK BUSINESS PURCHASE AGREEMENT

past ____ years. Seller represents that the books and records are those maintained in the ordinary and normal course of business and used by Seller in the computation of federal and state income tax returns. If examination of the books and records of the business discloses conditions or information inconsistent with the representations made, Buyer may cancel this agreement. If not disapproved in writing by Buyer and delivered to Seller within ____ working days of receipt of books and records this condition shall be deemed waived.

14. **RISK of LOSS:** Any risk of loss to the property shall be borne by the Seller until title has been conveyed to the Buyer. If the leasehold property or any part of the business assets in which the business is situated is destroyed or materially damaged prior to the closing, then, on demand of Buyer any such deposit, down payment, or any other consideration paid by Buyer shall be returned to Buyer and this contract thereon shall terminate, unless Seller or lessor are willing and able to repair such damage.

15. **SALES and USE TAX:** Any sales tax due for the sale of the personal property shall be paid by Buyer through escrow or closing agent.

16. **TITLE to BUSINESS:** In the event Seller is unable to convey good title to said business and property, all rights and obligations hereunder may, at the election of the Buyer, terminate and end, and the deposit shall be returned to Buyer.

17. **FURTHER TERMS and CONDITIONS:**

_____
_____
_____
_____
_____

EXPIRATION: This offer shall expire unless a copy hereof with Seller's written acceptance is delivered to the buyer or his agent on or before _____ A.M./P.M., on _____, 19__

TIME: Time is of the essence of this agreement. The term "days" as used herein means calendar days unless otherwise specified.

DATED: _____   **TIME:** _____

Exhibit 4.1 (Continued)

_____   _____

Buyer   Buyer

ACCEPTANCE: The undersigned Seller agrees to sell the herein-described business for the price and on the terms and conditions herein specified. The undersigned seller hereby covenants that he is the owner of the above business and property and has the legal right to sell same.

DATED: _____ **TIME:** _____

_____   _____

Seller   Seller

Exhibit 4.1 *(Continued)*

EXHIBIT 4.2 COMPLETED BUSINESS PURCHASE AGREEMENT

Business Purchase Agreement

Received From, <u>Robert S. Lee</u> herein called Buyer, the sum of **$5,000.00** (Five Thousand Dollars) by Personal Check payable to **Mission Valley Escrow,** to be deposited in escrow after completion of due diligence, as a good faith deposit on account of and to be applied toward the Purchase Price of **$298,000.00** **(two hundred ninety-eight thousand dollars**) for the assets setforth herein and for the business situated in the City of <u>San Diego,</u> County of <u>San Diego,</u> State of <u>California,</u> located at <u>2145 Fur Street,</u> known as <u>Bob's Furniture Warehouse</u> owned and operated by <u>Philip Warner</u> hereinafter known as Seller, on the following terms and conditions precedent:

I. CLOSING: To be held on <u>August 1, 1996</u> or **sooner;** both parties shall deposit with Mission Valley Escrow, all funds and instruments necessary to complete the sale in accordance with the terms hereof including the balance of the purchase price for the benefit of the Seller, a valid bill of sale of said business, and property together with any lease or assignment thereof of the premises on which the business is located.

II. CLOSING COSTS: Any transfer tax—any tax other than Sales tax pursuant to paragraph 15 shall be paid **by Seller, if any.**

III. COVENANT NOT TO COMPETE: Seller, individually shall execute, prior to close of escrow, a covenant not to compete wherein Seller shall not operate, invest in, manage, be employed by, or consult for a business which competes with the business sold to the Buyer, within San Diego County, for a period of 60 months from close of escrow, so long as Buyer or his successor in interest are operating the business in said area. Seller recognizes that this agreement not to compete is a material inducement to the Buyer concerning the purchase of their business.

IV. CLOSING AGENT or ESCROW and ASSOCIATED FEES: Shall be paid by **Buyer 50% and Seller 50%.**

V. INSPECTIONS: Seller represents that he knows of no defects in the premises, in the equipment of the business which is being conveyed in connection with this agreement, or in any factors regarding the premises or business which would materially affect the decision of the Buyer to enter into this agreement, Furthermore, Seller represents that he knows of no defects in the premises or in matters regarding environmental issues or of anything pertaining to the business which would interfere with the lawful operation of the business by Buyer, and agrees that he will advise Buyer in writing of any defects which come to his attention prior to completion of the sale.

Exhibit 4.2 Example of a Completed Business Purchase Agreement

VI. LEASE ASSIGNMENT: This sale is contingent on Buyer's approval of the existing lease, and assignee, assignor, and landlords consent to the assignment of said lease. Seller shall provide Buyer with a copy of the lease and all modifications and amendments thereto within five days of acceptance of offer.

VII. LEGAL NOTICES: Seller shall obtain any approvals and give any notices required by law or necessary to avoid liens on the property sold.

VIII. LICENSES: The sale is contingent on approval of transfer of any licenses by state or local agencies or on issuance of any new licenses required by Buyer. The Buyer thereof shall pay all costs.

IX. MAINTENANCE: Until possession is delivered, Seller agrees to continue to operate the business in the same manner in which it is being operated at the date of the offer, and to maintain the goodwill of the business and all personal property in good working condition.

X. NAME: Title to be taken in the name of <u>Robert S. Lee</u> or a corporation to be named during escrow.

XI. PHYSICAL POSSESSION: Physical possession shall be delivered to Buyer after 6:00 P.M. on the day preceding the closing date and following the completion of a physical inventory of all merchandise held for resale.

XII. PRORATIONS: Personal property tax, rents, franchise or other taxes, if any, equipment leases, premiums on insurance acceptable to Buyer, and other expenses of the property to be prorated as of the date of change of possession of the business. Security deposits or advance rentals, if any, shall be credited to the Seller and charged to the Buyer of the business through escrow or closing agent.

XIII. REVIEW of RECORDS: Seller shall furnish or cause to be furnished to Buyer or Buyer's representatives all data for the past five years and other operational information concerning the business that may reasonably be requested by Buyer, within <u>five</u> days of acceptance. Buyer and Buyer's legal counsel, accountants, or other designated representatives shall be given access to Seller's original books, bank records, payroll records, employee records, and business tax returns for the past five (5) years. Seller represents that the books and records are those maintained in the ordinary and normal course of business and used by Seller in the computation of federal and state income tax returns. If examination of the books and records of the business discloses conditions or information inconsistent with the representations made in the business-marketing package, Buyer may cancel this agreement. If not disapproved in writing by Buyer and delivered to Seller within <u>five</u> working days of receipt of books and records this condition shall be deemed waived.

Exhibit 4.2 *(Continued)*

EXHIBIT 4.2 EXAMPLE OF A COMPLETED BUSINESS PURCHASE AGREEMENT

XIV. RISK of LOSS: Any risk of loss to the property shall be borne by the Seller until title has been conveyed to the Buyer. If the leasehold property or any part of the business assets in which the business is situated is destroyed or materially damaged prior to the closing, then, on demand of Buyer any such deposit, down payment, or any other consideration paid by Buyer shall be returned to Buyer and this contract thereon shall terminate, unless Seller or lessor are willing and able to repair such damage.

XV. SALES and USE TAX: Any sales tax due for the sale of the personal property shall be paid by Buyer through escrow or closing agent.

XVI. TITLE to BUSINESS: In the event Seller is unable to convey good title to said business and property, all rights and obligations hereunder may, at the election of the Buyer, terminate and end, and the deposit shall be returned to Buyer.

XVII. FURTHER TERMS and CONDITIONS:

1. The purchase price includes: Trade Name, all leasehold improvements, furniture, fixtures, and equipment, inventory, goodwill, lease, training/consulting, noncompete covenants, customer lists, telephone listing, and software.

2. The sales price does not include the accounts receivable and accounts payable.

3. This offer is contingent on Buyer obtaining financing through the SBA. Buyer's approval for said financing shall be obtained within 30 days of a complete purchase agreement being accepted between the parties. Seller shall provide to Lender all requested and necessary information within five calendar days of receipt of request for such information.

4. Provided that financing is not approved within the 30 days, Buyer offers the following substitutionary terms: the down payment shall be one hundred thousand dollars ($100,000.00); included therein is the five thousand ($5,000.00) dollar good-faith deposit. Buyer shall execute a note in favor of Seller for the balance of the purchase price which is approximately one hundred ninety-eight thousand dollars ($198,000.00). The note shall be fully amortized over 60 months with interest of 10 percent (10%) annually. Payments of $4,206.91 shall be made monthly on the 1st of each month beginning September 1st, 1996. The note shall bear no prepayment penalty. The interest shall begin to accrue at close of escrow with the first payment becoming due on the first of the month following close of escrow. The note shall be secured by a security agreement and UCC-1 financing statement covering all securable assets of the business. The note shall be personally guaranteed by Buyer.

5. Buyer shall submit to Seller within five working days of acceptance, a per-

Exhibit 4.2 *(Continued)*

sonal financial statement, credit report, and verification of funds. Seller's acceptance is contingent on Seller approving Buyer for the financing requested in the preceding paragraph # 5.

6. Inventory to be taken the evening before close of escrow between Buyer and Seller or by a mutually agreed on inventory company. The inventory used in the normal course of business shall be priced at cost. The inventory held for clients shall be priced at cost plus the value of the added labor and material. The inventory is approximately fifty-five thousand dollars ($55,000.00) but in no case shall the inventory exceed eighty-two thousand dollars ($82,000.00) or be less than fifty-five thousand dollars ($55,000.00). Both Buyer and Seller agree to submit to escrow a signed copy of both inventories. The amount of the note shall be adjusted according to the final amount of inventory.

7. Accounts Receivable shall be accounted for at the change of possession. The Buyer shall execute through escrow an interim note in favor of Seller for the accounts receivable and the amount of prorated work-in-process. The note shall be all due and payable within 60 days of close of escrow. The Buyer shall then receive the incoming accounts receivable and disperse the same to Seller as it is received. If the Buyer does not receive all of the monies due from the accounts receivable, then the responsibility to collect the delinquent accounts shall be the Seller's responsibility and the note shall be reduced by the amount of any uncollected monies.

8. All work-in-process remaining at change of possession shall be prorated for costs incurred up to the point of change of possession. When the monies due for the work-in-process have been received, Buyer shall then reimburse Seller for the amount that was prorated at change of possession less any deposits that were made on each job.

9. After due diligence is completed satisfactorily, escrow is opened, all required documents are signed, and buyer's down payment has been deposited into escrow, then buyer shall be allowed to begin the 30 day instruction/consulting period. Seller agrees to provide free of additional charge, said instruction/consulting in the familiarization of existing operating policies and procedures of the business operation during normal working hours, a minimum of 25 hours per week.

10. Seller agrees to not increase any employee hourly wage and/or salary from the date of this offer including during the escrow period and to inform the Buyer of any verbal or written promises to do so.

11. Workmans' Compensation claims, Unemployment Insurance claims, Vaca-

Exhibit 4.2 (Continued)

EXHIBIT 4.2 EXAMPLE OF A COMPLETED BUSINESS PURCHASE AGREEMENT

tion pay, pension funds, bonuses, or other fringe benefits accrued and/or due employees are to be paid by Seller, prior to change of possession.

12. Buyer is aware that there is an existing contract for yellow page advertising in the telephone book and hereby agrees to assume same outside of escrow.

13. Buyer shall either assume the existing insurance on the business or procure their own prior to close.

14. Notwithstanding anything contained herein to the contrary, any controversy or claim between the parties arising out of or relating to this contract, or the breach thereof, or any resulting transaction shall be settled by arbitration in accordance with the rules of the American Arbitration Association or in such form to which the parties may mutually agree, and not by court action except as provided by California law for judicial review of arbitration proceedings. Judgment on the award rendered by the Arbitrator(s) may be entered into any court having jurisdiction thereof. Reasonable attorney's fees and costs shall be awarded to the prevailing party (as determined in the arbitration).

15. The statements made and information given by Seller to Buyer concerning said business and on which Buyer has relied in agreeing to purchase said business are true and accurate and no material fact has been withheld from Buyer. Should Buyer discover during the due diligence, information that is construed by Buyer to be detrimental to the on-going successful operation of the business, then Buyer may cancel this agreement, receive a full refund of the deposit, and be relieved of all obligations herein.

16. The telephone number for the subject business will remain the same and Seller is instructed not to take or change the following number or additional lines (619) 453-2000, fax (619) 453-6666

17. Seller shall submit to Buyer a complete list of all furniture, fixtures, leasehold improvements and equipment included in this sale as represented in the offering, as Exhibit B, within seven (7) days of acceptance. The list is to be submitted to escrow and approved by both parties to this transaction prior to close. The Buyer shall have the right to a final inspection prior to close and any furniture, fixtures, and equipment found to be in need of repairs, or missing, shall be repaired or replaced at Seller's expense prior to close.

18. There are to be no contractual changes concerning the subject business during the process of sale period unless disclosed to Buyer and Buyer shall so agree to accept responsibility.

19. The Seller herein warrants that she has no knowledge of any developments or threatened developments of a nature that would materially be adverse to the subject business.

Exhibit 4.2 *(Continued)*

20. Seller warrants that the financial statements and other documentation provided to Buyer in relation to the business are substantially true and correct and are not materially misleading in any respect.

21. Seller shall individually indemnify, defend, and hold harmless Buyer against any and all claims, demands, losses, and reasonable attorney fees that Buyer shall incur or suffer which arise or result from, or relate to the conduct of the business, any breach or failure of Seller or its agents or employees during the period which seller operated the business being sold herein.

22. Seller warrant that the premises will meet all city, county, and state codes, standards, and regulations as exist at the time of close of escrow or change of possession which ever is sooner.

23. The close of escrow is contingent on the transfer of the business and all assets thereof to Buyer free and clear of any encumbrances or claims of third parties except as setforth herein.

24. Both Seller and Buyer shall agree on the allocation of purchase price based on generally accepted accounting and tax principles, prior to close and will submit the allocation in writing as Exhibit A of this contract prior to change of possession.

25. Buyer at change of possession shall receive from Seller all business records of any kind of character, including but not limited to: customer lists, personnel records, contracts, and financial records, on which the Buyer must rely for the continuing successful operation of the business. Seller agrees to not retain any copies or duplications of the customer lists except as needed for record retention per IRS regulations, specifically the accounts receivable reports.

26. Buyer acknowledges the existence of equipment leases that are to be assumed. They are as follows: ABDick 87 Folder, 9800 T-Head T-51, 9800 Crestline Dampener, 5390 Xerox Duplicator, and a 5334 Xerox Duplicator. A list of the leases with the balances due, payment amounts, and terms shall be approved by both parties in conjunction with the close of escrow.

EXPIRATION: This offer shall expire unless a copy hereof with Seller's written acceptance is delivered to Buyer or his agent on or before _____, 19____ at ____ A.M./P.M.

TIME: Time is of the essence of this agreement. The term "days" as used herein means calendar days unless otherwise specified.

ACKNOWLEDGMENTS: Buyer and Seller acknowledge receipt of a copy of pages 1 through 5

Exhibit 4.2 *(Continued)*

EXHIBIT 4.2 EXAMPLE OF A COMPLETED BUSINESS PURCHASE AGREEMENT

ACCEPTANCE: The undersigned Seller agrees to sell the herein-described business for the price and on the terms and conditions herein specified. The undersigned Seller hereby covenants that he is the owner of the above business and property and has the legal right to sell same.

DATE: _____   **TIME:** _____

_____   _____
Buyer   **Seller**

Exhibit 4.2 *(Continued)*

Counteroffer

This is a counteroffer to the Business Purchase Agreement, to purchase the business known as _____. Offered by _____ (referred to as Buyer) Dated, _____ Time _____ A.M./P.M. The following counteroffer is hereby submitted by _____ (referred to as Seller):

Seller accepts all of the terms and conditions of the above referenced Business Purchase Agreement, which remain in full force and effect, with the following changes or amendments: _____

_____

_____

_____

_____

_____

_____

_____

_____

_____

_____

RIGHT TO ACCEPT other offer: Seller reserves the right to continue to offer the subject business for sale and accept any other offer prior to Buyer's written acceptance of this counteroffer. Acceptance shall not be effective until personally received by _____.

EXPIRATION: This counteroffer shall expire and be deemed revoked unless a copy hereof with Buyer's written acceptance is delivered to Seller or his agent on or before _____, 19____ at _____ A.M./P.M.

Date: _____ **Time:** _____

_____   _____

Seller   Seller

Exhibit 4.3 Blank Counteroffer Form

EXHIBIT 4.3 A BLANK COUNTEROFFER FORM

Counteroffer

❏ The undersigned Buyer accepts the counteroffer as set out on page one of this two page counteroffer OR

❏ The undersigned Buyer accepts the above counteroffer with the following changes or amendments:

Unless the following changes or amendments are accepted and a copy duly accepted and signed by Seller is personally delivered to Buyer or his agent on or before _____, 19_____ at _____ A.M./P.M., it shall be deemed revoked and deposit shall be returned to Buyer. Receipt of a copy is acknowledged.

_____
_____
_____
_____
_____
_____
_____
_____
_____
_____
_____

Receipt of Acceptance is hereby acknowledged. Dated: _____ Time: _____

_____   _____

Buyer   Buyer

Receipt of signed copy on _____, 19_____ at _____ A.M./P.M. is acknowledged/accepted.

_____   _____

Seller   Seller

Exhibit 4.3 (Continued)

THE LEGAL VALIDITY OR ADEQUACY OF ANY PROVISION CON-
TAINED HEREIN IS NOT GUARANTEED OR IMPLIED. IF YOU
HAVE QUESTIONS ABOUT A PARTICULAR CLAUSE, YOU SHOULD
SEEK LEGAL ADVICE FROM AN ATTORNEY AND ANY TAX
ADVISE NEEDED FROM A COMPETENT PROFESSIONAL.

The following paragraphs include a variety of contingencies and conditions
that have been compiled over many years. A majority of contingencies and
conditions that are commonly used in the sale of small businesses are contained herein. In some of the paragraphs the word escrow, or escrow holder is
used. If you do not use an escrow holder (company) in your state, then replace
the word(s) with the appropriate noun, such as closing agent.

All you have to do is to choose the clause or clauses that you want to see in
the contract between you and the buyer and add them into a counteroffer you
make to the buyer, or when you have the final contract written. You can also
use any of the following clauses in an offer you may make for someone's business:

1. Except as specified herein, buyer assumes no liability or obligation of
   seller or of its business or properties of any kind of character.
2. Vacation pay, pension funds, or other fringe benefits accrued and/or due
   employees are to be handled outside of escrow by seller, prior to change
   of possession.
3. The statements made and information given by seller to buyer concerning said business and on which buyer has relied in agreeing to purchase
   said business are true and accurate and no material fact has been withheld from buyer.
4. The telephone number for the subject business will remain the same and
   seller is instructed not to take or change the following number or additional lines (____) _____-_____.
5. Buyer and seller recognize that the telephone bill for telephone number
   (____) _____-_____ and any additional lines are to be prorated outside
   of escrow. Buyer to retain the same phone number and will assume
   responsibility for the telephone. Seller agrees to reimburse buyer for his
   prorated share of the telephone bill.
6. Seller shall submit to buyer a complete list of all furniture, fixtures, and
   equipment included in this sale, within days of acceptance. The list is to
   be approved by both parties to this transaction prior to close. The buyer
   shall have the right to a final inspection prior to close and any furniture,

Exhibit 4.4 Purchase Agreement Conditions and Contingencies List

EXHIBIT 4.4 PURCHASE AGREEMENT CONDITIONS AND CONTINGENCIES LIST

fixtures, or equipment found in need of repair shall be repaired at seller's expense prior to close.

7. There are to be no contractual changes concerning the subject business during the escrow period unless disclosed to buyer and buyer shall so agree to accept responsibility.

8. Seller to assist buyer in the familiarization of the business operation during normal working hours for a period of *30* days, to begin no later than close of escrow.

9. Notwithstanding anything contained herein to the contrary, any controversy or claim between the parties arising out of or relating to this contract, or breach thereof, shall be settled by arbitration in accordance with the rules of the American Arbitration Association, and judgment on the award rendered by the arbitrator(s) may be entered in any court having jurisdiction thereof.

10. The seller herein warrants that he has no knowledge of any developments or threatened developments of a nature that would materially be adverse to the subject business.

11. Seller warrants that the financial statements and other documentation provided to buyer in relation to the business of the corporation, are substantially true and correct and are not materially misleading in any respect.

12. Seller agrees to not increase any employee wages or salaries during the time in which the business sale is taking place, and seller agrees to inform buyer of any verbal or written promises to do so.

13. Seller shall individually indemnify, defend, and hold harmless buyer against any and all claims, demands, losses, and reasonable attorney fees that buyer shall incur or suffer which arise or result from, or relate to the conduct of, the business or any breach or failure of seller or its agents or employees during the period which seller operated the business being sold herein.

14. Seller warrants that the premises will meet all city, county, and state codes, standards, and regulations as exist at the time of close of escrow or change of possession, whichever is sooner.

15. Both seller and buyer shall agree on the allocation of purchase price prior to close of escrow or consummation and will submit the allocation in writing to escrow prior to change of possession.

16. **DEFAULT:** Buyer recognizes that it would be difficult, if not impossible, to determine the exact amount of damages which would result if buyer

Exhibit 4.4 *(Continued)*

herein should fail to complete this purchase. Buyer acknowledges that by entering into an escrow and in order to complete this escrow the seller may be required to notify employees, creditors, suppliers, and similar parties; sellers goodwill may be affected; seller may have engaged accountants and attorneys; and seller will be required to publish notices and will be required to perform other acts which will prove detrimental to him and his business should this sale not be completed. Therefore, in the event buyer should fail to complete this sale for any reason whatsoever (other than the contingencies contained in the definitive agreement), buyer agrees to pay the sum of $ _____ to the seller as consideration for executing these documents. Both the seller and the buyer agree as of the date hereof the amounts provided herein are reasonable if buyer fails to complete the purchase.

Seller's initial _____ Buyer's initial _____

17. Seller recognizes that it would be difficult, if not impossible, to determine the exact amount of damages which would result if seller herein should fail to complete this sale. Seller acknowledges that by entering into an escrow and in order to complete this escrow the buyer has expended time and effort to analyze and understand this business; buyer may have forborne from the pursuit of other business acquisitions or gainful employment; buyer may have engaged accounts, consultants, or attorneys; and buyer will be required to perform other acts which will prove detrimental to him and his economic betterment should this sale not be completed. Therefore in the event seller should fail to complete this sale for any reason whatsoever (other than the contingencies contained in the definitive agreement), seller agrees to pay the sum of $ _____ to buyer as consideration for executing these documents. Seller and buyer agree as of the date hereof the amounts provided herein are reasonable if seller fails to complete this sale.

Seller's initial _____ Buyer's initial _____

18. The Board of Directors of seller shall have duly authorized and approved the execution and delivery of this agreement and all corporate action necessary or proper to effectuate the fulfillment of the obligations of seller to be performed herein on or prior to the closing date.

19. The consummation of the sale contemplated hereby shall be subject to the satisfactory completion of a due diligence review of the Corporation by Buyer. Promptly after the execution of this letter of intent and continuing until consummation of the sale contemplated hereby, the Seller will

Exhibit 4.4 *(Continued)*

EXHIBIT 4.4 PURCHASE AGREEMENT CONDITIONS AND CONTINGENCIES LIST

cause the Corporation (a) to provide Buyer and their representatives with access to the offices and facilities of the Corporation together with such records as are reasonably requested by Buyer for the purpose of reviewing the business and operations of the Corporation, (b) to provide Buyer and their representatives with information reasonably requested by them concerning the facilities, assets, records, financial condition, legal compliance, if any, and (c) to otherwise cooperate with and assist Buyer and their representatives in connection with their review thereof.

20. Without express written consent of all parties hereto, each of the parties hereto agrees to maintain in confidence and not disclose to any person the existence of this letter, the terms of the proposed sale, or the information delivered in connection with the proposed due diligence investigation, other than disclosures required to obtain the approvals for the sale contemplated hereby, disclosures to those professionals and advisors who have a need to know, or any other disclosure required by applicable law.

21. Promptly after the date of Seller's acceptance of this letter of intent, Buyer and Seller shall have a definitive Agreement of Sale drawn up. The definitive Agreement of Sale shall contain covenants, conditions, and indemnities of the Seller which are customary to sales of the type described herein including, but not limited to, representations as to the accuracy and completeness of the financial statements of the Corporation, disclosure of all contracts, commitments, and liabilities, direct or contingent, the compliance by the Corporation with applicable provisions of law and regulation, including, without limitation, provisions of environmental law and regulation, and similar provisions. The agreement of sale shall also contain representations and warranties of the buyer which are customary to sales of this type described herein including, but not limited to, representations as to the due organization and proper capitalization of Buyer, and the compliance by Buyer with applicable provisions of law and regulation.

22. The corporation will not (1) amend its articles of incorporation or bylaws (except to remove the name _____); (2) issue any shares of its capital stock; or (3) issue or create any warrants, obligations, subscriptions, options, convertible securities, or other commitments under which any additional shares of its capital stock of any class might be directly or indirectly authorized, issued, or transferred from treasury. Unless specifically set forth herein, the Corporation will not do, or agree to do, any of the following acts: (1) make any changes in compensation payable to any

Exhibit 4.4 (*Continued*)

277

officer, employee, sales agent, or representative; (2) make any changes in benefits payable to any officer, employee, sales agent, or representative under any bonus or pension plan or other contract or commitment; or (3) modify any collective bargaining agreement to which either of them is a party or by which either may be bound.

23. Without Buyer's consent, the Corporation will not agree to enter into any contract, commitment, or transaction except in the usual and ordinary course of its business.

24. The Corporation shall not declare, set aside, or pay any dividend or make any distribution in respect of its capital stock; or directly or indirectly purchase, redeem, or otherwise acquire any shares of its capital stock.

25. The Corporation shall not modify, amend, cancel, or terminate any of its existing contracts or agreements, or agree to do any of those acts.

26. Seller shall comply with the provision of Division 6 of the Uniform Commercial Code and shall publish and record such notices as required under the code. (See Chapter Five for an explanation of the "Bulk Sales Law.")

27. Seller herein grants buyer the right, at buyer's expense, to select and hire a licensed contractor(s) or other qualified professional(s) to inspect and investigate, including but not limited to, the subject business's furniture, fixtures, equipment, machinery, and premises (business assets and property). Buyer shall keep the subject business free and clear of any and all liens, indemnify and hold seller harmless from all liability, claims, damages, or costs, and repair all damages to the business and its assets and/or property arising from the inspection. All claimed defects concerning the condition of the business assets and/or property that adversely affect the continued use of the business's assets and/or property for the purpose for which it is presently being used shall be in writing, supported by written reports, if any and delivered to seller within _____ calendar days after seller's acceptance of the offer. Buyer shall furnish seller with copies at no cost, of all reports concerning the business assets and/or property obtained by Buyer. When such reports disclose conditions or information unsatisfactory to buyer, which seller is unwilling to correct, buyer may cancel this agreement. Seller agrees to make the premises available for all inspections. Buyer's failure to notify Seller of unsatisfactory conditions of the business assets and/or property shall conclusively be considered approval and acceptance of the condition.

28. Seller agrees that on or before close of escrow all liabilities and long-term debts owed by the company shall have been paid in full by the seller.

Exhibit 4.4 *(Continued)*

EXHIBIT 4.4 PURCHASE AGREEMENT CONDITIONS AND CONTINGENCIES LIST

29. Buyer is aware that there is an existing contract for yellow page advertising in the telephone book and hereby agrees to assume same.
30. Buyer at change of possession shall receive from seller all business records of any kind or character, including but not limited to, customer lists, personnel records, contracts, and financial records, on which the buyer must rely for the continuing successful operation of the business.
31. Buyer will either assume the existing insurance on the business or procure their own prior to consummation of the sale and seller shall provide buyer with a copy(s) of the policy of insurance.
32. Seller shall have all equipment in good working condition prior to the closing.
33. As this is a "service-type business" there should be no sales tax due on this transaction; unless State Board of Equalization should determine that some of the subject fixtures and equipment are taxable, in which event buyer shall pay _____% of the taxable fixtures and equipment so determined. Seller warrants to buyer that this is not, nor will be, one in a series of three (3) within a one (1) year period; thus making this sale and others taxable.
34. The seller herein guarantees to have all equipment in good working condition at the time buyer takes possession of the business and to warrant the equipment good working condition for *30* days from close of escrow. Unless Seller is notified in writing within *30* days after the date possession changed, it shall be accepted as final that all equipment is in good working condition. Should any repair work be necessary during the warranty period, Seller agrees to pay the cost of repairs or replacement.
35. Buyer shall submit to Seller within five working days of acceptance, a personal financial statement, credit report, and verification of funds. Seller's acceptance of Buyer's offer is contingent on Seller approving Buyer for the financing requested in the preceding paragraph #_____.
36. Workmans' Compensation claims, Unemployment Insurance claims, Vacation pay, pension funds, bonuses, or other fringe benefits accrued and/or due employees for the time Seller operated the subject business are to be paid by Seller by the closing.
37. $_____ to be in the form of a promissory note executed by buyer in favor of the seller, payable in monthly installments of $_____, or more, including interest at the rate of ____% per annum. Interest to commence from the date of buyer's possession of the subject business with the first payment of principal and interest becoming due one month from

Exhibit 4.4 (*Continued*)

such date of possession and continuing thus until _____. Escrow holder is instructed to inset dates in the note at the close of escrow. *This note is to be secured by a Security Agreement and UCC-I financing statement covering fixtures, equipment, and all securable business assets, including, but not limited to, those items listed on an exhibit to be attached to the Security Agreement and UCC-1 financing statement with the office of the Secretary of State, Sacramento (or other state capital), (state), at the close of escrow or within ten (10) days of buyer's possession, whichever date occurs first. (Please note: If selling/buying a business outside of California, the italicized portion of this paragraph should be modified according to that state.)*

38. $_____ being the approximate unpaid balance of an encumbrance of record in favor of _____, payable in monthly installments of $_____, including interest at the rate of __% per annum. Buyer herein to assume liability for and pay said encumbrance in accordance with the terms and conditions contained therein, and escrow holder is instructed to obtain a Beneficiary Statement from the lender to verify the exact unpaid balance and terms thereof. In the event the actual unpaid balance is more or less than $_____, the _____ to be adjusted accordingly.

39. The allocation of the consideration is as follows: fixtures and equipment $_____; goodwill $_____; convenant not to compete $_____; lease $_____; leasehold improvement $_____; license $_____; total $_____; inventory of stock (approximate) $_____.

40. The buyer has read and approved the lease. The seller agrees to personally effect the transfer of the lease to buyer and to deliver the lease and assignment into escrow. Seller agrees to cooperate with buyer in obtaining landlord's consent thereto. This escrow is contingent on the escrow holder's receipt of the landlord's written consent to the assignment of the lease and deposit into escrow of this written consent and assignment by the landlord shall constitute satisfaction of this contingency.

41. Buyer is aware that there is no lease and has made satisfactory rental arrangements outside of escrow.

42. Buyer acknowledges having negotiated with lessor the terms of a lease, which are satisfactory to both parties. This lease is to be executed by the parties prior to the date of possession with a copy of same delivered to respective parties and buyer shall pay the landlord direct for the rent deposits and other payments as called for thereunder.

Exhibit 4.4 *(Continued)*

EXHIBIT 4.4 PURCHASE AGREEMENT CONDITIONS AND CONTINGENCIES LIST

43. It is understood that the seller is also the real estate owner of the property on which the subject business is located. Buyer and seller acknowledge having negotiated the terms of a new lease which are satisfactory to both parties. This new lease is to be executed by the parties prior to the date of possession with a copy of same delivered to escrow holder. Buyer shall pay seller direct for the rent deposits and other payments as called for thereunder, all outside of escrow with which escrow holder and/or broker is to be in no way concerned or liable.

44. The buyer acknowledges that the business is being sold without his examination of books and records and buyer is not relying on any representations relevant thereto. Buyer's purchase is based solely on buyer's contemplation of future earnings and this business is being sold without records of income and expenses of prior operations.
    (   ) Buyer's initial

45. The buyer herein acknowledges that he has examined all relevant business records including records of income and expenses and hereby approves the same, and seller certifies that these records are correct.

46. The buyer is purchasing furniture, fixtures, and equipment in "as is" condition and acknowledges there is no warranty made by the seller as to operation or other condition related thereto.
    (   ) Buyer's initial

47. The seller herein guarantees to all equipment in working condition at the time of buyer's possession. Unless seller is notified in writing with a copy to escrow holder 48 hours after possession, it shall be accepted as final that all equipment is in good working condition.

48. Buyer and seller have approved the itemized inventory of all fixtures and equipment being conveyed herein. A list of same approved in writing by both parties is attached to the Bill of Sale.

49. The seller warrants and the buyer acknowledges that the books of accounts of the corporation are a true representation of the financial condition of the corporation. The buyer further acknowledges that he has made his own independent investigation of the business and understands that on the transfer of corporate assets for the consideration and terms stated herein he is accepting the assets of the corporation.

50. Seller warrants that the premises will meet all city, county, and state codes, standards, and regulation as exist at the time of buyer's possession.

51. Inventory of stock to be taken on _____, between buyer and seller or by a mutually agreed on inventory company. Inventory of stock

Exhibit 4.4 (Continued)

to be priced at _____. In the event the value of inventory is more or less than $_____, escrow holder is authorized to adjust the note to seller accordingly.

52. All inventories comprised of finished goods or lay-away are to be included in the inventory at no cost to buyer.

53. The inventory of merchandise used for resale and supplies that are consumed in the normal course of operation of the business shall be included.

54. All the silverware, kitchen utensils, dishes, glassware, and linens are fixtures and equipment.

55. All opened bottles, containers, and perishables do not have to be accepted as inventory at the option of the buyer. If not accepted by the buyer, seller may remove them from the premises.

56. All used parts are to be included in the inventory at no cost to buyer.

57. All inventory out on loan or on rental with a deposit thereon, is to be included in the inventory.

58. All the inventory is to be acceptable to buyer at current wholesale prices.

59. All inventory comprised of work-in-progress is to be included in the inventory at no cost to buyer.

60. Inventory of stock to be taken on _____ between buyer and seller, or by a mutually agreed on inventory company. Inventory of stock to be priced at _____. In the event that the inventory of stock is more or less than $_____, the buyer's cash is to be adjusted through escrow accordingly.

61. Inventory to be taken on _____ between buyer and seller or a mutually agreed on inventory company. Stock to be priced at _____. Seller guarantees to deliver to buyer an inventory valued at least $_____, or agrees to adjust cash in escrow back to buyer accordingly and buyer and seller agree to submit a statement to that effect to escrow.

62. Cash for the estimated closing costs is to be deposited into escrow before the date of possession. In the event the date of possession is such that there is insufficient time for verification of items being adjusted hereunder, escrow holder is to estimate such adjustable items on the basis of information submitted by Seller at the opening of escrow.

63. Cash for closing costs shall be deposited in escrow on demand on date amount is known.

64. Cash for closing costs shall be deposited in escrow before the date of possession.

Exhibit 4.4 *(Continued)*

EXHIBIT 4.4 PURCHASE AGREEMENT CONDITIONS AND CONTINGENCIES LIST

65. If an outside inventory service is used, cost of the service will be paid one-half by seller and one-half by buyer.

66. Buyer does acknowledge that he has made his own independent investigation of the business and that he has satisfied himself that he can properly conduct the same; and that the buyer is purchasing subject business in contemplation of future profits only and seller has not made any representation to buyer concerning the future profits of this business. (   ) Buyer's initial

67. Seller agrees that his representative will instruct buyer, free of additional charge, in the operation of the business for a period of _____ days commencing _____.

68. Possession to be given on _____ if all funds are on deposit.

69. Possession is to be given on _____, if all funds required are on deposit and the lease assignment executed by the landlord has been received or a waiver signed by buyer. Seller agrees to be personally and financially responsible for any indebtedness prior to date of possession.

70. It is mutually understood and agreed between buyer and seller herein, that on their own initiative and suggestion, the seller will grant possession of the subject business to the buyer prior to the _____ becoming effective, providing all funds required are on deposit. The buyer herein agrees to be personally and financially responsible for any fines and/or indebtedness incurred by him while operating the business during the interim period pending all final approvals and the seller shall be relieved of any liability after such date of possession.

71. Stock to be maintained at the normal level during the escrow period.

72. Seller agrees to keep the business in operation during regular business hours until buyer takes possession.

73. Seller, individually, shall indemnify, defend, and hold buyer harmless against any and all claims, demands, losses, and reasonable attorney's fees that buyer shall incur or suffer, which arise as a result from, or related to, any breach or failure of seller or its agents or employees during the period seller operated the business being sold herein.

74. Seller warrants that there are no known or alleged accusations, citations, or violations pending against the subject ABC license and that he has the right to convey the same.

75. In the event this escrow is contingent on the transfer or acquisition of any license, permit, interim appointment, bond, or any document requir-

Exhibit 4.4 (Continued)

ing the approval of a third party, buyer and seller agree that all necessary steps to expedite such transfers or acquisition of such document will be taken in good faith by _____.

76. This escrow is contingent on the buyer obtaining a state license to operate the subject business. Buyer recognizes that it would be difficult, if not impossible, to determine the exact amount of damages which would result if buyer herein should intercede though his own efforts to cancel the application for said license, or if license is denied for any reason because of the acts of buyer; therefore, in such event or events, buyer agrees that the amount of $_____, deposited herein shall be paid to the seller as a consideration for executing these documents. Buyer and seller agree that as of the date hereof the amounts called for herein are reasonable.
     (   ) Seller's initial (   ) Buyer's initial

77. This sale is not contingent on buyer obtaining a state license (or _____), however, buyer is aware that he must obtain said license (or _____) in order to operate said business.

78. Buyer and seller will file with the State of _____, in good faith, all necessary documents required for the transfer of the following State Licenses on or before _____, 19____.

79. Seller guarantees there is no contract existing on games, neon signs, jukebox, cigarette machines, or similar agreements binding the business in a continuous manner.

80. Seller herein guarantees that there are no rental contracts, lease, or other agreements of any kind existing on any of the fixtures and equipment being conveyed to buyer (except as set forth herein).

81. Seller herein guarantees there no contracts existing for yellow page advertising or promotional contracts or agreements, coupon offers, or similar agreements binding the business in a continuous manner.

82. Buyer acknowledges the existence of a contract on games and/or jukebox and agrees to assume same outside of escrow.

83. Buyer is aware there is an existing contract for yellow page advertising in the telephone book and hereby agrees to assume same outside of escrow.

84. Seller guarantees there are no warranties or guarantees existing on any products sold or services rendered.

85. Seller has revealed there are warranties and guarantees existing on products sold or services and will honor them as follows.

86. Buyer acknowledges the existence of a contract on _____ with _____ and hereby accepts the terms and conditions of said contract and agrees to assume same outside of escrow.

Exhibit 4.4 *(Continued)*

EXHIBIT 4.4 PURCHASE AGREEMENT CONDITIONS AND CONTINGENCIES LIST

87. Buyer recognizes that it would difficult, if not impossible, to determine the exact amount of damages which would result if buyer herein should fail to complete this escrow. Buyer acknowledges that by entering into this escrow and in order to complete this escrow the seller may be required to notify employees, creditors, suppliers, and similar parties; seller's goodwill may be affected; seller may have engaged accountants and attorneys; and seller will be required to publish certain notices and will be required to perform other acts which will prove detrimental to him and his business should the escrow not be completed. Therefore, in the event buyer should fail to complete this escrow for any reason whatsoever (other than any contingencies set forth herein), buyer agrees to pay the sum of $_____ to seller as consideration for executing these documents plus escrow cancellation fees and expenses. Buyer and seller agree that as of the date hereof the amounts called for herein are reasonable if buyer fails to complete this escrow.

   (   ) Seller's initials (   ) Buyer's initial

88. Seller recognizes that it would be difficult, if not impossible, to determine the exact amount of damages that would result if seller herein should fail to complete this escrow. Seller acknowledges that by entering into this escrow and in order to complete this escrow the buyer has expended time and effort to analyze and understand this business; buyer may have forborne from the pursuit of other business acquisitions or gainful employment; buyer may have engaged accountants and attorneys; and buyer will be required to perform other acts which will prove detrimental to him and his economic betterment should this escrow not be completed. Therefore, in the event seller should fail to complete this escrow for any reason whatsoever (other than any contingencies set forth herein), seller agrees to pay the sum of $_____ to buyer as consideration for executing these documents. Seller agrees to pay escrow cancellation fees and costs. Seller and buyer agree that as of the date hereof the amounts called for herein are reasonable if seller fails to complete this escrow.

   (   ) Seller's initials (   ) Buyer's initials

89. The buyer and seller herein recognize that it would be difficult, if not impossible, to determine the exact amount of damages which would result if buyer herein should fail to complete this escrow. Therefore, in the event buyer should fail to complete this escrow for any reason whatsoever (other than any contingencies set forth herein), buyer agrees to pay the sum of $_____ to seller as consideration for executing these documents plus escrow cancellation fees and costs. The seller

Exhibit 4.4 (Continued)

agrees that should seller fail to complete this escrow for any reason what-soever (other than any contingencies set forth herein) seller shall be responsible for buyer deposits and pay to buyer the sum of $_____ plus escrow cancellation fees and costs. The parties herein agree that as of the date hereof the amounts called for herein are reasonable if either party should fail to complete the escrow.

(   ) Seller's initial (   ) Buyer's initial

90. Except as otherwise specified herein, Buyer will not, without the written consent and permission of Secured Party, sell, contract to sell, lease, or encumber the collateral until the indebtedness to Secured Party has been completely discharged.

91. If for any reason the buyer is not approved by the beneficiary of the encumbrance of record, seller agrees to remain responsible for said encumbrance as Guarantor for the buyer.

92. The transfer of vacation pay, pension funds, or any other fringe benefits accrued as of the date of possession are to be handled and arranged between buyer and seller prior to the closing.

93. The undersigned debtor/seller, as consideration, hereby assigns to buyer herein all right, title, and interest as debtor in that certain security agree-ment dated _____ in which (prior seller or other secured third party) is the secured party and the undersigned is the debtor covering that cer-tain personal property situated in the County of _____, State of _____, on the premises known as _____ located at _____.

94. The undersigned buyer, in consideration of the foregoing assignment, hereby promises and agrees to assume all obligations of said agreement and note and agrees to keep and perform all of the terms, covenants, and provisions of said agreement and note and further agrees that he is obli-gated to the secured party therein by reason of said assignment to the same extent as of he was the original debtor named in said agreement and note. (Prior seller or other secured third party), secured party named in the foregoing mentioned agreement and note, does hereby consent to the assignment thereof with the understanding that all the terms, condi-tions, provisions, and convenants of said agreement and note shall remain and continue in full force and effect.

95. The purchase of the business does not include accounts receivable.

96. The accounts receivable of the business herein are included for the con-sideration of $_____. Seller agrees to furnish up-to-date accounting

Exhibit 4.4 *(Continued)*

EXHIBIT 4.4 PURCHASE AGREEMENT CONDITIONS AND CONTINGENCIES LIST

of all accounts receivable on the date of possession and deposit same into escrow. Buyer reserves the right to audit the accounts and verify the existence thereof, unless escrow holder is notified in writing by _____, it shall be deemed by escrow holder and seller that the buyer herein has approved the accounts receivable in their entirety.

97. Seller shall, in instructions mutually agreeable to buyer and independent hereof, authorize collection of accounts receivable owing at close of escrow on seller's behalf.

98. In consideration for the purchase of the business, the seller grants to buyer the right of first refusal of the sale of the real property to be leased to the buyer in connection with the purchase of the business. This right of first refusal is to be effective for the duration of: (a) the present lease period, or (b) the present lease period and subsequent renewal periods. In the event the seller receives a bonafied offer to purchase, seller will give the buyer herein fifteen (15) days to match the offer to purchase held by the seller and purchase the real property pursuant to the terms and conditions of said offer to purchase.

99. Inasmuch as the parties hereto have determined the business is a "service" type business, the parties have determined no sales tax is due the State Board of Equalization. In the event the State Board of Equalization determines some of the fixtures and equipment taxable, buyer shall pay __% sales tax based on the determined value of such fixtures and equipment.

100. The parties herein acknowledge and understand that the personal property tax bill will be required to be paid to the tax collector's office prior to closing. On receipt of such tax bill, seller shall immediately pay same and submit the tax bill showing receipt of such payment into escrow. On delivery of said paid bill, escrow holder shall charge buyer for said amount and credit seller through escrow. In the event seller has not received the tax bill by the close of escrow, seller shall immediately, on receipt of same, deliver the bill to buyer for buyer's payment outside of escrow. In such event, escrow holder shall not be concerned, responsible nor liable in any manner whatsoever regarding the personal property tax bill.

101. The Escrow holder is directed to order and obtain from the Secretary of State, or at such office and in such state(s) as may be applicable, a certificate that said corporation is "in good standing" as defined in the State of California (*state in which sale is occurring*) and may fully exercise all rights of a corporation pursuant to this transaction. In the event such cer-

Exhibit 4.4 *(Continued)*

tificate is not forthcoming the escrow holder shall immediately notify the party responsible for having such certification of the cause for the failure to obtain certification and that party shall forthwith cure any such cause or causes.

102. The seller warrants and buyer acknowledges the books of accounts of the corporation are a true representation of the financial condition of the corporation. The buyer further acknowledges he has made his own independent investigation of the business and understands, on the transfer of corporation securities for the consideration and terms stated herein, he is accepting the assets and the liabilities of said corporation. The buyer agrees to hold harmless the escrow holder for any conditions not specifically stated herein.

103. The seller and buyer acknowledge they have the responsibility of personally obtaining clearance from the Department of Corporations of the State of California (*state in which sale is occurring*) for any and all rulings effecting the transfer of the corporate securities of the corporation named herein.

104. Seller and _____, individually, shall indemnify, defend, and hold buyer harmless against any and all claims, demands, losses, and reasonable attorney's fees the buyer may occur or suffer which arise as a result from, or related to, any breach or failure of seller, his agents, or employees, during the period seller operated the business sold herein.

105. The undersigned seller agrees not to compete as an owner, investor, or employee in the same or a similar business within a ____ mile radius of the subject business for a period of _____ years from the date of possession of the undersigned buyer, with the exception of the following location _____. Seller recognizes that this agreement not to compete is a material inducement to buyer concerning the purchase of this business.

106. The undersigned seller agrees not to compete as an owner, investor, or employee in the same or a similar business within a _____ mile radius of the subject business for a period of _____ years from the date of possession of the undersigned buyer. Seller recognizes that this agreement not to compete is a material inducement to buyer concerning the purchase of this business.

107. Seller agrees to execute a noncompete agreement for _____ miles and _____ years to be evidenced by a separate agreement to be deposited in escrow prior to close of escrow. Execution of this agreement

Exhibit 4.4 (*Continued*)

EXHIBIT 4.4 PURCHASE AGREEMENT CONDITIONS AND CONTINGENCIES LIST

by buyer and seller shall constitute their approval of the terms and conditions of the agreement.

108. As a material inducement for this transaction, the seller agrees to refrain from carrying on, engaging in, advising, investing, or otherwise being connected with a similar business as is being sold hereunder within a radius of _____ miles from said business for a period of _____ years from the date of possession by buyer hereunder. For the purpose of this paragraph, business shall be deemed carried on by seller himself as owner, employee, manager, investor, consultant, or in any other capacity, or by a partnership of which he is a general or limited partner or a corporation or association of which he is a shareholder or member, and agrees to execute a separate agreement to this effect. In the event seller should carry on or engage in the operation of a business as contemplated herein, within the time and distance contemplated, seller shall pay to buyer and/or assigns one hundred dollars ($100.00) for each day such activity occurs. Seller recognizes that this agreement not to compete is a material inducement to buyer concerning the purchase of this business and buyer and seller have agreed that as of the date hereof the amounts called for herein are reasonable.

109. The undersigned seller agrees not to compete as an owner, investor, or employee in the same or a similar business within a _____ mile radius from the business for a period of _____ years from the date of possession of the undersigned buyer. In the event seller should engage in the operation of a similar business within the time and distance designated, seller will pay to buyer and/or assigns the sum of _____ dollars ($_____) for each day such activity occurs. The buyer and seller agree that it would be difficult, if not impossible, to ascertain the amount of damages which would result if this agreement were violated; however, each agrees that it would be reasonable for seller to pay the buyer and/or assigns the sum of $_____, as liquidated damages in the event of violation of this convenant not to compete. Seller recognizes that this agreement not to compete is a material inducement to buyer concerning the purchase of this business and buyer and seller have agreed that as of the date hereof the amount called for herein is reasonable in the event of violation of this agreement.

110. The undersigned seller agrees not to compete as an owner, investor, or employee in the same or a similar business within a _____ mile radius from the business for a period of _____ years from the

Exhibit 4.4 (Continued)

date of possession of the undersigned buyer, excepting at_____.
In the event seller should engage in the operation of a similar business
within the time and distance designated, seller will pay to buyer and/or
assigns the sum of _____ dollars ($_____) for each day such
activity occurs. The buyer and seller agree that it would be difficult, if not
impossible, to ascertain the amount of damages which would result if this
agreement were violated; however, each agrees that it would be reasonable for seller to pay the buyer and/or assigns the sum of $_____,
as liquidated damages in the event of violation of this convenant not to
compete. Seller recognizes that this agreement not to compete is a material inducement to buyer concerning the purchase of this business and
buyer and seller have agreed that as of the date hereof the amount called
for herein is reasonable in the event of violation of this agreement.

111. The seller agrees that neither it nor any officer or shareholder shall
compete directly or indirectly, in the same or similar business within
_____ mile radius of the business sold for a period of
_____ years from the close of escrow. Parties recognize that it
would be difficult, if not impossible, to determine the exact amount of
damages which would result if seller breaches this convenant not to compete; and therefore agrees to pay the buyer the sum of $_____
as liquidated damages in the event of this violation of this convenant not
to compete. The seller recognizes that is agreement not to compete is a
material inducement to buyer concerning the purchase of this business.
Buyer and seller agree that as of the date hereof the amounts called for
herein are reasonable in the event of violation of this agreement.

THE LEGAL VALIDITY OR ADEQUACY OF ANY PROVISION CON-
TAINED HEREIN IS NOT GUARANTEED OR IMPLIED. IF YOU
HAVE QUESTIONS ABOUT A PARTICULAR CLAUSE, YOU SHOULD
SEEK LEGAL ADVICE FROM AN ATTORNEY AND ANY TAX
ADVICE NEEDED FROM A COMPETENT PROFESSIONAL.

Exhibit 4.4 *(Continued)*

5

DUE DILIGENCE, ESCROW, AND CLOSING THE SALE

DUE DILIGENCE: WHAT YOU NEED TO DO

This is the final segment of the journey to successfully selling your business. This phase begins with the first task after achieving an agreement with the buyer. Some people refer to this next task as "checking the books" or performing due diligence. Due diligence is the process of investigating the business and the claims that have been made about it. More transactions never close because of a failed due diligence than any other factor. Why? Because the business's records and operations were misrepresented to the buyer.

From the time the negotiations are completed and the agreement has been signed, both you and the buyers should begin to act as though you were are on the same team. The promotion of this attitude is important. During the negotiations you were adversaries, now you have a common goal, and that is to get the transaction closed. Supposedly, they want to own the business and you want them to own the business. Sometimes the negotiations are brutal and we develop attitudes of animosity toward the buyer, now is the time to put all that aside and do your best to cooperate the rest of the way.

The seller's due diligence is usually easier than the buyer's; the buyer in almost every sale has more to investigate. What you should be concerned about is the buyer's ability to qualify for the financing; bank, Small Business Administration (SBA), or seller's note. If you have not received and reviewed the buyer's personal financial statements yet, ask for them now. You can use the form provided in Exhibit 3.10. You should also have the buyer provide a current credit report. If you would prefer to have someone on your side request the credit report, you will need the buyer's authorization. There is such an authorization form provided in Exhibit 3.11 at the end of Chapter Three.

CHECK THE BUYER'S PERSONAL FINANCIAL STATEMENT

When you receive the buyer's personal financial statement, be sure that the buyer has signed the statement. Look the statement over carefully to see the various assets and liabilities. Look at the types of cars listed, the make, model, and year: see if the value stated for the items seems correct. The cars listed are not usually very significant to the overall net worth, but the stated value can give you an indication of how truthful the buyer has been on the statement.

Look carefully at all the real estate listed on the form. Call a real estate broker or sales agent you know or one that works your neighborhood. Ask them to provide you with a Competitive Market Analysis (CMA) for the neighborhood where the buyer lives. You can also ask them if they know a title representative. If so, ask the real estate broker to ask the title representative for a property profile on the buyer's property address. Do this for all property listed on the buyer's personal financial statement. Tell the real estate broker the actual address you are looking up. Tell them how many bedrooms, bathrooms, square footage, pool, and so on, the house has (ask the buyer if you do not know). They can get the Competitive Market Analysis from the local real estate multiple-listing computer. The CMA will show what the houses in the neighborhood are on the market for, and what the recent sales of homes similar to your buyer's actually sold for. Compare the results of your research to what the buyer stated his house is worth. If the title representative was able to get a property profile, compare the information to what else you have learned about the buyer's property. Be sure to check whose name the title is in. If the name is unfamiliar to you, ask the buyer why. I had an experience where a buyer's home was in his brother's name. The buyer had bad credit. I then insisted that the brother also guarantee the note the seller was going to carry-back. The brothers shortly thereafter quit-claimed or deeded the property to another family member. I caught the change and we put that person on the note, too.

The buyers' cash in their bank accounts, and so on, which they show on the personal financial statement, should be more than is needed for the down payment on your business. Be sure the money is either in cash or is able to be liquidated on request. If not, you should ask the buyer to explain where the funds are coming from. You can also call the buyer's bank and check to see if you could cash a check for an amount that would demonstrate to you that they indeed have the balance in the account they said on the personal financial statement. This would be the same as merchant check verification. You can get the account number from the check they gave you as a good-faith deposit or from the personal financial statement, if they included it on there.

By checking the few items as mentioned, you should be able to get a feel for the validity of the buyer's financial statement. If all is good, no problem. If the statement is full of values inconsistent with the facts as researched, you must get satisfactory answers or go no further with the sale.

CONFIRM WHAT YOU ARE TOLD

Sometimes the buyers say they own other businesses. You may want to see recent tax returns for their businesses. This would help you to be sure that the income from the other businesses would aid the financial qualification of the buyer. Perhaps they could give you a lien on those businesses as well as on your own. If you are in a situation where you need and receive tax returns, ask the buyer to fill out and sign an Internal Revenue Service (IRS) form 4506. This is a request to the IRS to send out a copy of the tax return filed by the taxpayer (the buyer). If the buyer fills out the form and signs it, you can be fairly sure that they filed a duplicate of what they provided you. Check it out, though.

I once ran into a buyer who had three businesses and was trying to buy my client's business. The buyer gave us three tax returns signed by him and his CPA. I asked him to fill out and sign an IRS form 4506. He refused. He finally admitted that the tax return we would receive from the IRS would look nothing like the one he provided to us. You can ask a tax attorney or CPA for the IRS form 4056. Exhibit 5.1 is a copy of a blank IRS form 4506 and is provided for your use if you feel it is needed.

Besides the items discussed already, there is not much more for you to check out about the buyer. If the buyers made any other claims about themselves, try to confirm what you were told.

BE AWARE OF WHAT THE BUYER NEEDS TO DO

The buyers have more to investigate in their side of the due diligence than you do. I would recommend allowing the buyers to see anything and everything they want to see. In many letters of intent or offers to purchase, the buyer specifies what they want to review. Sometimes the buyers may perform the due diligence themselves. Sometimes they hire a CPA and attorney. It is a good idea to have the buyers and their advisors make a list of what they want to study. In that way, you can pull out the requested items. Sometimes the books and records are looked at on your business' premises; if so, have the buyer and his advisors make an appointment before coming into the business to see anything. Some buyers or their advisors want everything brought over to them. If that is the case, it is a good idea to make a list of what you are taking over and have the buyer or advisor sign for receiving the items.

Sometimes the buyer may ask to speak with employees, vendors, and customers. If there are some major contingencies still left to be fulfilled that could easily kill the sale, then you must weigh carefully the risks involved in exposing your employees, vendors, and customers to such a thing. Sometimes this subject is not brought up by the buyer until the due diligence phase. Sometimes it comes up in the negotiations. You must weigh the risks carefully no matter when the topic comes up. Perhaps this would be a time to include a liquidated damages clause or ask for a nonrefundable deposit, or even the release of some funds, nonrefundable.

When the buyers or their accountants have finished checking the books and records, have them sign to indicate that they have approved the books and records. A blank form is located in Exhibit 5.2 at the end of this chapter. By signing the approval, they are making an important statement. It is very important that you have them sign the form. If they balk, then you have a problem that needs to be dealt with right away. Find out why they will not sign, and do what you can to solve it. Once the books and records have been approved, it is time to open escrow or call the attorney to prepare all elements for the closing.

THE FUNCTION OF AN ESCROW COMPANY

An escrow company is a business acting as a neutral stakeholder. They perform a necessary and valuable function. They work for both parties and take care of holding all the money, all the vital ownership documents, and various releases needed from government agencies. Usually, the escrow company will provide all the necessary documents, such as the bill of sale, note, security agreement, bulk sales notice, and the UCC-1 and UCC-2s (personal property liens and releases), to name a few items. Additionally, the escrow company will perform lien searches, requests for beneficiary statements, requests of the Department of Corporations, and much more. The escrow company also serves as the place where any vendor, government agency, or person having a claim against the business can write, call, or put a claim. The escrow company will not allow the sale to close until all conditions are met and all legally required notices have been filed and complied with. The escrow company will not allow either party to change any condition or requirement without the approval of both parties. The buyer's money cannot be released without both parties' permission. Sometimes when buyers decide not to go through with a purchase, they try to quickly get their deposit or down payment out of escrow. If you have a valid escrow and have not overtly preapproved the release of funds, the buyer will not be allowed to withdraw any money without your written permission.

Unlike closings held by attorneys and other closing agents, when using an escrow company, all the documents are signed in advance of the closing. The note, the bill of sale, and the like, are all signed within a few days of opening the escrow. The escrow officer types in the final precise amounts where needed when they are closing the transaction. An escrow closing is anticlimactic in that all the documents have been signed in advance and there should be nothing else to do but perhaps sign a closing amendment. A closing amendment just tidies up any details that were adjusted near or at the closing. The process runs extremely smoothly if the escrow officers are competent, detailed, and conscientious (they should be). By following the checklist in Exhibit 5.3 and the instructions provided herein, the closing or escrow, if you use one, will go as smoothly as practical.

WHAT TO DO AFTER DUE DILIGENCE IS COMPLETED

When the due diligence has been completed and all parties are satisfied, make an appointment with an escrow company experienced with handling sales of businesses, or find an attorney who does real estate or business closings (preferably a neutral party). Take a copy of the purchase contract to the escrow company or closing agent along with the buyer's deposit check. In addition, take the information and papers as set forth in items 1 through 10 in Exhibit 5.3.

As soon as the escrow officers inform you that they have prepared the escrow instructions and the rest of the documents, get together with the buyer at the escrow office and sign everything. It is best to meet at the escrow or closing agent's office because any corrections or clarifications needed can be taken care of immediately.

Check with your Secretary of State's office to find out any particular laws that should be followed, such as the Bulk Sales Law. Usually a notice to creditors of a bulk sale must be published in a newspaper that is distributed in the area where the business is located. (Check with your escrow company or closing agent for specific guidelines for your state or county.) The transaction cannot close until the time limit imposed by the Bulk Sales Law has been completed; including weekends, the time in many states is 17 days. Almost all escrowed business transactions last 30 days. They typically last 30 days or longer to allow a nonrushed time to take care of all the necessary elements to transfer the ownership. If a lender other than the seller is involved, the escrow closing or a closing through an attorney or any other means can take as long as 60 to 90 days.

BUSINESSES THAT SELL ALCOHOLIC BEVERAGES

If the sale includes an Alcoholic Beverage Control license, make an appointment at the state office that controls the licensing as soon as possible. In some states the department of Alcoholic Beverage Control will govern the time to close the sale. Carefully follow what the department and the escrow officer or closing agent say to do in relationship to the transfer of the alcohol license. Generally, a public notice of the transfer of the Alcoholic Beverage Control license will be posted at the business. Therefore, all the employees and customers will be aware of the sale.

YOUR MAIN RESPONSIBILITY

Your main responsibility during escrow or in preparation to close the sale is to have all papers signed, documents gathered, loans approved, and leases assigned. Get everything done as quickly as possible. Use the checklist in Exhibit 5.3 as a guide. Follow up regularly with the buyers to make sure that they are doing what they need to do. Do not let a week go by without checking the buyer's progress. If a problem or snag occurs, deal with the problem right away.

WHEN TO TELL THE LANDLORD

When the due diligence is completed and you are ready to open escrow or go to a closing attorney, contact the landlord or the property manager personally and tell him that you have entered an agreement to sell your business. Do not tell him you sold the business. Ask the landlord or his representative if they have a lease assignment form they prefer to use; escrow companies and closing attorneys can provide a lease assignment form if the landlord does not prefer to use his own.

Ask the landlord what he wants to see from the buyer, and if he wants to meet the buyer; surprisingly, some do not need to meet the buyer. Since you have the buyer's personal financial statement and perhaps a credit report, you can supply a copy of them to the landlord. This will help expedite things. In some cases, you will have to really stay on top of the process of the lease assignment. This is an important part to closing the sale. Landlords typically do not feel the need to expedite the process; after all they are not profiting from the assignment. Follow up with the landlord or the property management frequently, but do not get him working against you.

WHAT TO DO ABOUT THE TELEPHONE AND OTHER UTILITIES

Do not call the telephone company and request that the service be discontinued as of a certain date. You just request to transfer the billing responsibility from you to the buyer. Some telephone companies call this a superseding, and can handle the process via the fax. You should call the utility company, too. Tell them when you are anticipating a change of ownership and request that the billing responsibility be changed as of that date. To expedite the process with both the telephone company and the gas and electric company, have any information you know about the buyer handy; tell them all they need for their records. Do not forget to transfer any pay phones at the business. There are a lot of businesses that do not pay a separate water bill. In that case, do nothing. If you do have a separate water bill, follow what was said about the other utility companies.

In many cases your buyers will have up to 30 days after they take over the business to obtain a new business license. If your business requires any special licenses, this should be taken care of as soon as possible, before closing. Nothing is worse than to find out that the buyers cannot qualify for, or for some other reason, obtain a necessary license or permit required. There are cases when the buyers can operate under your permit until they can obtain one for themselves. Be sure you understand the liability of doing such a thing before you agree to do so.

STATE SALES TAX CLEARANCE

For those businesses located in the state of California, a clearance from the State Board of Equalization will need to be gotten before escrow will close. In order to expedite obtaining this clearance, please do the following as described. As the date to close the escrow approaches, have your accountant bring all accounting current as it regards paying sales tax. Then on the day you change possession, have the accountant finish the sales tax accounting. Prepare a State Board of Equalization tax return form and write Final Return on it. Have the line that asks for the amount of tax due for the sale of furniture, fixtures, and equipment filled out with the tax due on the amount you allocated to those assets. Complete the form and get a cashier's check for the amount of tax due. Remember that the buyer will repay you through escrow for the tax due on the furniture, fixtures, and equipment. Take the form, the cashier's check, a photocopy of your two previous State Board of Equalization tax filings, and a photocopy of the front and back of the canceled checks that paid the tax on the last two filings all down to the State Board of Equalization office. There is a specific person who handles businesses being sold. Your tax clearance will be taken care of in the shortest amount of time possible. If you pay the taxes owed with a business check instead of a cashier's check, that can cause up to a two-week delay in getting your money out of escrow.

EMPLOYMENT DEPARTMENT CLEARANCE

You will also need a clearance from the Employment Development Department. The escrow officer or closing agents should call them and request the clearance. I would also suggest that you call them and find out what they want you to do to obtain the clearance. Sometimes if you have a payroll service, there is nothing for you to do except close the account. I have seen the clearance given if the business's account is up to date. If your account is not current, you will need to pay all employment taxes due before you get the clearance. Escrow will not disburse your proceeds until these clearances are obtained.

HOW TO HANDLE UNPAID BILLS OR ACCOUNTS PAYABLE

If your business owes any vendors and they submit a claim for payment into escrow or to the closing agent, there are two ways to handle the payment. One is to pay the bills yourself from the business, or have escrow or closing agent pay the bills when the closing takes place. You will be asked to confirm the amounts owed. If you pay the bills, it will take longer to get your money released from escrow. The reason is that the escrow company must have verification that the bills were paid and also receive a release from the claimant. This can take time. However, if the escrow pays the bills, they know that the bills were paid and will not hold up the payment of your funds until a release is received.

If you dispute a claim that says you owe someone, escrow will not give you any of the proceeds of the sale until the dispute is settled. At best, escrow will hold the amount in dispute and release the balance of the funds to you.

Typically, small businesses are sold free and clear of all liens and accounts payable. Therefore, you will need to clean up all bills and collect any money owed to you after the change of possession. If all vendors are satisfied and there are no outstanding conditions left to be fulfilled, the escrow will then close. Be sure to look at the checklist and see if everything was either checked done or checked nonapplicable. If you use an escrow company, they will take a few hours to a day or two to wrap up all the paper work and issue your check and all copies of the sale documents.

Have a successful business sale.

Form **4506**
(Rev. October 1994)
Department of the Treasury
Internal Revenue Service

Request for Copy or Transcript of Tax Form

▶ **Please read instructions before completing this form.**

▶ **Please type or print clearly.**

OMB No. 1545-0429

Note: *Do not use this form to get tax account information. Instead, see instructions below.*

1a Name shown on tax form	**1b** First social security number on tax form or employer identification number (See instructions.)
2a If a joint return, spouse's name shown on tax form	**2b** Second social security number on tax form

3 Current name, address (including apt., room, or suite no.), city, state, and ZIP code (See instructions.)

4 If copy of form or a tax return transcript is to be mailed to someone else, show the third party's name and address.

5 If we cannot find a record of your tax form and you want the payment refunded to the third party, check here . . . . ▶ ☐

6 If name in third party's records differs from line 1a above, show name here. (See instructions.) ▶

7 Check only one box to show what you want:

a ☐ Tax return transcript of Form 1040 series filed during the **current calendar year** and the **2 preceding calendar years.** (See instructions.) (The transcript gives most lines from the original return and schedule(s).) **There is no charge for a transcript request made before October 1, 1995.**

b ☐ Copy of tax form and all attachments (including Form(s) W-2, schedules, or other forms). **The charge is $14.00 for each period requested.**
   Note: *If these copies must be certified for court or administrative proceedings, see instructions and check here* . . . . . ▶ ☐

c ☐ Verification of nonfiling. **There is no charge for this.**

d ☐ Copy of Form(s) W-2 only. **There is no charge for this.** See instructions for when Form W-2 is available.
   Note: *If the copy of Form W-2 is needed for its state information, check here* . . . . ▶ ☐

8 If this request is to meet a requirement of one of the following, check all boxes that apply.
   ☐ Small Business Administration   ☐ Department of Education   ☐ Department of Veterans Affairs   ☐ Financial institution

9 **Tax form number** (Form 1040, 1040A, 941, etc.)	**11** Amount due for copy of tax form:	
	a Cost for each period	$ 14.00
10 **Tax period(s)** (year or period ended date). If more than four, see instructions.	**b** Number of tax periods requested on line 10	
	c Total cost. Multiply line 11a by line 11b .	$
	Full payment must accompany your request. Make check or money order payable to "Internal Revenue Service."	

Please Sign Here ▶

Signature. See instructions. If other than taxpayer, attach authorization document.   Date

Title (if line 1a above is a corporation, partnership, estate, or trust)

Telephone number of requester ( )

Best time to call

Instructions

A Change To Note.—Form 4506 may be used to request a tax return transcript of the Form 1040 series filed during the current calendar year and the 2 preceding calendar years. There is no charge for a tax return transcript requested before October 1, 1995. You should receive it within 10 workdays after we receive your request. For more details, see the instructions for line 7a.

Purpose of Form.—Use Form 4506 only to get a copy of a tax form, tax return transcript, verification of nonfiling, or a copy of Form W-2. But if you need a copy of your Form(s) W-2 for social security purposes only, do not use this form. Instead, contact your local Social Security Administration office.

Do not use this form to request Forms 1099 or tax account information. If you need a copy of a Form 1099, contact the payer. However, Form 1099 information is available by calling or visiting your local IRS office.

Note: *If you had your tax form filled in by a paid preparer, check first to see if you can get a copy from the preparer. This may save you both time and money.*

If you are requesting a copy of a tax form, please allow up to 60 days for delivery. However, if your request is for a tax return transcript, please allow 10 workdays after we receive your request. To avoid any delay, be sure to furnish all the information asked for on this form. You must allow 6 weeks after a tax form is filed before requesting a copy of it or a transcript.

Tax Account Information Only.—If you need a statement of your tax account showing any later changes that you or the IRS made to the original return, you will need to request tax account information. Tax account information will list certain items from your return including any later changes.

To request tax account information, do not complete this form. Instead, write or visit an IRS office or call the IRS toll-free number listed in your telephone directory.

If you want your tax account information sent to a third party, complete **Form 8821,** Tax Information Authorization. You may get this form by calling 1-800-TAX-FORM (1-800-829-3676).

Line 1b.—Enter your employer identification number **only** if you are requesting a copy of a **business** tax form. Otherwise, enter the first social security number shown on the tax form.

Line 2b.—If requesting a copy or transcript of a joint tax form, enter the second social security number shown on the tax form.

Note: *If you do not complete line 1b and, if applicable, line 2b, there may be a delay in processing your request.*

Line 3.— For a tax return transcript, a copy of Form W-2, or for verification of nonfiling, if your address on line 3 is different than the address shown on the last return you filed and you have not notified the IRS of a new address, either in writing or by filing **Form 8822,** Change of Address, you must attach either—

(Continued on back)

For Privacy Act and Paperwork Reduction Act Notice, see back of form.   Cat. No. 41721E   Form **4506** (Rev. 10-94)

Exhibit 5.1 IRS FORM 4506, Request for Copy or Transcript of Tax Form

- A **copy** of two pieces of identification that have your signature, or
- An original notarized statement affirming your identity.

Line 4.—If you have named someone else to receive the tax form or tax return transcript (such as a CPA, an enrolled agent, a scholarship board, or a mortgage lender), enter the name and address of the individual. If we cannot find a record of your tax form, we will notify the third party directly that we cannot fill the request.

Line 6.—Enter the name of the client, student, or applicant if it is different from the name shown on line 1a. For example, the name on line 1a may be the parent of a student applying for financial aid. In this case, you would enter the student's name on line 6 so the scholarship board can associate the tax form or tax return transcript with their file.

Line 7a.—If you are requesting a tax return transcript, check this box. Also, on line 9 enter the tax form number, on line 10 enter the tax period, and on line 11c enter "no charge." However, if you prefer, you may get a tax return transcript by calling or visiting your local IRS office.

A tax return transcript shows most lines from the original return (including accompanying forms and schedules). It **does not** reflect any changes you or the IRS made to the original return. If you have changes to your tax return and want a statement of your tax account with the changes, see **Tax Account Information Only** on the front. A tax return transcript is available for any returns of the 1040 series (such as Form 1040, 1040A, or 1040EZ) filed during the current calendar year and the 2 preceding calendar years.

In many cases, a tax return transcript will meet the requirement of any lending institution such as a financial institution, the Department of Education, or the Small Business Administration. It may also be used to verify that you did not claim any itemized deductions for a residence.

Line 7b.—If you are requesting a certified copy of a tax form for court or administrative proceedings, check the box to the right of line 7b. It will take at least 60 days to process your request.

Line 7c.—Check this box only if you want proof from the IRS that you did not file a return for the year. Also, on line 10 enter the tax period for which you are requesting verification of nonfiling, and on line 11c, enter "no charge."

Line 7d.—If you need only a copy of your Form(s) W-2, check this box. Also, on line 9 enter "Form(s) W-2 only," and on line 11c enter "no charge."

Forms W-2 are available only from 1978 to the present. Form W-2 information is only available 18 months after it is submitted by your employer. But you can get this information earlier if you request a copy of your tax return and all attachments. See line 7b.

If you are requesting a copy of your spouse's Form W-2, you must have your spouse's signature on the request. If you lost your Form W-2 or have not received it by the time you are ready to prepare your tax return, contact your employer.

Line 10.—Enter the year(s) of the tax form or tax return transcript you are requesting. For fiscal-year filers or requests for quarterly tax forms, enter the date the period ended; for example, 3/31/93, 6/30/93, etc. If you need more than four different tax periods, use additional Forms 4506. Tax forms filed 6 or more years ago may not be available for making copies. However, tax account information is generally still available for these periods.

Line 11c.—Write your social security number or Federal employer identification number and "Form 4506 Request" on your check or money order. If we cannot fill your request, we will refund your payment.

Signature.—Requests for copies of tax forms or tax return transcripts to be sent to a third party must be signed by the person whose name is shown on line 1a or by a person authorized to receive the requested information.

Copies of tax forms or tax return transcripts for a jointly filed return may be furnished to either the husband or the wife. Only one signature is required. Sign Form 4506 exactly as your name appeared on the original tax form. If you changed your name, **also** sign your current name.

For a corporation, the signature of the president of the corporation, or any principal officer and the secretary, or the principal officer and another officer are generally required. For more details on who may obtain tax information on corporations, partnerships, estates, and trusts, see Internal Revenue Code section 6103.

If you are **not** the taxpayer shown on line 1a, you must attach your authorization to receive a copy of the requested tax form or tax return transcript. You may **attach a copy of the authorization document** if the original has already been filed with the IRS. This will generally be a **power of attorney** (Form 2848), or **other authorization**, such as Form 8821, or evidence of entitlement (for Title 11 Bankruptcy or Receivership Proceedings). If the taxpayer is deceased, you must send Letters Testamentary or other evidence to establish that you are authorized to act for the taxpayer's estate.

Note: Form 4506 must be received by the IRS within 60 days after the date you signed and dated the request.

Where To File.—Mail Form 4506 with the correct total payment attached, if required, to the **Internal Revenue Service Center** for the place where you lived when the requested tax form was filed.

Note: You must use a separate form for each service center from which you are requesting a copy of your tax form or tax return transcript.

If you lived in:	Use this address:
New Jersey, New York (New York City and counties of Nassau, Rockland, Suffolk, and Westchester)	1040 Waverly Ave. Photocopy Unit Stop 532 Holtsville, NY 11742
New York (all other counties), Connecticut, Maine, Massachusetts, New Hampshire, Rhode Island, Vermont	310 Lowell St. Photocopy Unit Stop 679 Andover, MA 01810
Florida, Georgia, South Carolina	4800 Buford Hwy. Photocopy Unit Stop 91 Doraville, GA 30362
Indiana, Kentucky, Michigan, Ohio, West Virginia	P.O. Box 145500 Photocopy Unit Stop 524 Cincinnati, OH 45250
Kansas, New Mexico, Oklahoma, Texas	3651 South Interregional Hwy. Photocopy Unit Stop 6716 Austin, TX 73301
Alaska, Arizona, California (counties of Alpine, Amador, Butte, Calaveras, Colusa, Contra Costa, Del Norte, El Dorado, Glenn, Humboldt, Lake, Lassen, Marin, Mendocino, Modoc, Napa, Nevada, Placer, Plumas, Sacramento, San Joaquin, Shasta, Sierra, Siskiyou, Solano, Sonoma, Sutter, Tehama, Trinity, Yolo, and Yuba), Colorado, Idaho, Montana, Nebraska, Nevada, North Dakota, Oregon, South Dakota, Utah, Washington, Wyoming	P.O. Box 9953 Photocopy Unit Stop 6734 Ogden, UT 84409
California (all other counties), Hawaii	5045 E. Butler Avenue Photocopy Unit Stop 52180 Fresno, CA 93888
Illinois, Iowa, Minnesota, Missouri, Wisconsin	2306 E. Bannister Road Photocopy Unit Stop 57A Kansas City, MO 64999
Alabama, Arkansas, Louisiana, Mississippi, North Carolina, Tennessee	P.O. Box 30309 Photocopy Unit Stop 46 Memphis, TN 38130
Delaware, District of Columbia, Maryland, Pennsylvania, Virginia, a foreign country, or A.P.O. or F.P.O address	11601 Roosevelt Blvd. Photocopy Unit DP 536 Philadelphia, PA 19255

Privacy Act and Paperwork Reduction Act Notice.—We ask for the information on this form to establish your right to gain access to your tax form or transcript under the Internal Revenue Code, including sections 6103 and 6109. We need it to gain access to your tax form or transcript in our files and properly respond to your request. If you do not furnish the information, we will not be able to fill your request. We may give the information to the Department of Justice or other appropriate law enforcement official, as provided by law.

The time needed to complete and file this form will vary depending on individual circumstances. The estimated average time is:

Recordkeeping	13 min.
Learning about the law or the form	7 min.
Preparing the form	25 min.
Copying, assembling, and sending the form to the IRS.	17 min.

If you have comments concerning the accuracy of these time estimates or suggestions for making this form more simple, we would be happy to hear from you. You can write to both the **Internal Revenue Service**, Attention: Reports Clearance Officer, PC:FP, Washington, DC 20224; and the **Office of Management and Budget**, Paperwork Reduction Project (1545-0429), Washington, DC 20503. **DO NOT** send this form to either of these offices. Instead, see **Where To File** on this page.

 Printed on recycled paper

Exhibit 5.1 *(Continued)*

305

Approval of Books and Continuous Warranty

The Buyer herein has examined all records of income and expenses of _____
_____, which were requested
by buyer to review for the due diligence investigation in the acquisition of the
aforementioned business and hereby approves same, and Seller certifies to
Buyer that all the records are correct.

_____   _____

Buyer   Date   Seller   Date

Exhibit 5.2 Form for the Buyer's approval of the Books and Records

EXHIBIT 5.3 CHECKLIST OF THINGS TO DO

Checklist of Activities to Be Done

OE = To Open Escrow   **DE** = During Escrow
CE = To Complete Escrow   **ACP** = After Change of Possession

BEFORE YOU OPEN AN ESCROW: Have the books and records approved by the buyer (due diligence). If the buyer is forming a new corporation to purchase the business, the Articles of Incorporation must be back from the Department of Corporations before the application to ABC is made. Any new corporation being formed should be started before opening escrow; this will expedite the time it takes to close. It usually takes two plus weeks to become incorporated.

✔ Check off when Done or mark the item N/A or nonapplicable.

OE _____ 1. Obtain correct names, addresses, and social security numbers of seller and buyer.

OE _____ 2. Obtain correct name, address, etc. of lessor (landlord).

OE _____ 3. Obtain copies of any notes and contracts assumable, also copy any leases and give escrow and buyer copies.

OE _____ 4. If the seller is a corporation, have a corporate resolution drawn up and submit to escrow or closing agent.

OE _____ 5. Obtain resale number, business license number, Federal Tax number, and copy of latest personal property tax bill from seller and submit to escrow or closing agent.

OE _____ 6. If an ABC license is involved, obtain license number and submit to escrow or closing agent.

OE _____ 7. Find out how the buyer wishes to take title and inform escrow or closing agent.

OE _____ 8. If inventory is retail, get value or percent discount for inventory established and written into contract.

OE _____ 9. Order escrow instructions, deposit earnest money.

OE _____ 10. All parties must approve escrow instructions and sign all escrow documents.

DE _____ 11. All partners must sign off the liquor license, but it needn't be done at the same time (at ABC office).

DE _____ 12. If outside financing is going to be used, make applications and get prequalified (ASAP). Find out exactly what the lender will want to see of the business and get it ready.

Exhibit 5.3 Checklist of Things to Do in Preparation of Closing

DE _____ 13. Be sure to clarify and point out any fixtures and equipment not worth repairing and don't include these on the list of fixtures and equipment.

DE _____ 14. Make a list of items that don't go with the business (submit to buyer and escrow).

DE _____ 15. Make a list of fixtures, furniture, and equipment; have both parties approve this list with signatures and submit to escrow or closing agent.

DE _____ 16. If an inventory company is being used, make an appointment with the company for the day you want the final inventory taken, prepare the store, make sure all the merchandise is marked, have departments defined and let the inventory company know the department titles to use for the inventory.

DE _____ 17. Determine the allocation of the purchase price (CPA or tax advisor should be consulted). Both parties should agree to allocation. Submit allocation to escrow or closing agent. See Exhibit 5.2 for a form to use for the allocation.

DE _____ 18. Contact landlord or property management to have lease assigned (follow their requirement for assignment). Do this as soon as you have opened escrow or completed the due diligence.

DE _____ 19. If health and/or a fire inspection is necessary, telephone health and fire department and request inspection.

DE _____ 20. If required, fill out and mail in health permit application.

DE _____ 21. Are there any special licenses particular to this type of business which are needed? If so, file applications.

DE _____ 22. Contact insurance company to establish coverage for the business, submit proof of insurance to escrow or closing agent.

DE _____ 23. Make sure escrow has notified State Board of Equalization of sale.

DE _____ 24. Contact Employment Development Department regarding closure of employment benefits account of seller. Be sure they send clearance to the escrow company or closing agent.

DE _____ 25. Check with seller regarding any Yellow Page ads or other on going advertising account or outstanding coupons, etc., with which the buyer will be responsible.

Exhibit 5.3 *(Continued)*

EXHIBIT 5.3 CHECKLIST OF THINGS TO DO

DE _____ 26. Has seller promised any wage increases or salary raises? Find out.

DE _____ 27. Are there any obligations on behalf of the business to be performed in the future? Find out, disclose, and discuss how they are to handled.

DE _____ 28. Secure all mailing lists and customer lists being sold with the business (seller is not to retain copies).

DE _____ 29. If applicable—buyer should make application with state lottery.

DE _____ 30. Buyer should obtain new resale permit from State Board of Equalization.

DE _____ 31. Buyer should have their CPA open an account with Employment Development Department and obtain a registration number. Also have them obtain reporting forms or State Income Tax withholding, State Disability Insurance, and Unemployment Insurance.

DE _____ 32. Buyer should (or CPA for buyer) obtain Federal Employer Number and reporting forms or Social Security and Federal Tax Withholding.

DE _____ 33. Buyer, when you receive "Golden Rod" copy of Fictitious Business Name Filing from escrow, you can then open your business banking account.

DE _____ 34. If the business takes credit cards, then consult with your business bank to get credit card ID plates, or set up electronic verification and authorization.

DE _____ 35. Submit application for a city business license (if bank needs proof of license, give copy of paid-for application until you receive the actual license).

DE _____ 36. Discuss how cash in cash drawer or register will be handled (also in house coin reserves). The cash is usually purchased by the buyer who brings a personal check for the amount kept in the business.

DE _____ 37. Contact Gas & Electric Co. to change billing name. Do not order cut off! (For Gas & Electric, Telephone company, and water department, all will want to know effective date).

DE _____ 38. Contact telephone company and have supersedure arranged and new account set up for buyer. They will fax necessary forms.

Exhibit 5.3 *(Continued)*

DE _____ 39. If there are any pay telephones at the business be sure to include the change over of those accounts.

DE _____ 40. If the business actually pays for the water bill and not the landlord, then contact water department and have billing name changed.

DE _____ 41. Seller should have business clean and in good shape before change of possession.

DE _____ 42. Inform employees and others who should know that the business is being sold and introduce buyer to crew.

CE _____ 43. To close out the State Board of Equalization, seller must submit their final tax return along with a cashiers check for the taxes due plus a copy of the last two tax returns made (either monthly or quarterly) along with copies of both sides of the canceled checks for the same period. Take all this personally to State Board of Equalization.

DE _____ 44. When a vehicle is to change ownership, a Smog Check is usually required, unless the vehicle has received a Smog Check certificate within 60 days prior to the change of ownership. The seller must provide the buyer with a Smog Check certificate prior to the transfer of ownership.

DE _____ 45. If the business receives 1099s from contractors, be sure to have them notified about the change of ownership.

CE _____ 46. Have buyer deposit balance of funds into escrow.

CE _____ 47. Decide on a day to take inventory and change possession on same day.

Exhibit 5.3 (*Continued*)

EXHIBIT 5.4 BLANK ALLOCATION FORM

Allocation

The following sets forth the values as allocated and agreed to by the under-signed:

Furniture, Fixtures, & Equipment $ _____

Covenant Not To Compete   _____

Lease   _____

Leasehold Improvements   _____

License   _____

Customer Lists   _____

Goodwill   _____

Inventory   _____

TOTAL $ _____

Agreed to: _____ 19_____

_____   _____

Buyer   Seller

Exhibit 5.4 Blank Allocation Form

BIBLIOGRAPHY

Berger, Lisa, Donelson Berger, and William C. Eastwood. *Cashing In: Getting the Most When You Sell Your Business.* New York: Warner Books, 1988.

Desmond, Glenn. *Handbook of Small Business Valuation Formulas and Rules of Thumb, Third Edition.* Camden, NJ: Valuation Press, 1993.

Desmond, Glenn and John Marcello. *Handbook of Small Business Valuation Formulas and Rules of Thumb, Second Edition.* Marina del Rey, CA: Valuation Press, 1988.

Desmond, Glenn M. and Richard E Kelley. *Business Valuation Handbook.* Los Angeles: Valuation Press, 1988.

Miles, Raymond C. *Basic Business Appraisal.* New York: John Wiley & Sons, 1984.

Powell, Tim. *Analyzing Your Competition.* New York: Find/Svp, 1992.

Pratt, Shannon P. *Valuing Small Businesses and Professional Practices.* Homewood: Dow Jones-Irwin, 1986.

Pratt, Shannon P. *Valuing a Business: The Analysis and Appraisal of Closely Held Companies, Second Edition.* Homewood: Dow Jones—Irwin, 1989.

Pratt, Shannon P., Jay E. Fishman, Clifford J. Griffith, and Keith D. Wilson. *Guide to Business Valuations, Fifth Edition.* Fort Worth, TX: Practitioners Publishing Company, 1995.

Pratt, Shannon P., Robert F. Reilly, and Robert P. Schweihs. *Valuing a Business: The Analysis and Appraisal of Closely Held Companies, Third Edition.* Chicago: Irwin, 1996.

Russel, John J., ed. *National Trade and Professional Associations of the United States.* 23rd Annual ed. Washington, D.C.: Columbia, 1993.

Troy, Leo. *Almanac of Business and Industrial Financial Ratios.* Englewood Cliffs, NJ: Prentice Hall, 1995.

Tyran, Michael R. *Handbook of Business and Financial Ratios.* Englewood Cliffs, NJ: Prentice Hall, 1986.

SOURCES FOR BUSINESS SALES COMPARISONS

John Wiley & Sons, Inc., Bizcomps Business Sales Statistics (electronic form) and various business valuation software products. Call 1-800-825-8763.

Sanders, Jack R., BIZCOMPS®. Write P.O. Box 711777, San Diego, CA, 92171 or call (619) 457-0366.

Internet sources: Check what current asking prices are for various businesses. Remember, asking prices are not prices that businesses were sold for.

Business Exchange Network: The Internet address is www.biz-exchange .com or call (925) 831-9925.

INDEX

R

Relative-employees, market value of labor of, 51–53
Rent:
    and location of business, 19–20
    payments for, on financial statements, 50
Reputation, business, 16–18
Request for Copy of Transcript of Tax Form of (IRS Form 4506), 296, 304–305
Response log, marketing, 225
Risk factor, *See* Capitalization rate

S

Sales tax, 301–302
SBA (Small Business Administration), 294
SDCF, *See* Seller's Discretionary Cash Flow
Security, loan, 103
Seller:
    financing by, 245, 257–258
    responsibilities of, 293–296
Seller's Discretionary Cash Flow (SDCF), 30–33, 34–41, 43–44
Service businesses:
    equipment of, 29
    questions to ask about, 193–195
    reputation of, 17–18
SIC codes, *See* Standard Industrial Classification codes

Small Business Administration (SBA), 294
Small-business ownership, perceived benefits of, 97–98
Spouse-employees, market value of labor of, 51–53
Standard Industrial Classification (SIC) codes:
    by major industry group, 78–80
    in numerical order, 81–88
Sub-Chapter S corporations, 92

T

Tangible assets, 46
Taxation:
    of corporations, 46
    sales tax, 301–302
Telephone:
    interviews over, 218–220
    transfer of, 301
Trade publications, 213
Transfer of ownership, 256
Transitional training and consulting, 258–259
Trends, multiyear, 11–12, 36–37
Trendy businesses, 26
Two-owner businesses, valuation of, 41

U

UCC-1/UCC-2, 298
Unique businesses, multiple for, 14–16